W9-BBR-064

# IN THE NINETIES

# IN THE NINETIES

JOHN STOKES

THE UNIVERSITY OF CHICAGO PRESS

The University of Chicago Press, Chicago 60637

Harvester Wheatsheaf, Hemel Hempstead

© 1989 John Stokes

All rights reserved. Published 1989

Printed in Great Britain

98 97 96 95 94 93 92 91 90 89   5 4 3 2 1

ISBN 0–226–77538–0

*Library of Congress Cataloging in Publication Data are available from the publisher.*

This book is printed on acid-free paper.

FOR LORAINE FLETCHER
AND IN MEMORY OF IAN

What's the good of losing heart now, that's what I say. We should have thought of it when the world was young, in the nineties.

Samuel Beckett, *Waiting for Godot*

# CONTENTS

# FOREWORD

I wasn't the only one who arrived at Reading University a teenager and left it a would-be scholar. I was simply the least deserving and, for a time, the least grateful. No one had told me that the study of literature can last a lifetime – the lesson I eventually learned from two remarkable men.

Donald Gordon is rightly remembered for his inspired teaching and his awesome knowledge. I remember too his tolerance, his humour, the pleasure he took in the visible world. There were times when he was the best company that I could ever hope for.

Ian Fletcher is known to countless students – and not just from Reading – as the man who rediscovered the *fin de siècle* for the post-war generations. In the nineties, Ian, prodigious of memory and imagination, would have been seen as the complete 'bookman'. His boundless generosity continued to keep me in ideas, more, perhaps, than he ever realized.

After such examples, what excuses? Add to my Reading debts my colleagues at the University of Warwick, especially John Goode who read an early draft of this book; my instructive graduate students, Bill Greenslade and Steve Attridge in particular; and my American collaborators on a bibliography of Arthur Symons – Karl Beckson and Wayne Markert – and I'm at a loss.

As for Faith Evans: in this as in all things only the mistakes were made without her.

# ACKNOWLEDGEMENTS

We would like to thank the following for permission to reproduce illustrations: the British Library for pp. xvi, 6, 36, 58, 59, 64, 72, 80, 83, 87, 88, 90, 92, 117, 140, 147, 162; the Board of Trustees of the Victoria and Albert Museum for pp. 2, 69, 70, 78; the William Andrews Clark Memorial Library, Los Angeles, for pp. 4 and 5; the Tate Gallery, London, for p. 39; the Gallatin Beardsley Collection, Princeton University Library, for p. 40; the National Portrait Gallery for p. 41; Geoffrey Verdon-Roe for p. 75.

Quotations from the works of Bernard Shaw appear by permission of the Society of Authors on behalf of the Bernard Shaw Estate; quotations from the works of Arthur Symons by permission of his literary executor; quotations from the letters of Oscar Wilde by permission of Merlin Holland, Oxford University Press and John Murray Ltd.

# INTRODUCTION
## Topics and Texts

In February 1898 the Empire music-hall in Leicester Square offered a
new entertainment. Entitled 'The Ballet of the Press', it told an
exhilarating story that began with Caxton, the inventor of the printing
press, and ended with a parade of dancers, costumed as newspapers, led
by the *Daily Mail*, the very latest product of print. In the interim, a
guardian angel, 'The Liberty of the Press' (danced by a new star, Adeline
Genée), presented two historical tableaux: first, Doctor Johnson
correcting proofs, then the bustle around a modern railway bookstall.
From which the scene moved to a large room in Fleet Street, with a view
of the railway bridge over Ludgate Hill and St Paul's Cathedral,
somewhat obscured by smoke.

Here, in the offices of 'The Metropolitan Press', crammed with
typists, war correspondents, special artists and a troop of eager
newspaper boys, the parade took place. Daily and evening papers in
their actual colours (green for the *Westminster Gazette*, pink for the
*Globe*) entered to a polka that changed to a gallop for the sporting
prints. The picture papers, the finance journals, the comic sheets and the
society reviews – over seventy in all – followed them on to the stage, and
the whole sequence culminated with the papers in a pyramid, each
waving a copy of its own latest edition. It was, as the poet, critic, and
balletomane Arthur Symons confessed, 'one of the most original,
fantastic, intricate, and amusing ballets which even the Empire has ever
given'. 'Even the most humble of the most lofty-minded "gentlemen of
the Press",' he thought, 'could not but feel individually flatered by a ballet
the whole of which is one long glorification, one long hymn in praise.'[1]

Time and place, medium and message combined to make 'The Ballet
of the Press' the quintessential late nineties event. Popular and skilled,
as up-to-date as its subject, the Empire ballet was a living picture of the
times. It demonstrated the energy of *laissez-faire* production: a topical
theme for a decade which placed unprecedented value upon 'topicality',

and was as spectacularly propagandist as the Jubilee celebrations of the previous year.

'The Ballet of the Press' belongs to an atmosphere that all the professional writers discussed in this book knew well. Most of them had contributed quite directly to the expansion of the newspaper industry. Oscar Wilde and Bernard Shaw wrote for the *Pall Mall Gazette*. Arthur Symons wrote for the *Star*, along with Shaw, A. B. Walkley and Richard Le Gallienne. The *Daily Chronicle*, most literary of the liberal dailies, used Lionel Johnson, William Archer and, again, Shaw. These were all learned writers (educated either by institutions or by themselves), ambitious, and committed to their own creative projects. Symons kept up a ferocious rate of reviewing but devoted what time was left over to introspective and fragmentary poems. Wilde notoriously kept himself in the foreground of the public view while exploring the 'criminality' of art in his fictions. Shaw boasted that the functions of political journalism were inseparable from his plays. Only Henry James managed to keep himself apart from the papers – and even he wrote continually about the problems of finding an attentive audience in the age of the headline.

Such pressing predicaments have been recognized by much of the recent critical work on the period which has concentrated upon the economics of literary production as they affected the activity of writing overall.[2] We are becoming more prepared to place writers according to their professional circumstances, as well as to their professed allegiances. Soon we may even improve upon the wide vision of Holbrook Jackson's *The Eighteen Nineties* which, although it was published three-quarters of a century ago, remains the only truly comprehensive survey. In 1913, when it first appeared, the nineties were recent enough to seem like interesting business not altogether finished. Feelings of both intimacy and distance enabled Jackson to provide a sweeping account that held in a single volume Wilde, Yeats, Shaw, Beardsley and Kipling, that put minor poets alongside best-selling novelists and mixed members of the Fabian Society with those of the Rhymers' Club.

After the First World War, a pervasive sense of national trauma, together with new cultural polarizations, meant that the nineties had to fall into place according to a narrowly selective range of predetermined convictions. There were the subterfuges of High Modernist 'tradition' which, as Eliot and Pound designed it, was always antagonistic towards social realism but nervously ambivalent towards 'Decadent' myth; there were revivals of dandyism among the West End novelists, and ritual commemorations of martyrdom in the literary catacombs where sexual and bibliographical interests sometimes met. These were cults, not true continuity. Later still, when literary criticism had been taken over by the universities, the nineties remained a field for partisans: Dr Leavis, determined to establish an uninterrupted line between the mid-nineteenth century and a few, a very few, Moderns; Frank Kermode, deftly filling the missing years with nothing but Symbolist theory. Where a literary historian like Jackson looked for synchronic interaction, modern critics have isolated the discrete thread, the significant 'tendency', and judged the nineties according to the preferences of their own time.

Of course, most literary history is written according to its consequences, or rather according to what these are assumed to have been. The nineties are no exception to the rule and we are always at risk from our knowledge of how every author at work in the period later turned out. When Jackson was writing, some of his subjects were still alive and some, it was reasonable to think, had yet to reach their prime. Although enthusiastic about Yeats and Shaw, Jackson could hardly have predicted *Responsibilities* (1914) or *Heartbreak House* (1919), gaunt milestones of middle age achieved by men who had begun their serious output in the nineties, and he was certainly in no position to foresee *Women in Love*, *The Waste Land* and *Ulysses*. As a professional observer he was naturally very much aware of those figures from the nineties who were currently in the ascendant: Shaw and Wells still seemed unstoppable, James close to the ineffable; Kipling had received the Nobel Prize and Beerbohm's retreat from London must, in 1913, have seemed less final than it was to prove.

If death and failure were no longer as fashionable as they had recently been, then that simply made the long list of mortal casualties in the nineties all the more striking. It was a marvel to Jackson 'how Death has gathered to himself so many of the period's most characteristic and most interesting figures',[3] and he intoned their names: Oscar Wilde, Aubrey Beardsley, Ernest Dowson, Charles Conder, Lionel Johnson, Hubert Crackanthorpe, Henry Harland, Francis Thompson, John Davidson. Two, at least, had brought about their own ends by deliberate means, two or three others were certainly responsible, through careless living, for their premature deaths. Jackson speculated that 'perhaps all that was mortal of them felt so essential to the Nineties that life beyond the decade might have been unbearable',[4] a thought that perturbed him more than it did those who had survived. In old age Arthur Symons actually liked to boast that he had known twelve men who had killed themselves.[5] That's the kind of flourish that makes Symons at once the most authentic and the most unreliable of memorialists. But Yeats, too, enjoyed the game, recording later that, in 1900, 'everybody got down off his stilts; henceforth nobody drank absinthe with his black coffee; nobody went mad; nobody committed suicide; nobody joined the Catholic Church; or if they did I have forgotten'.[6] The joke was at Yeats's own expense and that of his whole generation, with its habit of regarding the extremism of its own decadent youth as a special episode, a perverse preparation for the rigours of the modern world.

For Jackson, who was still young in 1913, the important idea was that the nineties had been – in a phrase he shared with Yeats – 'an age of transition' that prepared the way for his own contemporary Edwardian milieu, with its penchant for vitalist or Nietzschean philosophies. Jackson was particularly scrupulous in documenting Nietzsche's arrival on the English intellectual scene (prophetic allusions by George Egerton and John Davidson, a study by Havelock Ellis in the *Savoy* of 1896), but rarely mentioned the far gloomier Schopenhauer, the one philosopher every nineties' writer knew of and had occasionally read. 'Transition' logically implied some kind of continuance, though Jackson didn't hold that the process was always smooth – a view of events aided, in his case, by a comparative innocence of methodology. By abstracting history into 'mood' or 'culture' or 'the spirit of the age', words and phrases everywhere implicit in his book, he was able to explain change in a pseudo-Nietzschean way, as produced by the clash of opposing tendencies, 'decadence' against 'imperialism' most obviously.

The essential difference between *The Eighteen Nineties* and *In the Nineties* is that by contrast with Holbrook Jackson I attempt to observe the period from within, by looking first of all at how the nineties saw themselves. I search for the origins of literary forms and ideas in the material conventions of the moment. By starting with the news rather than with moods all too easily imposed by posterity, I try to allow for immediacy of response, for both common ground and divided opinion, to foreground the world the writers knew and the means by which they came to know about it. Fact is compared with fiction, journalism with literature, in the certain knowledge that the papers were omniverous and omnipresent.

So much so that only one day after his release from gaol Wilde was already making jokes about journalism: 'Do you know of the punishments that happen to people who have been "away"?' he asked his friends. 'They are not allowed to read the *Daily Chronicle*.' On the

train up from Reading he had been forbidden to read his warder's copy.
Might he, perhaps, be permitted to read it upside down? 'This they
consented to allow ... I read the *Daily Chronicle* upside down all the way
and never enjoyed it so much. It's really the only way to read
newspapers.' Wilde's underlying point may have been that the *Chronicle*
(a personal favourite, in fact, sometimes smuggled into his cell by a
kindly officer) made headlines out of minor matters that should, in his
aesthetic view, have been dismissed as the dreary and inconsequential
'facts' of the modern world. 'The impossible in art,' he had once noted, 'is
anything that has happened in real life.'[7] It followed that a paper which
claimed to reflect the order of things should be read by artists only in an
upside-down way, that the higher truth would lie outside, in their
imaginative response.

The essays that make up *In the Nineties* amount, in all, to an
experiment in inter-disciplinary criticism inspired by the period they
study: a decade that was preoccupied by the relations between high and
popular culture, one medium and another, art and life. For although they
range over many subjects and are designed to be read individually, what
they share is the 'upside-down' approach. Each essay starts with a 'topic'
as it was presented in the press, and then moves out among 'texts': some
pictorial – paintings and prints; some fictional – novels, poems and
plays; some critical – books, articles and extended reviews.

In my selection of topics I have been guided by the papers themselves.
Some issues were longstanding matters of concern; the papers made
them all seem equally new. Topics are public events as well as public
debates, and can reduce conviction to controversy. They enter into
promiscuous relationships with their neighbours on the page: in the
terminology of Roman Jakobson, subsequently adopted by David Lodge,
their mode is 'metonymy' while that of 'texts' is 'metaphor'.[8] Texts are
intrinsically patient: though open to suggestion, they are cautious about
the supposedly corporate voice and resist the pressures of production.
All the writers, painters and critics who are commemorated here have it
among their otherwise disparate achievements that they were capable of
recreating topics as texts.

Not that my desire to write about how the arts functioned at the time,
in the nineties themselves, has meant that I have ignored more recent
historians and critics. There have been many mentors and many guides,
and I have deliberately provided footnotes of unusual fullness, as well as
an introductory booklist for each chapter so that *In the Nineties* might
also offer a working bibliography for the newcomer.

Chapter 1 considers how the decade addressed itself in the correspondence columns: the papers are both topic and context. This chapter also serves as an introduction to the book as a whole because it provides the historical information that underlies my empirical approach. The presiding spirit is Raymond Williams who, more than any other modern critic, appreciated the complex interaction between developments in the media and social change. The letters page, along with other innovations of the so-called New Journalism, is analysed as a form of cultural production through which ideas were put into general circulation. The threat of 'degeneration', the menace of 'morbid' art, the confidence of 'The Philistine': these and other journalistic inventions are explained in context and are shown to be counters in a political and economic struggle.

Arguments about the appreciation of the visual arts, subject of Chapter 2, also involved the relationship of minority to mass, popular to 'advanced'. How could an artist paint what many denied was there to be seen? What was the true relation of 'subject' to 'treatment'? Such questions were tackled by those who were known as the New Critics. Men like D. S. MacColl and R. A. M. Stevenson took it upon themselves to uphold modern painting, Impressionism in particular, in the face of hostility from those who claimed to speak for the public. Out of this confrontation came a number of new and polemical theories of art which, although now superseded in turn, retain their force because of the vigour and depth with which they were expressed, the literary qualities that have given them the lasting power of texts, albeit critical ones.

Chapter 3 opens with reported scandals in the running of the music-halls, but the emphasis soon shifts to the manner in which certain writers tried to communicate their own mixed feelings about modern entertainment. These self-styled 'amateurs' of the variety stage, most notably Arthur Symons, sought a vantage point that would allow aesthetic appreciation without moral judgement or social commitment. Their imaginative prose, their poems and their pictures contrast tellingly with the contemporary pronouncements made by public bodies. And, as the music-hall is a field that has attracted much attention of late from theatre historians and sociologists, there are further contrasts to be made between modern cultural ideologies and the professed values of the time.

In the papers, crusades to clean up places of entertainment attracted as much moral fervour as campaigns to reform the prison system. The 'criminal', protagonist of Chapter 4, was one of those instances of deviance by which the *fin de siècle* diagnosed itself. But deviance from what? Reformers argued that if material conditions inside the prisons were to be radically improved, offenders would have a better chance of rehabilitation. They might re-enter the society that had condemned them. A more radical wing – Oscar Wilde included – felt the irony in that proposal and reacted accordingly. Wilde's *Ballad of Reading Gaol*, traditionally criticized for its mixture of realism and romance, is revealed as an authentic product of conflicting impulses, and as a protest against the extended movement in modern criminology, charted by Michel Foucault, whereby 'punishment' has come to appear as 'therapy'.

The suicide, ambiguous hero of the following chapter, was another exception who proved unpalatable rules. Much has been written from a sociological standpoint about the nineteenth-century interest in this subject, partly because of Emile Durkheim's great work *Le suicide*, which appeared in France in 1897, a landmark in the growth of the discipline. A recent scholar, Olive Anderson, has re-opened the fascinating question of the validity of statistical evidence in the reconstruction of historical 'mentalités'. How the nineteenth-century preoccupation with suicide related to literary structures has been less adequately treated. There are complex links between the ways in which suicides presented themselves in their notes of farewell, the ways in which they were accounted for by coroners, and the ways in which writers took suicide as a point of departure for elaborate fictions.

The upsurge in suicide rates was not only supported by statistics, it coincided with the growth of popular journalism. In Henry James's long short story *The Papers*, published in 1903 and discussed in the last chapter, the topic of suicide is subordinated to the power of the press, as if journalists had the means to bestow or withhold existence itself. This is an early stage in the Edwardian concern with establishing distinctions between literature and journalism, an issue James debated with Wells and with Shaw. Already, in the nineties, neither James nor, in fact, Shaw and Wilde, could live with the thought that writers might become entirely dependent upon the press. All three took journalism's most intrusive technique, the 'interview', and appropriated it for their own ends, using textual inquisition as a means of concealing and disclosing their professional presence. Once again, the insistence of the topic was countered by the deceptive autonomy of the text.

# 1

# 'IS IT A REVOLUTION?'
## The economics of the New Journalism and the aesthetics of the body politic

The press is at once the eye and the ear and the tongue of the people.

W. T. Stead

## 'UNKNOWN QUANTITY'

Most literary historians agree with the contemporary journalists in proclaiming that the truly notorious nineties ended halfway through the decade. 'The aesthetic cult, in the nasty form, is over,' announced the *News of the World* on 26 May 1895, as Wilde was led from court.[1] According to Holbrook Jackson, writing in 1913, the decade fell into two almost precise halves – the first 'remarkable for a literary and artistic renaissance, degenerating into decadence; the second for a new sense of patriotism degenerating into jingoism'.[2] The first ended with the fall of Wilde, the second with the war in South Africa. In 1987, Richard Ellmann put it this way: 'The Nineties began in 1889 and ended in 1895. At least the Wildean Nineties did so, and without Wilde the decade could not have found its character.'[3] This essay sets out to reconsider a long established view, and looks again at the spring of 1895 as it was represented in the press at the time.

NEW YEAR.

" RING out, wild bells." We hope that you,
  With '94 that's rung out,
Will kindly ring out just a few
Of all those things entitled " new "
Which plagued us till quite mad we grew
  As mad as dog with tongue out.

Those novelties ! The newest kind—
  With turned up nose and weird, slee-
-py eyes, that told of vacant mind,
And monstrous chignon massed behind—
Were those appalling things designed
  By Mr. AUBREY BEARDSLEY.

Yes, "things"; for nought of human shape,
  However strangely bizarre,
Is there portrayed ; there's not an ape,
That feeds on cocoa-nut or grape,
Between Morocco and the Cape,
  So hideous as these are.

For goodness' sake, don't let us see
  New Art which courts disaster !
We much prefer to Mr. B.
VELASQUEZ, REMBRANDT, even P.
P. RUBENS or VANDYKE, for we
  Like oldness in a master.

And then " New Humour." Heavens, why
  It's but a pleasure killer !
A cause of weary yawn and sigh,
Which makes us almost long to fly
To those old jokes collected by
  A certain Mr. MILLER.

In politics Newcastle, too,
  With programme was prophetic ;
And now Leeds leads, and shows who's
  who.
The Grand Old Man — there's age for
  you.!—
Has found much better things to do,
  Not prosy but poetic.

But all the things, so new in time,
  Are nothing to the woman,
Who now is " new," and seeks to climb
To heights which seem to her sublime ;
(Excuse the execrable rhyme)
  She is indeed a rum 'un.

Of course we know that youth is sweet ;
  Old women are not charming ;
But no old woman we could meet,
With featless form and formless feet,
This wild New Woman now could beat,
  She's perfectly alarming.

Ring out, wild bells, wild belles like these
  New-fangled fancies screaming ;
Ring in the woman bound to please,
A lady, always at her ease,
Not manlike woman, by degrees
  More man that woman seeming.

Old '94, who now has fled,
  Encouraged blatant boldness
In things called " new," as we have said ;
New '95, now he is dead,
Might bring some things which are instead
  Remarkable for oldness.

*Punch* celebrates the coming of 1895 with a parody of Tennyson that mocks all things 'New'.

A terminus for the career of Oscar Wilde, it was, after all, only a turning point in the lives of others. For Wilde it brought litigation, arrest, trials, sentence and, eventually, imprisonment. The greatest talker of the age found his name first whispered in gossip, then shouted in headlines, finally rendered 'unspeakable'. For Henry James, the public catastrophe of his play *Guy Domville* in January simply put a stop to his siege of the London theatre. Retreating to his study, James went back to fiction and contributed to *The Yellow Book* a short story entitled 'The Next Time' about an author who finds it almost impossible to write badly enough for a best-seller. Two nights before the opening of *Guy Domville*, James had endured the triumph of Wilde's *An Ideal Husband*, which had been positively received by, among others, H. G. Wells, drama critic of the *Pall Mall Gazette* – a job that James had turned down in 1883.[4] Wells was to the fore: his first great success, *The Time Machine*, was to come out in June.[5] Alongside Wells in the audience at the St James's for *Guy Domville* were Arnold Bennett and George Bernard Shaw. Bennett was still primarily a journalist, though he had a short story in the July issue of *The Yellow Book*. Shaw was at his energetic peak. In July he published a devastating reply (later reprinted as *The Sanity of Art*) to Max Nordau's tirade against European decadence, *Degeneration*, which had appeared in England in February.[6] Discussion of *Degeneration* preoccupied the newspapers for days on end.[7]

A great deal happened to literary London in 1895, but not all of it was to do with literature. The Liberal government was already floundering badly – the party's inevitable decline had perhaps been sealed with Gladstone's resignation in 1894. Indeed it is said that Lord Rosebery, the Prime Minister, might have come to Wilde's aid had he not feared that his own implication in the homosexual world would be revealed, and had he not been warned by Asquith, the Home Secretary, that he would risk losing the June election. As Ellmann drily records, 'In the event, he lost the election anyway.'[8] Political speculation, a mood of apprehension, was in the air. For a London press more sensitive than ever to 'the mood of the times', the unprecedented range of simultaneous cultural events in the year of 1895 offered a priceless opportunity for social homilies. And its readers were fully prepared to participate, in the only way they could, in the way they knew best: with letters to the correspondence columns.

Some letters bore an urgent signature; others, often the most magisterial, were pseudonymous. 'Unknown Quantity', for example, whose long letter to the *Daily Chronicle* of 6 August carried the headline 'Is it a Revolution?', provided a comprehensive explanation of recent

# OH! OSCAR WILDE,
## WE NEVER THOUGHT
# That You Was Built That Way.

Now wonders they will never cease, and
   as each day we read,
The papers, why we of't say, well, "I am
   surprised" indeed,
For people who we think are 18 carat
   turn out brass,
And what we thought a Lion's roar's the
   braying of ass,
We read of pious preachers who turn out
   to be sad rakes,
But Oscar Wilde, he fairly earns the
   bakery and the cakes,
He's got into a mess, and he will take
   some getting out,
You've climbed Jane's ladder, Oscar but
   you've got stuck up the spout.

### Chorus.

Oh! Oscar, you're a Daisy, you're a Sun-
   flower and a Rose,
You're a thick old "Dandylion," from
   your pimple to your toes,
You're the sweetest lump of "Boy's Love"
   that's been picked for many a day,
Oh! Oscar Wilde, we never thought, that
   you was built that way.


You've been "An Ideal Husband," in your
   tin pot way no doubt,
Though "A Woman of no Importance,"
   was your wife, when you were out,
At least that's what the papers say, of
   course they can't be wrong;
They seemed to say that Oscar's fun was
   very, very, strong,
He would'nt treat a "Lady" no not even
   Totty Fay,
But with the pretty boys, he liked to
pass his time away,
Champagne, and Chicken suppers, and
   he'd also give them pelf,
He was fond of manly beauty, he's so
   beautiful himself.


The Marquis of Queensberry, it would
   seem got Oscar "Wild(e)"
He must have been a silly little silly, to
   get riled,
You know there is a saying Oscar, "hard
   words break no bones,"
And folks who live in houses made of
   glass, should not throw stones.
The Marquis got the best of it, and
   knocked poor Oscar out,
They did'nt use no 4 oz gloves, 'twas "raw
   uns" there's no doubt,
He got one in the windbag, and he cussed
   the "Queensberry Rules"
For Oscar, and his second, Taylor looked
   a pair of fools.


At Hollaway our only "Oscar," does his
   fate bewail,
And says he'd rather be at the "Savoy"
   than be in jail,
The Idol of Society, the Poet and the Pet
Can't get a Hock and Seltzer, or yet
   smoke a cigarette,
The "Golden Haired Divineties," seen in
   the Strand each night,
Are quiet excited at the news, and says
   it serves 'em right,
For blacklegging in any trade, is very
   mean and wrong,
And the papers say, that Lord knows who,
   they'll have before so long.

*Street ballads sold at the time of the Wilde trials take their information from 'the papers' which threaten 'Lord knows who they'll have before so long'.*

# OSCAR'S
# WORKING ON A FRESH
# JOB NOW.

The Oscar trial is ended, and his dream of love is
  o'er,
And now in jail, he does bewail,
His funny little capers, he won't cut for two
  years more,
He'll have to start upon a job, he's never done
  before,
His very tender feelings will be mangled now and
  torn,
When he has to rise each morn, and grind the
  golden corn,
And instead of ham and chicken, and such dainty
  bits of scran,
For dry toke and pint of skilly, he'll be putting out
  his can:

Chorus.—

Oh! Oscar Wilde your tricks, has got you in a fix,
You've lost your precious liberty, and got to live
  on skilly go-lee,
Instead of going to plays, you'll have to go to
  prayers,
Then "All in a row" off you'll go, climbing the
  golden stairs.

Well, Oscar cannot grumble, that he's not been
  tried enough,
For twice should be, a fill say we,
The lawyers on each side no doubt, have done
  their best to bluff,
The juries bit the second one, for Oscar cut up
  rough,
The evidence no doubt, was pretty hot
Of letters, such a lot, and mostly tommy rot;

For when men write of rose leaf lips, and say
  they're kissing mad,
About another man, why! you can bet they've got
  it bad.

There's no doubt some of the witnesses, were quite
  as bad as he,
And did not fail, to claim which man
With Wilde, and Taylor, safely lodged in jail they
  ought to be,
And to carry on the same old game, should not
  be free,
The case has caused a lot of blood and hair to fly,
For the Marquis had a try, and blacked Lord
  Thingumys eye,
Although a lot of people seem to say, they must be
  fools,
To start in Piccadilly, fighting under Queensberry
  rules.

For two long weary years, from business Oscar has
  retired,
To sleep alone, and break some stone,
The public of his plays and poetry, seem to soon
  have tired,
Although his company by them, till lately was de-
  sired,
When he his sentence got 'tis said that Oscar
  seemed quite dazed,
In fact was quite amazed, and seemed to be going
  crazed,
And no doubt for the next two years, he will need
  all his pluck,
When instead of dainty bits, he has to tackle
  Indian buck.

*Crowds in Fleet Street struggle to read election results as they appear on electric scoreboards outside newspaper offices.*

history: an account still worthy of examination because it displays so many representative concerns. The moral decline of the nation had all begun, decided 'Unknown Quantity', in the eighties, with the spread of agnosticism and the birth of the Aesthetic Movement, a combination which had rapidly led to a 'new gospel' in which 'we were told to ransack life for pleasurable sensations, to live and enjoy to the uttermost'. A period of material and intellectual 'extravagance' had followed, its style set by a London 'Society' which enjoyed 'the unintelligible verses of obscene French lunatics and criminals', while the lower classes applauded music-hall songs that 'had for their refrain not words but a string of absolutely meaningless syllables hyphenated together'. Changes in aesthetic taste had diminished decorum to the extent that 'the young lady who talked about her soul had given place to the young lady who talked about her sex in its relationship to your own'. Even the middle-classes had become infected, their newspapers taken over by discussions of the failure of marriage and the rights of women. As for business, previously respectable transactions were now conducted in the spirit of the gambling table. 'Extravagance and levity – a restless and morbid spirit – all that was implied by that tawdry, borrowed, used-out, detestable word *fin de siècle* – these things,' warned 'Unknown Quantity', 'have brought us to the point of departure for revolution.'

Disarmingly, this fearful scenario was no sooner mooted than it was withdrawn. The real news, 'Unknown Quantity' then revealed, was not of morbid revolution so much as of vital reaction. The fall of the Liberal government, brought about in part by working-class apathy to decadent 'progress', was an unmistakable sign of a changing mood. So, too, was the new enthusiasm for sport. An immensely successful benefit for the cricketer W. G. Grace ('I have read serious proposals that the honour of knighthood should be conferred upon him') and the popularity of cycling ('of the New Woman nothing is left but her bicycle') were both clear indications of 'a more healthy and manly spirit'. In literature, the outlook was equally promising. Max Nordau's *Degeneration* may have 'contained a fair amount of the very quality that it was written to expose and condemn', but it had nevertheless 'opened the eyes of many people to the real character of extravagance and levity, and the Nemesis that awaits them'. Wilde had been safely convicted and 'we have seen *The Yellow Book* turn grey in a single night, and lose Mr Aubrey Beardsley'. All things considered, the public was entitled to hope that 'the sex-problem will in future be approached rather differently – more in the spirit of a decent man of the world and less in the spirit of a curious schoolboy', that romance might return to replace the 'novel with a purpose', and that 'in its general tone literature may become more restrained, healthier and brighter'. 'Unknown Quantity' confidently concluded that 1895 would be 'an important year in the history of our politics, art, and morals'.

He had certainly touched on sensitive issues. For days afterwards the correspondence columns of the *Daily Chronicle* were taken up with comments on his views; twenty-four letters and one sonnet. Some saw this as an opportunity to make their contribution to an established debate on the weakening effect that modern science had had upon Christianity. There were plenty of recent books on the subject – works like Charles H. Pearson's *National Life and Character* (1893), A. J. Balfour's *The Foundation of Belief* (1895), Henry Drummond's *The Ascent of Man* (1894) and Benjamin Kidd's *Social Evolution* (1894), while the issue had only just been rehearsed in a previous controversy in the *Daily Chronicle*, 'Is Christianity a Failure?' Initiated by the poet and journalist Richard Le Gallienne, this series of articles and letters formed the basis of his book *The Religion of a Literary Man*, also published in 1895.[9]

The supposed spiritual crisis obviously carried social implications but, despite the provocation of the election result, replies to 'Unknown Quantity's' leading question were rarely political, at least not in the parliamentary sense. 'The revolution, if one there be,' asserted a reader, 'is among the thinkers.'[10] No one disagreed and, on the evidence of this correspondence alone, one might have to conclude that in the summer of 1895 there was little interest in the idea that political change could come about through class conflict. 'Unknown Quantity' and his fellow letter-writers were more concerned with a shared consciousness, what they called 'the spirit', an idealistic vision that suited their transcendental view of literature. 'If there is any question on which a wise man will be slow to give an opinion', one of them wrote, 'it is the connection between literary and political phenomena.'[11] Literature was the most accurate index of the times only when it rose above them, a contemporary truism that only the literate could fully appreciate. The point was reiterated by the several literary personalities who shared their opinions with 'Unknown Quantity'. Not surprisingly, the Darwinist philosopher Grant Allen thought that the 'reaction' was illusory. Allen had recently made a notorious name for himself with a lecture advocating sexual liberty called 'The New Hedonism' in 1894,[12] followed by a polemical novel in defence of free love, *The Woman Who*

*Did*, published earlier in 1895. Distinguishing between fluctuations in political mood, measured quantitatively by votes, and an increased moral understanding, sustained by a permanent minority of serious readers and writers, Allen now stayed confident that 'the school of revolt' (Hardy, Meredith, William Morris) would continue unshaken.[13] Unfortunately, his attempt to explain that even the fate of Wilde did not affect his essential optimism never saw the light of day, as the portions of his letter referring to 'a certain lamentable trial' were, as he later complained, censored by the *Chronicle*.[14] Which left Max Beerbohm to invoke Wilde's sacrifice with a fit of general disdain. In Beerbohm's view, the reaction of 1895 was simply a revival of philistinism in a public that, even at the height of the Aesthetic craze, had never much cared for art.

> The tragedy and ruin of the most distinguished of the aesthetes has given the public its cue. 'Art,' it cries, 'is all wickedness.' It dives into the pages of the genial Nordau. 'Art,' it cries, 'is all madness. We were quite right after all. . . .' Now this, it seems to me, is the extent of the revolution – that the public need pretend no longer.[15]

Soon after that the controversy died out or, more likely, was brought to a halt by the paper. It serves now as a plausible guide to current attitudes towards modern art halfway through the nineties, a time when the 'correspondence column' was widely offered as providing the ideal structure for democratic debate, a newspaper forum which would allow individuals to express themselves in a manner entirely appropriate to modern conditions. That invitation was to be kept open long after the 1890s. Writing in the 1930s, Walter Benjamin was still brooding on the significance of the correspondence column. It was, he thought, a siphon for feelings that had been stirred up by the literary confusion of the modern newspaper in the first place.

> Its content eludes any form of organisation other than that which is imposed upon it by the reader's impatience. And this impatience is not just the impatience of the politician waiting for information or that of the speculator waiting for a tip-off; behind it smoulders the impatience of the outsider, the excluded man who yet believes he has a right to speak out in his own interest. The editorial offices have long ago learned to exploit the fact that nothing binds the reader to his newspaper so much as this impatience, which demands fresh nourishment every day; they exploit it by continually throwing open new columns for reader's questions, opinions and protests. Thus the unselective assimilation of facts goes hand in hand with an

unequally unselective assimilation of readers, who see themselves elevated instantaneously to the rank of correspondents.[16]

Already on the letters pages of nineties newspapers Benjamin's 'impatience' was meeting with reassurance. 'Unknown Quantity' had chosen his name wisely. He could be almost anyone. Genial yet concerned, confident yet perturbed, informed yet dispassionate, he made instinctive connections between different areas of behaviour and different sections of society. Ever ready with opinions and generous with generalizations he was, above all, a man who knew how to create a stir in the press, and, at the same time, how to damp it down.

### 'LUMPING THINGS TOGETHER'

Expansion of the correspondence column was one of the consciously 'democratic' policies adopted by the liberal editors of the self-styled New Journalism as they set about remodelling the British press in the 1880s and early 1890s. The professed intentions of such men – they include, most famously, W. T. Stead of the *Pall Mall Gazette*, T. P. O'Connor of the *Star* and H. W. Massingham of the *Daily Chronicle*[17] – are contained in Stead's high-minded pronouncement that it was the duty of the press 'to interpret the knowledge of the few to the understanding of the many',[18] an ambition that had as its ostensible aim the widening of the intellectual franchise for political ends. Consequently the ideal of reader participation came to play an important part in the propaganda that the New Journalists put forward about themselves.

H. G. Wells went so far as to prophesy that the correspondence columns would become 'the most ample, the most carefully collected, and the most highly paid of all developments in the paper',[19] anticipating a revolutionary future when the newspaper would become a kind of corporate text, and the divisions between producer and consumer, editor and contributor, reader and writer would finally dissolve.

This was already unrealistic because for some time 'minor "advanced" figures and newspaper editors' had, as a modern historian unquestioningly asserts, 'co-operated to whip up heated debate in the correspondence columns of popular newspapers, in order to advertise themselves and their views, and to boost circulations'.[20] So skilled were they at exploiting their readers' 'impatience' to participate, that editors would on occasion issue bogus invitations. It was not unknown for specially composed letters, full of 'controversy', to be inserted in the columns simply in the hope of provoking a large response. In the early days of the *Star* A. B. Walkley wrote to Shaw mentioning William Archer's idea

'that I should aim at starting topics from time to time likely to provide a correspondence; a capital way of getting one's copy done *gratis*. Your name occurs to me as that of the greatest Impolite Letter Writer of the day ... Is there any topic you would like to write about? If so, I would insert the necessary paragraph next week'.[21]

The correspondence columns also presented opportunities to professional writers. Wilde, in particular, was adept at finding himself drawn protestingly into epistolary debate – a device for the generation of personal publicity that he developed for his American visits in the early 1880s, and refined in a long series of letters objecting to the response to *Dorian Gray* in 1890.[22] In short, in order to give readers the illusion that they were writers (and to drum up some free column inches), writers would sometimes pretend to be readers. It is more than likely that in the editorial offices of the *Daily Chronicle* 'Unknown Quantity' was in truth a well-known character.

Whether 'Unknown Quantity' was a professional writer or a bona fide reader, he undoubtedly constructed his argument in the manner of someone who had seriously studied the papers: that is to say, through an aggregate of examples. The unlucky coincidences of 1895 – in particular, the publication of Max Nordau's *Degeneration* and the fall of Wilde – did much to encourage this cumulative way of thinking. So, for instance, the *Westminster Gazette* could write at the time of Wilde's disgrace: 'In view of recent events, Nordau's summing up of his case against Oscar Wilde as the typical English "decadent" comes with all the force of a fulfilled prophecy.'[23] Or, rather, as a fortunate opportunity for newspaper intervention.

What the journalists saw in *Degeneration* was an intoxicating if distorting reflection of their own habit of arguing by collocation. For all its special notoriety Nordau's tirade was part of an intellectual current, widespread in Continental Europe, deriving from the example of the earliest Darwinists, Herbert Spencer in particular, which purported to study social misfits – the insane, the suicidal and the criminally inclined – in the context of the modern environment as well as of heredity.[24] Nordau's Continental predecessors, all of whom he acknowledged, included Krafft-Ebing, Ribot, Féré, Morel, Charcot and the Italian criminologist Cesare Lombroso – to whom *Degeneration* was, in fact, dedicated. English influences were less in evidence, though Henry Maudsley, the psychologist and theoretician of 'criminal insanity', was cited on occasion.

Nordau's book was distinguished by its apocalyptic tone and the originality of its chosen sample. By piling instance upon instance its author sought to demonstrate a universal thesis that modern artists were driven by pathological needs to portray in their work only the ugly and vicious aspects of life, an abnormal impulse which they then attempted to conceal with the fraudulent 'Aesthetic' tenet that art had nothing to do with ethics. It's true that Nordau pursued this theory with obsessive vigour ('I do not share Lombroso's opinion that highly-gifted degenerates are an active force in the progress of mankind'),[25] but *Degeneration*, with its insistence upon the close ties between biological behaviour and social conduct, between technology and psychology, between deviancy and a moral vacuum, seemed at the time to be interestingly extreme rather than woefully eccentric. And it made at least one strong appeal to empirical evidence: there had indeed been a massive increase in the possibilities of communication in the nineteenth century, and one of the most obvious examples was the modern newspaper, with its widening circulation, its competitive spirit and its built-in ephemerality. How these developments related to the products and personalities of artists was, of course, quite another matter, and one that was to be the focus of prolonged and heated dispute.

Nordau's diagnosis of the present malaise had a double focus: the population of the civilized world as a whole, and the artists who offered themselves as its elite. Man's capacity for the production and dissemination of ideas had, according to Nordau, developed so rapidly that it had outstripped the physical capacity of human organs to adapt to changes in function. Everyone had suffered from the coming of railways, telegrams and newspapers, but the symptoms were most clearly to be observed in the art and literature produced by those who were more susceptible to the pressures because they were more sensitive in their natural organization. These, the 'degenerates', with their malfunctioning nerves and, sometimes, even their malformed bodies, were a 'morbid deviation from the type', as the strangeness of their art revealed. In Ibsen, Wagner, Tolstoy, Nietzsche, the Impressionist painters and above all in Oscar Wilde, the weariness and irrationality of modern 'progress' had come home to roost. 'Great wits are sure to madness near allied' – never so much as now.

*Degeneration* proclaimed its authority by cataloguing the world according to an impressive set of clinical terms – 'echolalia' (a compulsion to repeat words), 'graphomania' (an uncontrollable urge to write) and so on, and it concealed its simple binary system of sane against insane, healthy against diseased, with an endless multiplication of categories. Naturally the comment was made, time and again, that Nordau was simply participating in the very phenomena he was describing ('Let us be grateful to Dr Nordau for his display of graphomania. It is not every higher degenerate whose passion for writing had made him so entertaining a critic'[26]), and it was often remarked that his enthusiasm for his own ideas was itself 'hysterical'. In his reply to Nordau, Shaw demonstrated that the castigation of artists for their failure to adapt to society might equally well be directed at the failure of society to adapt to the insights of art, while Dr T. Clifford Allbutt, a friend of Thomas Hardy and a specialist in nervous diseases, spotted the other essential fallacy:

> To say that an increase of insanity is an indication of stress in modern life and to urge, the other way around, that the stress of modern life must be increasing insanity, is too circular an argument.[27]

Allbutt pointed out that according to statistics 'insanity' was more prevalent among agricultural workers than city dwellers, that syphilis was more common among soldiers and sailors than 'brainworkers' (Nordau had made much of Baudelaire), and that it was the health of the urban working class that was deteriorating rather than that of society aesthetes. But his most original claim was that the determining factor in the outbreak of nervous disease was not the condition itself so much as the spread of information concerning it.

> To turn now from insanity ordinarily so called, to other nervous maladies – to nervous debility, to hysteria, to neurasthenia, to the fretfulness, the melancholy, the unrest due to living at a high pressure, to the whirl of the railway, the pelting of the telegrams, the strife of business, the hunger for riches, the lust of vulgar minds for coarse and instant pleasures, the decay of those controlling ethics handed down from statelier and more steadfast generations – surely at any rate, these maladies and these causes of maladies are more rife than they were in the days of our fathers?[28]

Allbutt believed that improved treatments paradoxically drew fresh attention to the illnesses they cured, and that it was now all too easy for complaints to become fashionable. 'One of the features of nervous disease', he concluded, 'is restlessness, quackishness and craving for sympathy', and that 'the intellectual acuteness of many of these sufferers, the swift transmission of news by the press and the facilities of modern locomotion all favour the neurotic traffic'.

Whether neurosis was thought to be caused directly by modern communications (as Nordau said), or indirectly by the publicity they created (as Allbutt countered), it was generally felt that the sheer onslaught of ideas was a determining factor in modern life and that quantity obscured and synthesised quality. Commenting on Allbutt, the *Speaker* volunteered that contemporary pessimism should be attributed to 'the persistent habit of looking at things too much in the bulk'.

> It is a natural mistake, especially for sensitive people; and it becomes easier every day as the number of sensitive people grows, and as the press, with a view to their pennies, heightens the lights and darkens the shadows amid which the world-comedy is presented to us.[29]

Speaking for itself, the press freely acknowledged the temptation to simplify and magnify the processes of history, its own dangerous capacity to turn events into an exhilarating kaleidoscope of facts and opinions that could, at times, overwhelm the powerless and solitary reader. Even journalists could concede that in 1895 'looking at things too much in the bulk' had served to reinforce the pessimist's vision of national or global degeneration. *Punch*, which had made its own contribution to Wilde's tragedy, celebrated the event with 'a Philistine's Paean':

> I am not *quite* sure that I *quite* understand
> How they've suddenly found all our fads
>     are degenerate,
> Why MAETERLINCK, IBSEN, VERLAINE, SARA GRAND,
>     TOLSTOI, GRANT ALLEN, ZOLA, are 'lumped'
>     but at any rate,
> I know I'm relieved from a horrible bore
> *I need not admire what I hate any more.*[30]

The prime victim of this habit of seeing things 'in the bulk' and 'lumping' them together was Wilde himself. 'For many years past Mr Wilde has been the real leader in this country of the "new school" in literature – the revolutionary and anarchist school which has forced itself into such prominence in every domain of art,' pronounced the *Speaker*.[31] But the 'new school' was an umbrella label sheltering many with whom Wilde would not have cared to be seen in public. 'The new criticism, the new fiction, the new poetry, even the new woman, are all, more or less the creatures of Mr Oscar Wilde's fancy,' the *Speaker* went on. That was

*Another instance of 'lumping things together'. In a contemporary cartoon Wilde acts the ideal housewife while a cigarette-smoking New Woman gets on with her reading.*

too generous even to Wilde, and probably less a tribute to one man than to the rhetorical magnetism of the single word 'new'.

## 'EYE AND EAR AND TONGUE'

In the nineties, to be 'new' was to be challenging, because it was to promise or to threaten further change. The 'New Journalism' shared in this ambience, claiming to provide a form of communication that would contribute to the coming world. It did so on the grounds that its approach was personal: it spoke directly to its readers, and even gave them the chance to reply. An 1895 contributor to the modishly named *New Review* tried to sum it all up when she concluded that

> By the New Journalism, I take it, we mean that easy personal style, that trick of bright colloquial language, that wealth of intimate and picturesque detail, and that determination to arrest, amuse, or startle, which has transformed our Press during the last fifteen years.[32]

This was true, but insufficient. The New Journalism did have a certain influence upon newspaper style, but that was not what made it a novelty. As Stephen Koss says, 'What was new about it was the extent to which it evoked comment, invited speculation and engendered passions.'[33] It had ideological pretensions that set it quite apart from the 'Yellow Press', an American influence best represented by the *Daily Mail*, which of course it predated, as well as from the more contemporaneous *Tit-Bits*, founded in 1881. *Tit-Bits*, as its full title implies (*Tit-Bits From All the Most Interesting Books, Periodicals, and Papers in the World*), was an unashamedly opportunistic venture, parasitic upon an industry that was already undergoing considerable international expansion in the number and kind of periodicals and papers published. The essential feature of the New Journalism was that it represented that growth as part of the spread of democracy.

Which is why the earliest references to the New Journalism are permeated with a note of real alarm. Such hostility underlies Matthew Arnold's pointed allusion to W. T. Stead in 1887 (usually thought to be the first public application of the phrase), which arises out of an airy dismissal of 'the new voters, the *democracy*, as people are fond of calling them'.

> They have many merits, but among them is not that of being, in general, reasonable persons who think fairly and seriously. We have had opportunities of observing a new journalism which a clever and energetic man has lately invented. It has much to recommend it; it is full of ability, novelty, variety, sensation, sympathy, generous instincts; its one great fault is that it is *feather-brained*. It throws out assertions at a venture because it wishes them true; does not correct either them or itself, if they are false; and to get at the state of things as they truly are seems to feel no concern whatever. Well, the democracy, with abundance of life, movement, sympathy, good instincts, is disposed to be, like this journalism, feather-brained....[34]

Like his more famous admonishment to the literary critic that he should strive 'to see the object as in itself it really is',[35] Arnold's objection to the New Journalism – that it feels no concern for 'the state of things as they truly are' – seems to assume an absolute criterion for truth that makes no allowances for either individual subjectivity or corporate disagreement. His edicts on the press betray a characteristic refusal to weigh what he saw as the vulgarity of its democratic manner, and its sheer circulation, against the gains in expressive freedom and general awareness its proponents claimed.

Sometimes the complaint was made that too many cheap words were in evidence, as if language were a coinage that could be debased, made lightweight, through over-production. And indeed that metaphor had its basis in economic reality, since the key to the expansion and multiplication of the publications lay in reduced costs. There were several factors at work. First, the introduction of web rotary presses in the 1860s, which reduced labour (though they required a large initial investment), and then, later, in the 1890s, of mechanical typesetting. Secondly, changes in the cost of paper brought on by changes in taxation and the shift in raw material from rags and esparto to cheap wood-pulp. In addition there were reductions in the costs of telegraphy and of advertisement. The increase in the number of new publications had more to do with basic changes in the economics of newspaper manufacture than the increase in potential new readers had to do with the Education Act of 1870 – whatever Matthew Arnold may have thought, or feared.[36]

In the early 1880s London already had six morning papers: *The Times*, the *Morning Post*, the *Standard*, the *Daily Telegraph*, the *Daily Chronicle*, the *Daily News*, and four evening papers: the *Globe*, the *Evening Standard*, and the so-called 'Clubland' papers, the *Pall Mall Gazette* and the *St James's Gazette*. These were joined by the *Evening News* (1881), the *Star* (1887), and another 'Clubland' paper, the *Westminster Gazette* (1892).[37] It's said that by the end of the century a London journalist had two dozen daily outlets from which to choose, many of them new or at least refurbished. There was also a considerable increase in the number of monthly and quarterly journals. *Macmillan's Magazine* (1859), the *Cornhill* (1860), the *Fortnightly Review* (1865), the *Contemporary Review* (1866), the *Nineteenth Century* (1877) and the *National Review* (1883) joined the much longer established *Edinburgh*, *Quarterly* and *Westminster* reviews. Then there were the intellectual weeklies: the *Saturday Review*, the *Athenaeum*, the *Speaker*, the *Spectator*; the illustrated periodicals: the *Sketch*, the *Graphic*, *Black and White*, the *Illustrated London News*; and, a symptomatic market development, new titles like *The Bookman* and *The Studio*, aimed at an audience of literate customer–enthusiasts.

And changes in the economics of production not only increased the number of titles but, in some instances, reduced the retail price or caused alterations in format:

> The halfpenny paper, which in 1870 was a small evening sheet, of columns lifted from morning publications, by the end of the century was a self-supporting and profitable institution: the *Daily Mail* was sold at a halfpenny, and other national dailies were shortly to follow suit. Where papers were not reduced in price, the cheapening of paper opened up a variety of

opportunities – to increase size without an increase in price, to improve or expand the coverage of news, to be less dependent on advertisements, perhaps to adopt less overcrowded layouts ...[38]

Different publications served different functions and looked to different readerships, but the effect of the sheer demand for output was felt at the time – by professional writers quite acutely. The most painful testimony is George Gissing's novel *New Grub Street* (1891), with its cast of hacks, researchers, editors and aspirant authors, all of them trying to serve a number of publishing masters. Expansion challenged the resources of high art and low journalism alike. Holbrook Jackson has not been alone in hazarding some connection between *The Yellow Book*, which appeared in 1894 and the *Daily Mail*, which made its début in 1896; and as seeing them, in however unlikely a way, as market rivals:

> The one was unique, individual, a little weird, often exotic, demanding the right to *be* – in its own way even to waywardness; but this one was really an abnormal minority, and in no sense national. The other was broad, general, popular; it was the majority, the man-in-the-street awaiting a new medium of expression. In the great fight the latter won. *The Yellow Book*, with all its 'new' hopes and hectic aspirations, has passed away, and the *Daily Mail*, established two years later, flourishes. In a deeper sense, also, these two publications represent the two phases of the times. The characteristic excitability and hunger for sensation are exemplified in the one as much as the other, for what after all was the 'brilliance' of Vigo Street but the 'sensationalism' of Fleet Street seen from the cultured side?[39]

There is some truth in that, but the liberal New Journalism came to the fore at a slightly earlier time, when the need to divide up the market accompanied a growing centralization of investment and unprecedented entrepreneurial vigour. It tried to capitalize on the situation with a specific programme: with an appeal to the liberal values of the whole, with open information, democratic debate and consensus decision-making, in the professed belief that these were the necessary preconditions for progress towards a more just society. Though there was continuous disagreement about alignment with particular political parties or factions, T. P. O'Connor, editor of the *Star*, could quite plausibly maintain that 'in the domain of charity, philanthropic effort, amusement and society, we find common ground, however bitterly we may be divided on political questions'.[40]

'Everything that is of human interest is of interest to the press,'[41] declared Stead in 1886. The aim of the *Star* was, according to T. P. O'Connor, to be 'as readable and as humorous and as full of human interest as possible'.[42] 'In our reporting column', he wrote in the very first issue, 'we shall do away with the hackneyed style of obsolete journalism; and the men and women that figure in the forum or the pulpit or the law court shall be presented as they are – living, breathing, in blushes or in tears – and not merely by the dead words that they utter.'[43] This emphasis on human interest actually affected the nature of news, tending to turn reports into narratives, political events into human incidents, and their agents into personalities. So much so that it is possible now to claim that at the close of the late nineteenth century,

> the 'story' became the basic molecular element of journalistic reality; a structured nugget of information – the basic unit through which the reader was to be presented with events. The techniques of journalism became analogous to those of fiction, and lay partly in the ability to discern those elements which could be made into a transmittable artefact.[44]

Simple gossip played an obvious part in the creation of these 'stories' and the *Star* was well known for its front-page column composed of brief items, headed 'Mainly About People'. But there were several other ways in which the New Journalism embodied its own ideology within a structured format. They included the use of signed articles and banner headlines, and the development of features such as 'investigations' and 'interviews' which, when the technology allowed, were frequently accompanied by pictorial illustrations.

Each innovation made its own quantitative contribution to the 'human interest' of the whole, indicating the relative significance that the paper accorded to an item quite as much as the item's innate importance. The increasing appearance of signatures came at exactly the same time as journalists were asking for greater professional recognition, on the grounds that they possessed unique skills that were as valuable as, though perhaps different from, those of any other writer (the Institute of Journalists was founded in the 1880s). But in another way, the signed article was a typically double-edged advance, because it paid tribute to its author's objective expertise by asserting his individuality. The enlarged headline was equally indicative of human involvement, a spatial sign of emotional concern. Stead maintained that the journalist must sometimes print in capitals because 'if you print in ordinary type, it is as if you had never printed at all'.[45]

It was with the sensational 'investigation' that the creative possibilities of journalism were exploited to the full, at least once it had been established that it was feasible for papers to instigate events that they subsequently reported. The definitive instance was Stead's famous 'The Maiden Tribute of Modern Babylon' campaign of 1885, in which he set about demonstrating the need to raise the age of consent for young girls by actually purchasing one himself.[46] Stead not only lost some advertising[47] but ended up in jail, having set a cautionary precedent that went several fatal steps beyond his inaugural investigative campaign at the *Pall Mall Gazette* in 1883, which had followed up Andrew Mearns's 'The Bitter Cry of Outcast London',[48] a pamphlet protesting against slum conditions, with articles, features and correspondence.

The arguments against Stead and his followers were not obscure. There was Arnold's claim that they were not above misrepresenting facts, and there was the persistent feeling that sensational means debased moral ends. Stead's reply, echoed ever since, was that dramatic techniques – shock, suspense and crisis – were sometimes needed to keep democracy awake.[49] Be that as it may, the function of journalism was now being called radically into question. Was the journalist the finder or the producer of truth? When moral enquiry relied on rhetorical skill, might not it be thought that journalism was beginning to depend, like fiction, upon its power to persuade? Would the truth of a report ultimately depend upon the number of people who read it?

The pros and cons of pictorial illustration could be debated on much the same terms. First sketches and, later, photographs were presented as a means of enlivening the actual, making it present and undeniable, as if multiple reproduction was itself a form of verification. 'There is ... an uncanny fascination about the huge, almost human monster which seizes a roll of blank paper and in a moment transforms it into a finished, vital, living, universally read, illustrated print,'[50] confessed Joseph Pennell, one of the first artists to see the full possibilities of illustrated daily journalism.

More insidiously there was the interview, which Stead defended as 'the most interesting method of extracting the ideas of the few for the instruction and entertainment of the many which has yet been devised by man', and as 'a form of influencing public opinion' that 'supplied, as the phrase goes, a real want'.[51] Stead was by no means the inventor of the interview, but he did give it particular prominence, and he made considerable use of the device of interviewing famous people in their domestic surroundings.[52] In the first six months of 1884 the *Pall Mall Gazette* published some seventy-nine interviews, their subjects ranging from the Archbishop of Canterbury to Emile Zola. Stead boasted, with some justice, of the number of other papers that were following suit.

Of all the supposed innovations brought about by the New Journalism, the interview was the most 'humanizing' and, at the same time, potentially the most distorting. By encouraging the belief that every event originated with an individual and that public activities could best be explained by hidden motives, the interview was soon paying the price of its own techniques. In spite of Stead's stress on the educational function, interviewing was consistently said to breed a spirit of cynical curiosity in readers and to foster a dishonest ambivalence in inter-viewees, who protested at the invasion of their privacy whilst wel-coming the commercial or political advantages of a free platform.

The letters, the bye-lines, the headlines, the enquiries, the pictures and the interviews – the New Journalism used them to devise for the modern newspaper a 'miscellany' structure that reached way beyond parliament and the magistrates' court to accommodate sporting occasions and artistic events. All sections of the paper were, to varying degrees, treated to a more personal style of reporting that aimed to facilitate the reader's involvement. And the public underpinning of this reform remained the liberal creed that society could only develop as a whole and according to principles of self-awareness and self-restraint, and that the newspaper must therefore strive to become its daily offspring, equally organic. The press, as Stead poeticized, was to be 'the eye and the ear and the tongue of the people', receiving and giving, responding and expressing. Journalism must be a natural process for the redistribution of knowledge: 'A newspaper must palpitate with activity.'[53] Or, as Massingham, the advanced editor of the radical-liberal *Daily Chronicle*, wrote of the updated *Times*:

> A newspaper, like society, is an organism which has a soul as well as a body. Its sustenance is drawn from the four quarters of the globe. Its nerves run in delicate fibres over two hemispheres.[54]

Committed to progress, eager to represent the entire corpus of public opinion, the New Journalism in the early nineties should have become the ideal medium for the dissemination of modern ideas. Why, then, did it sometimes turn out to be the watchdog for forces immediately hostile to anything else that claimed the sobriquet 'new'? Why should some of the liberal press have feasted upon Oscar Wilde along with other less civilized organs? The *Daily Chronicle* is said to have 'used a skilful blend of liveliness, variety, seriousness, and thoroughness to make itself a very acceptable mouthpiece of advanced opinion, much read by trade unionists and the upper working classes as well as by middle-class people'.[55] Why then did it need, in 1895, to make space for 'Unknown Quantity'?


## 'PART OF WHILE APART FROM'

The shortest answer in terms of newspaper ideology, the longest in terms of their political history, involves various manipulations of the organic analogy in which the modern media are still so deeply implicated. In the late nineteenth century organic presuppositions were everywhere, and if, as was generally agreed, social progress was like some form of organic growth, then the newspapers had to appear to be part of it. And that claim to natural social function required urgent reaffirmation as parliamentary Liberalism lost its strength, and circulations wavered.

When 'Unconvinced' replied to 'Unknown Quantity' in the *Daily Chronicle* correspondence of 1895, he quite instinctively resorted to organicism to explain recent events. 'Coarseness, slanginess, noisiness and vulgarity,' he said, 'are as natural excrescences in the life of a people as the growth of fungi in the lives of plants.'[56] A related metaphor was adopted by another correspondent, who took a quite different view. The New Women, he wrote, were but a natural outcome of modern materialism, and therefore 'signs of healthy growth rather than causes of danger'.[57]

It might be incontrovertible that society evolved according to natural laws, but they did not always seem to be visible and their workings were always open to debate. The New Journalism had tried to establish itself through its appeal to one liberal version that depended upon majority agreement and a degree of equality among people: in a word, consensus. But most of the other bearers of the label 'new' were intellectual minorities – feminists, 'New Hedonists' (frequently a term for homosexuals), decadents and pessimists – whose alternative voices not only disrupted the confident tone of editorial opinion but actually undermined the papers' public rationale for their own existence. They, too, laid claim to the future, but according to other 'natural' laws: the laws of either 'natural excrescence' or 'natural outcome'. Their art, whether symbolist or realist, clearly said as much by turning its back on the normative view to concentrate upon the shocking and unexpected. It made good commercial and political sense for a liberal paper to show interest in this 'advanced' work, to borrow its sensational aspects, to capture the minority readership, while sometimes repudiating it in a show of egalitarian enquiry.

An obvious means was at hand: an initial attack, with copious examples, that would open up the correspondence columns for further comment. The master of this stratagem was the journalist J. A. Spender of the *Westminster Gazette*, who wrote under the name of 'The Philistine'.[58] In 1895 his 'controversies' were collected and reprinted as a book, *The New Fiction: (A Protest against Sex-mania) and Other Papers*.[59] Such made-up books were not unusual. Among the first was Harry Quilter's *Is Marriage a Failure?* of 1888,[60] based on the 27,000 letters reputedly sent to the *Daily Telegraph* in response to an article proposing that conventional marriage might not be appropriate to modern conditions. These are the letters, incidentally, with which the Pooters of *The Diary of a Nobody* (1892), whose marriage is, they insist, a notable success, console themselves in times of difficulty – some indication perhaps of the readership that the *Telegraph* was hoping for.[61]

The contents of Spender's *The New Fiction* amounted to a dossier of nineties obsessions: 'The New Art Criticism', dating from March 1893, an attack on the critic D. S. MacColl and his enthusiasm for a painting by Degas; 'A Rain of Geniuses', from January 1895, an exposure of the critical methods of Richard Le Gallienne; 'The New Fiction', also early 1895, a critique linking the New Woman novels of Sara Grand and George Egerton with Arthur Machen's fantastical *The Great God Pan* and Grant Allen's polemical *The Woman Who Did*. Spender was an expert when it came to 'lumping things together', seeing them 'in bulk'. In fact all that his targets really had in common were their apparent rejection of previous styles and their power to win the admiration of other young critics whose professional ingenuity rivalled that of Spender himself.

Spender was fighting battles about journalism in the medium of journalism. 'The New Art Criticism' challenges the right of critics to advance their own ideas irrespective of public taste; 'A Rain of Geniuses' maintains that an incestuous conspiracy of poets is intent upon boosting their own reputations by absurdly exaggerated praise for each other's work; 'The New Fiction' berates critics for their moral susceptibility. Thus Spender evoked the spectre of an insidious minority actually working within the New Journalism to corrupt its true purpose, like one of those diseased outgrowths that sometimes threaten progress. 'One of the chief defects of criticism just now', he warned, 'is a morbid fear of being out of date. It takes up with the new art which it does not understand, or with the decadent in literature which it positively dislikes, for fear some emancipated lad should pronounce it to be anile or moral.... In what respect, unless in pruriency, morbidity, degeneracy, are we 'advanced', when we become proud of our diseases, unreserved about our animalities, and boastful about our appetites?[62]

This should not, of course, to be taken at face value. Spender's background was one of Liberal reformism: he had begun writing for the *Pall Mall Gazette* when he was still at Oxford.[63] 'The Philistine' was simply the mask of a populist malcontent, one that allowed him to set in motion a lively, competitive and saleable scenario. At full strength, though, Spender became Thersites himself, and the columns of censorious disgust that he directed at 'advanced' behaviour went beyond merely discounting his professional rivals. They invoked a vision of profound disorder in the global discourse.

'Philistine's' views on the New Woman are a case in point. The objection is not to feminism itself (or so he says), nor does he wish to censor novels whose 'obscenity' he so vigorously denounces. What he attacks are the New Woman's efforts to monopolize attention. Repeatedly he flogs this male hobby-horse. Sex, he says, is only part of life: the New Woman wants to make it everything; social harmony depends on the views of 'the average man': the New Woman would subject him to her 'morbid analysis', her 'morbid egotism'. The argument is really about language – who possesses it and, more than that, who possesses the spaces it can occupy. And 'Philistine's' fit might have amounted merely to satirical bluster were it not that feminists themselves had recognized their need for publicity. Grant Allen's *The Woman Who Did*, for instance, confronts the problem by anticipating its own reception. Its heroine – significantly, a journalist herself – writes a book advocating free love. Allen invents some reviews to go with it, and has the *Spectator* pronounce:

Its very purity makes it dangerous. The book is mistaken; the book is poisonous; the book is morbid; the book is calculated to do irredeemable mischief; but in spite of all that, the book is a book of undeniable and sadly misplaced genius.[64]

To parody journalistic compromise and contradiction was one of Allen's better ideas, spoiled by an unctuous narratorial comment that 'the *Spectator* had noticed it because of its manifest earnestness and sincerity; for though the *Spectator* is always on the side of the lie and the wrong, it is earnest and sincere and has a genuine sympathy for earnestness and sincerity'.[65] Allen knew the world he was writing in as well as the world he was writing for, and it's this very over-familiarity that makes his own novel little more than a diatribe. No wonder that 'Philistine' could exonerate *The Woman Who Did* from 'that morbid analysis which is the special mark of sex-mania', even though he was 'in total disagreement with Mr Allen's conclusions'.[66]

Allen was a male journalist projecting himself as a feminist novelist, 'George Egerton' a female writer thinly disguised by a man's name. Egerton built press response into her fiction as well, but in contrast with Allen she has a wittily jaundiced sense of her identity as a female writer condemned to treatment by preening journalists. A story in Egerton's *Keynotes* (1893) features a Decadent critic, 'Larry Moore' of the *Vulture*, who sounds rather like Arthur Symons:

> one of the most wickedly amusing of men, prides himself on being *fin de siècle* – don't you detest that word? – or nothing, raves about Degas, and is a worshipper of the decadent school of verse, quotes Verlaine you know – well, he came in one evening on his way to some music hall.[67]

While *Discords* (1894) has a passing reference to the other type of critic, who has 'no temperament himself':

> The touch of egotism that one gladly pardons for the sake of the warm human blood flowing through the pages, the sympathy one feels lies in the writer's nature, offends some canon of taste peculiar to him.[68]

The journalist is the enemy upon whom the New Woman depends. By pitting the outspoken individual against the rest of the female sex, he can effectively drown her voice in silence. But how else could she be heard except through the papers? The Institute of Women Journalists was, we might remember, founded in 1895. In an article of the same year, Evelyn March Phillipps addressed herself to the highly topical issue of male ridicule, and imagined a journalist reading her while 'taking out his pocket pen and beginning in the time-worn strain "The New Woman has fallen foul of the New Journalist"'.[69] That is precisely what happened whenever women's demands to be heard clashed with editorial decisions about who spoke for whom. Phillipps took the orthodox position that it was unjust of the papers to concentrate upon a minority of extremists.

> Wholesome mockery clears the air; but to talk and write as if only a small and noisy band of womanhood were taking action, apart from the mass of womanhood, is to be grossly wanting in perception.[70]

This is the more conventional radical position, quite foreign to Egerton who, because she was well read in Nietzsche, made sure that her fictional heroines were pioneering women whose successful struggle for expression did indeed sometimes take the form of 'the triumphant doctrine of the ego'[71] so denounced by Spender. But for 'Philistine', needless to say, the prospect of a female Nietzsche remained irresistibly comic, allowing him to indict Egerton's New Woman on grounds of 'morbid egotism' alone – which was nothing less than the final judgement he had passed upon Impressionist painters and Decadent poets.

In the nineties, that single word 'morbid' – incorporating anything from the sluggish to the downright deathly – carried a burden of meaning greater than any other derogatory adjective. A frequent term of condemnation in earlier periods, it had by the end of the century achieved the definitive status of a cliché just toppling into parody. In 1893 Arthur Symons defined 'Decadence' itself as 'that morbid subtlety of analysis, that morbid curiosity of form',[72] while Vincent O'Sullivan contributed an article to the second issue of the *Savoy* entitled 'On the Kind of Fiction Called Morbid'. But paradox was never far away. 'Morbid? Of course it is morbid. Is there anything that is not morbid? Life is a disease: the moment we are born we begin to die!' remarks a character in a novel by John Davidson.[73] For Wilde, the word provided a running joke throughout *An Ideal Husband*: 'Marchmont and I have been married for seven years, and he has never once told me that I was morbid. Men are so painfully unobservant,' complains a fashionable aristocrat.[74] Yet, as Wilde most certainly knew, the word was also sometimes adopted as a provocative euphemism for homosexuality: as in the title of J. M. Stuart-Young's 1905 volume of poems, *An Urning's Love (Being a Poetic Study of Morbidity)*.[75] Wilde's usage may often carry this nudging meaning.

At a time when all the official moralities, endorsed either by science or by religion, trumpeted the positive virtues of vitality, progress and activity, to be 'morbid' was to be exceptional. 'Morbidity' was the enemy within, an internal threat to the organism whether it were society as a whole or the media through which society found expression. No wonder the word was so heavily laboured by journalists like Spender when they chose to attack artists and critics: minority views were to liberal opinion as morbid growths were to healthy development. Furthermore, 'morbidity' linked the artistic minority with those other social outsiders whose insidious activities corrupted the whole – the lunatics, criminals and sexual deviants of scientific treatise. Modern artists may not all have been, as Nordau was to argue, literally insane, but the lunatic still provided the best model as an anomaly. Nor did England have to wait for *Degeneration* to take up the idea that madness can be defined as an anti-social attitude.

It was the cornerstone of *The Pathology of Mind, magnum opus* of the influential English psychologist Henry Maudsley, first published in 1867 and revised in 1895. Maudsley offered a clinical definition of the lunatic that was based on two parallel sets of relationships, with nature and with society.

> Alienated from his normal self and from his kind, he is in the physiological organism: something which being a law unto itself, in the body but not of it, is an alien there, a morbid kind, and ought in the interests of the whole either to be got rid out of it or sequestrated and rendered harmless in it.[76]

As he freely acknowledged himself, there was a problem with Maudsley's definition. Man may be a social being, he is also a natural animal: he is therefore essentially 'part of while apart from nature'. Consequently,

> To describe a being as anti-social is not to say that he is anti-natural. Just as disease is as natural as health and to die as natural as to be born, so a madman, a criminal, an anarchist is just as true a social product as a philosopher or a saint.[77]

'Morbidity', in short, was natural – 'part of while apart from'.

Yet on the level of public discourse, that paradox could, if the 'morbid' minority were sufficiently articulate, be turned into a positive advantage, as Wilde, above all, was well aware. In 'The Soul of Man Under Socialism' (1891) he first listed the philistine's favourite words of condemnation: 'immoral', 'unintelligible', 'exotic', 'unhealthy', and then continued:

> There is one other word that they use. That word is 'morbid'. They do not use it often. The meaning of the word is so simple that they are afraid of using it. Still, they use it sometimes, and now and then, one comes across it in popular newspapers. It is, of course, a ridiculous word to apply to a work of art. For what is morbidity but a mood of emotion or a mode of thought that one cannot express. The public are all morbid because the public can never find expression for anything. The artist is never morbid. He expresses everything. He stands outside his subject and through its medium produces incomparable and artistic effects. To call an artist morbid because he deals with morbidity as his subject-matter is as silly as if one called Shakespeare mad because he wrote King Lear.[78]

Wilde's aim was to exploit, to invert, rather than directly to refute, the ideal of organic totality. He did so paradoxically, by insisting that it was the capacity of artists to express the morbid that guaranteed them a place in the universal discourse. This was a typically Wildean move, but not uncommon in the nineties, when many of the great aesthetic debates took their shape from the interaction between minority and majority, elite and mass, margin and centre.

Significantly, that same dialectical pattern of intellectual production was reflected in the phenomenon of the newspaper itself, which was centrifugal in its distribution but centripetal in its reception. Its very structure demonstrated a paradox of consumption. For it was, as Max Beerbohm, for one, well knew, the ambiguous gift of the wide-circulation paper that it granted its readers a sense of independence by allowing them to develop private habits of reading. 'I do not know what morning paper you read at breakfast', Beerbohm granted to his readers in 1910:

> but certainly, if you have read that particular paper every morning for many years, it has acquired a hold on you that none of its contemporaries could now relax. I do not know what is your method of reading it. My own newspaper I approach always through its outskirts, lightly lingering over the reviews of books on the one hand, and the law reports on the other, all the while listening to, but not obeying, the insistent call of the central page, which may or may not contain some tremendous piece of news to stir the very depths of my soul. Such is my procedure. Yours may be to envisage straightway the central page. Yours may be better.[79]

Beerbohm's polite concessions to his own readers sound genuine enough, but the fact is that, even at that late date, he was unusually sensitive to the effect of the papers upon contemporary consciousness. Announcing his imminent retirement from a literary career almost as he embarked upon it, Beerbohm had already declared, in 1895, when he was only twenty-three, that he would find imaginative stimulus within their protective sheets:

> Humanity will range itself in the columns of my morning paper. No pulse of life will escape me. The strife of politics, the intriguing of courts, the wreck of great vessels, wars, dramas, earthquakes, national griefs or joys; the strange sequels to divorces, even, and the mysterious suicides of land-agents at Ipswich – in all such phenomena I shall steep my exhaurient mind.[80]

More often the teasing structure of the paper escaped notice altogether. Writing in *The Yellow Book* in 1895, Hubert Crackanthorpe described a ritual that he had seen take place in a travelling circus where each morning the company doctor read out from his paper to the assembled company:

> He would begin at the top right-hand column of the inside page, reading mechanically almost right through the paper – the political speeches, the police news, the foreign telegrams, and the sporting intelligence – till he had come again to the advertisements.[81]

This scene, with its 'droll solemnity', struck Crackanthorpe as 'curiously pathetic', but he declined to follow up the implications of what he had witnessed: a mechanically linear reading of matter normally perused according to the particular impulses of an individual reader. And Crackanthorpe's blindness must be taken as typical; certainly few apart from Beerbohm seem to have been greatly interested at this stage in the effect of layout upon comprehension. There is no true English equivalent of *Un coup de dés*, Mallarmé's extraordinary poem of 1897 which responds to the spatial tension of newspapers with a complex arrangement of the spaces between words, an experimentation taken much further by Apollinaire, also fascinated by newspapers, and by Cubism as a whole. English literature had to wait for the seventh section of Joyce's *Ulysses* for anything comparable, and even then the parody is more to do with language than layout.[82]

What did take root among English intellectuals, especially the proto-modernists of the nineties, was a kind of nausea at the spectacle of newspapers which claimed to represent their readers as a whole while abandoning them as individuals to a daily round of triviality. Already in 1893 John Davidson's *Fleet Street Eclogues* were speaking of 'a traffic of lies', of 'Sweet rivers of living blood/Poured into an ocean of mud', of a benighted London where 'Newspapers flap o'er the land/And darken the face of the sky', where 'Beauty and truth are dead,/And the end of the world begun'.[83] This, in a way, was to be both behind and ahead of the times: Davidson's eighteenth-century vision of Fleet Street as a moral cess-pit wasn't to be entirely reinstated until a few years later.

In 1903, though, Arthur Symons could write in a review of a book on journalism that 'The newspaper is the plague, or black death of the modern world. It is an open sewer, running down each side of the street, and displaying the foulness of every day, day by day, morning and evening.'[84] So pleased was he by this review that Symons, who liked to open his books with a statement of intent, made it the prefatory essay to the collection he published in 1904 called *Studies in Prose and Verse*.

And he could quote his friend Yeats in his support: 'England, where journalists are more powerful and ideas less plentiful than elsewhere'. Like other Moderns, Yeats was to make the journalist a favourite whipping-boy, newspapers a concrete symbol of the heterogeneity that made up the degraded modern world. Symons differed from Yeats, however, in that when he had started out in the early nineties, he had been enraptured by his profession as a journalist, sometimes publishing two or three pieces in a single week. His later jaundice may have been prompted by his conversion at the hands of Yeats to a mystical brand of Symbolism which virtually demanded contempt for the mass; but it had a wider context as well. The press, Symons fulminated in 1903, was powerful because it was

> the fulfilment of the prophecy: that the voice of the people shall be the voice of God. It is the perpetual affirmation of the new law which has abolished all other laws; the law of the greatest wisdom of the greatest number.

At which point it becomes extremely hard to distinguish mistrust of the democratic spirit from hatred of its current agents.

A modern historian of the Victorian press has said that the difference between Northcliffe and Stead lay not in their methods but in the fact that 'Northcliffe was a successful entrepreneur and Stead was not'.[85] There is really no reason why the force of that distinction should have been any more lost upon their intellectual contemporaries than it is upon us – except that we have more evidence of its destructive potential. Once entrepreneurs like Northcliffe gain control then literary contempt for journalism, if sometimes as hysterical as its object, does at least become easier to comprehend. Economics certainly contributed as large a part to the weakening of the idealistically inclined New Journalism as they had to its emergence. The titles of the New Journalism had never been financially secure: Stephen Koss points out that the *Star*, launched in 1888 on £40,000, was the last economically successful radical paper; whereas Northcliffe was able to found the sensational *Daily Mail* on a mere £15,000.[86] Neither the *Daily News* nor the *Daily Chronicle* nor the *Westminster Gazette* made any money.[87] Liberal ideals, whatever their economic origin, did not in themselves pay bills.

It is possible that Symons saw the *Daily Mail*, with its bolder, more condensed style, as the illegitimate descendant of the New Journalism of the late eighties and the early nineties. Yet by comparison with later developments the split between the popular press and more respectable organs was still slight, even after the arrival of the *Mail*. Besides, Symons had never been much interested in politics, liberal or otherwise. What seems far more likely is that he was belatedly recoiling from an image of society in which his lone but somehow representative voice might be lost: responding to the use of the organic ideal, itself founded in economic growth, to insinuate consensus verdicts that he found menacing and distasteful. The New Journalism, while it had promised more democratic access than it could possibly have achieved, had done enough to undermine, at the same time as it made audible, any writer who attempted to combine professional energies with a sense of himself as a prophetic exception, the marginal voice at the centre of the paper. By the turn of the century, the newly created patterns of intellectual division were much more obvious: for Symons and his like the pulsing organism led inevitably to the corporate sewer.

Oscar Wilde, mirror and master of his age, might have been able to exploit the contradictions while exposing them, but Wilde's moment had passed in 1895, and with it the chance to manipulate the organic ideal with an entertaining contempt for the public that the public could hardly resist. By the end of the nineties it was becoming ever more obvious to less robust spirits like Arthur Symons that only with an accompanying hatred for the public itself, and not just for their supposed mouthpiece, the popular press, would modern artists and their admirers manage to advance.

'Unknown Quantity' was, then, right in his verdict, if misguided in his values. There had been no more of a cultural 'revolution' in the year of 1895 than there had been a political one. Notions like that live and die only in correspondence columns. What had taken place was more serious: a setback in the battle to establish a democratic relation between the community, its spokesmen, and the means of communication between them – the continuing process that Raymond Williams called 'The Long Revolution'. In 1895 to banish plump morbid Oscar was to banish, if only for a time, all the world.

# 2

# 'IT'S THE TREATMENT NOT THE SUBJECT'

### First principles of the
### New Art Criticism

Fine art is for fine eyes.

D. S. MacColl

## 'FIT WORDS'

The nineties were a perplexing time in English art. The inauguration the New English Art Club in 1886 had brought together young artists who were partially influenced by French Impressionism, and as much by Whistler, but who were already revealing a distinctly English cast. At least two members – Walter Sickert[1] and Wilson Steer[2] – showed promise of major work. Even so, Pre-Raphaelite traditions stayed strong, putting out a late flowering in the final work of Burne-Jones. The Arts and Crafts Movement of the 1880s, itself an outgrowth of Pre-Raphaelitism, lived on in the socially conscious work of William Morris and Walter Crane, while Charles Shannon and Charles Ricketts grafted *symbolisme* on to the English heritage. New media developed – the poster and the illustrated newspaper – and were taken in unpredictable directions by Aubrey Beardsley.

So much novelty inevitably brought with it some resistance from the public at large, or at least from its self-appointed representatives in the papers, such as A. J. Spender, 'The Philistine'. This external pressure compounded the problems of those serious critics who were already committed, by the sheer diversity of artistic activity, to a fundamental revision of their principles. Writers like George Moore[3] of the *Speaker*, R. A. M. Stevenson[4] of the *Saturday Review* and the *Pall Mall Gazette* and, above all, D. S. MacColl[5] of the *Spectator*, were faced with the challenge of endorsing recent art without losing their readers, of discriminating between individual works without betraying artists, of being both judge and advocate. Much later, these 'New Critics' were to be castigated for having prolonged a tepid Aestheticism resting on tired notions of 'beauty', at the very moment when art was starting off in revolutionary directions. But that was not how it felt at the time, when a basic belief that good painting must eventually find an understanding audience made them see their primary duty as enthusiastic explication. Mistrusting the principle that quality in art is proven by public consensus, they continued to insist that modern painting was like a natural language that the population had yet to learn.

The New Critics began by asserting that it was no longer possible to judge a painting by the moral intention which choice of subject implied. Whistler had already trounced that assumption in his 'Ten O'Clock Lecture' of 1885, but there were several last-ditch efforts to preserve the naive view. The New Critics rejoined the battle by shifting the emphasis of their writing from moral exhortation to visual instruction, from talent to technique, and often made use of slogans which stressed the indissoluble link between painting and perception. A phrase also employed by Mallarmé, 'effects not facts',[6] was one: a distinction often mooted by Walter Pater, 'character not proportion',[7] was another. Both became part of the rhetoric of critics who were as much concerned with setting out general ideas as with investigating the methods of individual artists. Of all their dicta, the most widely employed was 'It's the treatment not the subject'[8] – a premise which clearly indicated where the value of a picture might lie, though it still allowed for certain ambiguities: 'treatment' could refer either to the significant subject, or to the significant presentation of a morally dangerous one. In the first instance, it was commonly said that the treatment 'revealed' the subject; in the second, that the subject was 'dignified' by the treatment. In neither case was the critic saying that the picture had no subject at all. On the contrary, the stress on treatment implied that art was a means of representing a world whose essence could be discerned in its appearance.

Another way in which the New Critics expressed this idea was through their stricture that painting should on no account be confused with 'literature'. This idea, too, was fraught with ambiguities. A picture might be 'literary' either because it had an obvious historical reference, or because it seemed to invite transposition into words, or because it was anecdotal, preserving a single moment from an implied narrative. Then again, the 'literariness' might be a bias of the spectator rather than a quality in the painting. The New Critics certainly reiterated their hostility to the 'literary' over and over, yet their own writing often betrayed what looked very much like a literary approach of one kind or another.

The most notorious lapse was occasioned by the exhibition in London in 1893 of a Degas painting known as 'L'Absinthe'. It was to this event – or, rather, to the succeeding critical acclaim – that Spender, 'The Philistine', responded so virulently in the first of his aesthetic controversies in the *Westminster Gazette*. The object of his attack was D. S. MacColl, the *Spectator* art critic and Degas' most articulate admirer. MacColl, tempting providence perhaps, had referred to 'L'Absinthe' as showing 'two rather sodden people drinking in a café', giving Spender an ideal opportunity to assault a

*'L'Absinthe' by Degas as it appeared in* The
Pall Mall Budget *on 2 March 1893.*

fellow journalist and to exercise his own skill in polemic. 'We have',
wrote 'The Philistine', 'a band of critics teaching with great
unanimity a theory of art which either denies that art is concerned
with the beautiful or asserts that what a natural instinct calls
"repulsive" is in reality a standard of beauty'.[9] The gates then opened,
and the letters poured in. Twenty-six were published in all, including
statements by the painter Walter Sickert, the critic Harry Quilter
(victim of a newspaper skirmish with Whistler a decade or so
earlier), the illustrator Walter Crane, and the novelist and critic
George Moore.

What was remarkable about the great Degas row as it appeared in
the papers in 1893 was that everything was on show at once,
including the knots that the New Critics could get into when they
tried to praise paintings without primary reference to the reality of
the subject-matter or according to criteria dismissed as 'literary'. The

contortions of George Moore are a comical case in point, a curtain-
raiser to more extended intellectual spectacles. Moore's misjudged
tribute to 'L'Absinthe', part of his weekly column in the *Spectator*,
involved a prose reverie based on his own knowledge of the *vie de
Bohème* he believed Degas to have depicted.

> The woman that sits beside the artist was at the Elysée Montmartre until
> two in the morning, then she went to the *Ratmort* and had a *soupe aux
> choux*; she lives in the Rue Fontaine, or perhaps the Rue Bréda; she did
> not get up till half-past eleven; then she tied a few soiled petticoats round
> her, slipped on that peignoir, thrust her feet into those loose morning
> shoes, and came down to the café to have an absinthe before breakfast.
> Heavens – what a slut! A life of idleness and low life is upon her face; we
> read there her whole life.[10]

That in itself was enough to conflict with the central principle of
non-literariness to which Moore was committed as a New Critic. He
was even more unexpected when he concluded the passage with a
blatant piece of moralizing: 'The tale is not a pleasant one, but it is a
lesson.' A week later Moore was recanting absolutely, with a public
return to the extreme Aesthetic position which had come to be associated
with him. 'The picture is only a work of art', he swore, 'and therefore void
of ethical signification.'[11]

But it was the systematic MacColl rather than the shamelessly
volatile Moore that 'The Philistine' selected as his main target. Here
is the passage that particularly roused his ire.

> 'L'Absinthe', by Degas, is the inexhaustible picture, the one that draws you
> back, and back again... It is what they call a 'repulsive subject', two rather
> sodden people drinking in a *café* ... M. Degas understands his people
> absolutely; there is no false note of an imposed and blundering sentiment,
> but exactly as a man with a just eye and comprehending mind and power
> of speech could set up that scene for us in the fit words, whose mysterious
> relations of idea and sound should affect us as beauty, so does this master
> of form, of colour, watch till the *café* table-tops and the mirror and the
> water-bottle and the drinks and the features yield up to him their
> mysterious affecting note. The subject, if you like, was repulsive as you
> would have seen it, *before* Degas made it his. If it appears so still, you may
> make up your mind that the confusion and affliction from which you
> suffer are incurable.[12]

Writing in the *Westminster Gazette*, 'The Philistine' described that as
a 'rhapsody' exceeding even the 'great deal of nonsense' which critics
customarily directed at pictures.[13]

In truth, it was a fairly typical if somewhat high-flown piece of writing from a thirty-year-old man who was thoroughly acquainted with the dominant tendencies in Victorian art criticism, and was something of a painter himself. MacColl had two undergraduate degrees. At University College, London, in the late seventies, he studied classics; at Oxford, in the early eighties, he had attended Ruskin's lectures, heard Morris speak and become a favoured friend of Walter Pater. Where 'The Philistine' claimed to hear only empty pretension, others might have spotted a degree of conventionality: in, for example, MacColl's allusion to the man who 'could set up that scene for us in the fit words', much as Degas had found form and colour. Analogies between painting and elevated language were universally deployed in the nineteenth century and (a factor which undeniably adds to the general confusion of terms) they could even be directed against the assumption that painting was a form of literature. Ruskin held that 'painting is properly to be opposed to *speaking* or *writing* but not to *poetry*. Both painting and speaking are methods of expression. Poetry is the employment of either for the noblest purpose.'[14] Yet Ruskin's greatest enemy, Whistler, ended up using virtually the same comparison: 'As music is the poetry of sound, so is painting the poetry of sight.'[15] It was as if the 'poetry of painting' could mean whatever it was needed to mean as long as it exalted the art.

MacColl, at least, does seem to have been aware of the problems. 'By poetry', he had explained in 1892, 'I mean the bringing home of an image to the emotions by the arts of the sense: literature must do this by evocation, painting does it by direct presentment.'[16] The following year, under fire from 'The Philistine', he was obliged to develop the point further and to try to distinguish between 'poetry', a high ideal for painting, and 'literariness', a sure sign of inadequacy.

> The poetry does not exist if the technique is not sufficient to express it. And 'literary' is properly used to depreciate painting in which an allusion is made to a poem or story to bolster a feeble pictorial treatment of the theme. An allusion made to a sentiment to save a bad picture is just as much an evasion, so that 'literary' does not cover all the ground. A bad painter paints an association because he cannot paint the thing; a good painter paints the thing, and trusts to its beauty to compel the association.[17]

That was in answer to 'The Philistine's' contempt for his remark that in 'L'Absinthe' the table-tops, mirror, water-bottle and drinks yield up 'their mysterious affecting note'. As MacColl saw it, the poetry of painting lay in the painting of things, whatever they might be.

*'Boulogne Sands' by Philip Wilson Steer.*

But 'The Philistine' had also picked out two other aspects of MacColl's critical style for condemnation. One was his use of the terms 'metaphor' and 'symbol' when writing about painting. To understand why 'The Philistine' was so keen to mock this 'doctrine of symbols' it is necessary to go back to some seaside pictures that Wilson Steer had exhibited the previous year. 'Boulogne Sands' MacColl had described as

> the very music of colour in its gayest and most singing moments, and every character and association of the scene helps by suggestion in the merry fête of light. The children playing, the holiday encampment of the bathers' tents, the glints of people flaunting themselves like flags, the dazzle of sand and sea, and over and through it all the chattering lights of noon – it is like the sharp notes of pipes and strings sounding to an invitation by Ariel.[18]

An exhilarating effect certainly, but nevertheless, as MacColl had also explained, one that had been achieved by technical means.

> The sky of the beach scene, for example, if it be taken as representing form and texture, is ridiculous: it is like something rough and chippy, and if that suggestion gets too much in the way, the method has overshot its mark. Its

mark is to express by a *symbol* the vivid life in the sky-colour, the sea-colour, and the sand-colour, and it is doubtful if the richness and the subtlety of their colour can be conveyed in any other way.

'The Philistine', always speaking as one of the 'populace', was unconvinced, seeing 'disagreeable hard lines ... flecked with innumerable spots of detached colour'[19] where MacColl had claimed 'the very music of colour'.

MacColl was a sufficiently conventional Impressionist to consider light the crucial factor in perception as well as in painting, and to believe that the most compelling visual experiences involved 'the rain and beat of light upon things'. He thought that when painting recreated the effects of light it was mediating between self and object, operating much like the symbols and metaphors of verbal language. It seemed entirely appropriate, therefore, when writing about 'Boulogne Sands', to reciprocate with verbal devices – 'people flaunting themselves like flags' and 'the chattering lights of noon' – that were the equivalents of Steer's painting techniques.

Finally there was MacColl's theory of drawing. 'The Philistine' found this particularly risible, but MacColl, challenged about something he had

*Beardsley by MacColl.*

*Beardsley by Sickert.*

written in 1892 – 'for drawing is at bottom, like all the arts, a kind of gesture, a method of dancing upon paper'[20] – responded simply by reiterating his ideas:

> The essential element in drawing is the pleasure of describing on paper, as a dancer does on the floor, as a skater does on ice, lines and curves beautiful in themselves. The artist may proceed, if he likes, to represent an object by means of lines and curves beautiful in themselves. But he limits his imitation to the beauty of the object.[21]

Accompanying MacColl's rejection of the falsely literary in painting was a fundamental revision of priorities through which the muscular impulses of the artist and the material qualities of his medium played a major part in the creation of the pictorial image. What made MacColl a prime target for 'The Philistine's' literalism was his inability or unwillingness to adjudicate between two basic convictions: that the artist had an instinct for rhythmic patterns which might take on a representational element, and that the artist was unusually sensitive to the solid world around him. Sometimes MacColl pursued these two ideas separately, sometimes he tried to make them interact in dialectic. The subjective gift of the artist was the crucial factor and, in the early nineties, along with other New Critics, MacColl was much preoccupied with the ways in which the artists managed to sustain their moods of aesthetic delight.

'A HAPPY CONSPIRACY'

1893 was an expansive and elated year for the art coterie. The Degas row finally subsided in April. The following month MacColl was in Paris to review the Salons. Also in Paris were his fellow critic R. A. M. Stevenson; Alec Reid, the dealer who had handled the sale of 'L'Absinthe' in England; Joseph and Elizabeth Pennell, illustrators and friends of Whistler; Henry Harland, the American novelist, and his wife; Robert Ross, the friend of Oscar Wilde; and Aubrey Beardsley and his sister Mabel. They filled their time with exhibitions, romantic boat trips, meals and pilgrimages. MacColl visited Whistler's studio, saw Zola in a restaurant, had coffee at the Nouvelles Athènes (the very café which Degas had used for 'L'Absinthe') and once, at a Salon, glimpsed the man who had posed as one of the notorious 'two rather sodden people'. He also met Charles Conder, an Australian artist specializing in the decoration of silk fans, who was soon to become a close friend. Most of all, the English visitors to Paris talked and argued among themselves. Stevenson fell into violent discussion with Beardsley, whose art he found 'inimicable'.[22]

The Paris spring of 1893 is recalled in many subsequent memoirs, like the Normandy summer that followed it. From June to September most of the same crowd reassembled at Sainte Marguerite, a village near Dieppe. The Harlands were there, and so were Conder and MacColl, the painter Alfred Thornton and, for part of the time, the Beardsleys. Sickert was living slightly apart, in the fishermen's quarter of Dieppe, where, MacColl reported, 'he has invented three new and only ways of painting and devotes them to portraying the corner of a washerwoman's shop'.[23] Steer was to have joined the party but cried off upon discovering that MacColl would be there. 'If MacColl met God Almighty', he said, 'he would criticize Him to His face.'[24]

It was the summer in which the plans were laid for *The Yellow Book* and, in later years, it was remembered as quite literally Arcadian. MacColl swam, sketched, painted and wrote. He had been asked to contribute a preface to a book on Greek vase painting by Jane Ellen Harrison, and George Moore wrote urging him to review his collected essays, *Modern Painting*. The idyllic location provoked some suitably sensual behaviour. MacColl, probably with Mabel Beardsley in mind, 'had dreams of a Giorgionesque tea-party under the apple trees of an orchard'.[25] In the evening, they would gather at a small hotel for

*Satirical sketch of Joseph Pennell*
*by Beardsley, Paris, 1893.*

aperitifs. 'A romantic gateway without any gate gives upon a little lane', MacColl reported back to his family. 'We sit in a vine-covered tunnel or at a table on the lawn and in the rosy darkness the beds of white and violet petunias smoulder. On Sundays gay parties come over from Dieppe to lunch and flit about in the sun like great butterflies.'[26]

The friends also engaged in some primal games. One repeated scenario involved a threatened or fallen paradise. MacColl even found himself acting out a mystery play in which

> Mrs Harland, as the Lord, asked Adam (Conder), who had suddenly turned rather shy, to show Eve (Mabel) round the garden. This was trying for me, who was hanging downwards by my feet from the tree as the Serpent to whisper in her ear. Thornton with a broom played Gabriel.[27]

Conder had a dream in which he came to a place he thought must be paradise, but the Guardian Angel was asleep: his flaming sword extinguished, the Gates open, the path overgrown. He woke the Angel, who complained, 'No one ever comes.' Years later, MacColl wrote a poem in memory of Conder based on that dream, connecting Sainte Marguerite, 'sea-gates of summer, pearl and chrysopane', with the fragile illusions of his art.[28]

Sainte Marguerite was a wild garden, appropriate setting for a nineties fantasy of innocence penetrated by experience: a lost world glimpsed through present pleasure, a momentary yearning for permanent bliss.

The following spring, MacColl joined Conder at Giverny, where they 'bathed in the Epte, under the cavalcades of Monet's poplars, and saw Monet himself setting off one day trundling a barrowload of canvases, to snatch, in twenty-minute spells, the kaleidoscope of the sun's turnabout'.[29] Later that year they again tried to find paradise in France – at Vétheuil. This time they named their settlement the Abbaye de Thélène: MacColl, always morally responsible, was Abbot; Conder, permanently prone, made up the seminary. He fell disastrously in love with one of three American sisters staying nearby. Oscar Wilde was apparently also in the area, creating scandal with his bathing parties, while Alfred Thornton and Roger Fry were at nearby La Roche Guyon discussing art. Thornton was drawn to Fry because he, too, was dissatisfied with the 'naturalism of the later impressionists' and, like Fry, wanted to go beneath surface appearance, beneath 'the passing show of light and colour'.[30] They visited Giverny together but, says Thornton, despite the glamour of what they saw there, his companion was still doubtful, and compared Monet unfavourably with the Old Masters. Fry was of a younger generation, and already dissatisfied with Impressionist theory. At about this time he wrote an essay on 'The Philosophy of Impressionism', intended for *The Fortnightly Review* but never published, which, according to his biographer, would have earned him 'a position among the most advanced writers in England'.[31]

Imagining these 'pluperperfect and endless summers'[32] can help us to understand what, in contrast, MacColl and his friends were still looking for in art. It was if they set out to recreate the qualities of painting – light, colour, ease and vitality – in a pastoral life, with the corresponding hope that their own creativity would gain by the holiday spirit. The mood was all-pervasive. As Alfred Thornton recalls, in the nineties 'life held few problems. We were young, and, though we were hard-up, existence around us seemed assured, with British imperialism moving towards its zenith.'[33] Aesthetic hedonism suffuses their prose memoirs, turning recollection into a French painting: 'apples red and thickly in the orchards, and fields of flax burned blue, like another sky upon the ground'.[34] The summer idyll, most seductive of nineties' moods, casts a burnished glow over what was in fact an intellectual clique, in pursuit of an aesthetic that though based on the transformative powers of art would be sufficiently broad to encompass all its manifestations. After all, it was easier to believe in the importance of painting if you could feel that life would sometimes live up to it. The holiday pictures they produced themselves are always described as brief unambiguous moments. Criticism admits their fugitive mood with simple permutations of a small vocabulary, as if the writer were confessing his own disproportionate response to admittedly minor but vital achievements. Walter Sickert, for example, on an exhibition of pictures by MacColl held in December 1893:

> Mr MacColl evidently holds that unless a subject calls forth in you a thrill of emotion it is not worth rendering. There is in his work none of the depressing insistence on the merely boring realities of nature. Each drawing suggests a mood, and only a moment of that mood, a happy conspiracy of light and life and weather, in which the elements of form furnished by the skies and the trees, by the men and the beast, are only borrowed so far as they express the one idea which is the *raison d'être* of the drawing.[35]

The painter–critic shows his appreciation of the critic–painter by expressing his visual pleasure in a common language. Just as what MacColl enjoyed in Steer's 'Boulogne Sands' was a colourful moment, so what Sickert saw in MacColl's 'Whitby Harbour' was

> a charming impression of white boats in the sun, a white boat with a stripe of black, by another with a stripe of blue, by a third with three stripes of red, blue and green; the wharf behind, with houses, the blue jerseys of sailors, green balconies; a woman at a window with a red shawl. All the pleasure of the sun and the life and the colour, and no stupid anecdote hurled heavily at your head.[36]

'Log-rolling' was said by 'The Philistine' and others to be the curse of the nineties, yet one advantage of critical friendliness was that it allowed for enthusiasm without excluding – friends being what they are – opportunities for the telling reservation. Moore reviewed MacColl's paintings too,[37] just as Fry and MacColl both reviewed Moore's *Modern Painting*,[38] and MacColl reviewed the writings of his critical colleague R. A. M. Stevenson.[39] They all reviewed Sickert, and Sickert remarked on most of them.[40]

## 'THE HUMAN OUTLOOK'

In the middle nineties the situation changed. George Moore virtually retired from art criticism. Sickert moved permanently to Dieppe in 1898, depressed by the vicissitudes of his professional life in London. R. A. M. Stevenson published, in 1895, *Velasquez*, a comprehensive book which summed up his thinking on art in general by concentrating on a single great painter. And MacColl, who switched from the *Spectator* to the *Saturday Review* in 1896, continued with an intellectual inquiry that was beginning to lead him into ever widening circles as he struggled to embrace all manner of artists while maintaining his preferential distinctions.

The artists he most admired were still those who followed 'the natural procedure of the eye',[41] whose work was 'born of a strenuous marriage of the eye with fact'.[42] Among their ranks were Leonardo, Holbein and Velasquez, in his view the historical forerunners of Impressionism. Sometimes MacColl called them 'realists', sometimes 'interpreters', always contrasting them with the 'caricaturist', who 'coerces and distorts the fact in the interest of a personal fancy'. Examples of the 'caricaturist' were Botticelli, Blake, Hokusai, Lautrec, Crane and Beardsley.

Nevertheless, MacColl's attempt at stringency was countered by a new readiness to acknowledge the many determinants that had affected the evolution of painting. So, for example, in three long articles on 'The Old Masters' early in 1896, he put forward a history of painting based on the consideration that pictures were not only the records of visual acts but items of decorative furniture, their boundaries determined by architectural shapes: the pointed arches of the gothic style, for instance. Painters had had to find ways of answering to two demands: those that architecture imposed upon them, and those of their own perceptual field. The history of painting showed many solutions – dark shadows around the edge of a canvas or *vignettes* set in an open white space – but none so satisfying as that of the Impressionists, who dealt with the problem 'by following the natural procedure of the eye when it looks at a field enclosed by a rectangular frame – as, for example, at a view out of a window'.[43]

MacColl also took into account another determining aspect of architectural environment: the colour of walls and of furnishings. He noted the absence of large areas of blue in Renaissance work, attributing the preference for brown to its appropriateness for rich dark interiors.

The blue picture, he decided, was essentially modern, and suitable for the grey stone of public buildings. The danger, already apparent in the work of the Pre-Raphaelites and William Morris, was that painting might now be reduced to the simple arrangement of coloured patterns – unsatisfactory when compared with Impressionism, where pictorial significance had not capitulated to decoration. Hostility to 'decoration' always marked the outer edge of MacColl's aesthetic. External reality might be endorsed as in the Impressionist tradition, or distorted as in 'caricature', but external reality – call it 'subject', 'thing', or 'fact' – should always, in some sense, have been made visible.

A comparable trust in the capacity of an individual vision to comprehend the objective world governed the theoretical investigations of R. A. M. Stevenson. He was twelve years older than MacColl and from a different educational background, but in the nineties both men were in pursuit of the natural laws of painting which they connected with the laws of perception, and both were inclined to dismiss styles other than 'Impressionist' as deviations from an overall historical and scientific tendency. For Stevenson, 'angle of vision' was the fundamental principle of modern painting, while for MacColl, of course, the effects of light were of supreme importance. Unlike MacColl, Stevenson never wrote at very great length about contemporary French Impressionists, but he was a resolute critic when it came to analysing single great artists of the past, and the *Pall Mall Gazette* got it almost exactly right when it said that Stevenson's *magnum opus* would have been better titled, 'A Defence of Impressionist Painting as Illustrated by the Works of Velasquez'.[44] What Stevenson found in the seventeenth-century Spanish artist was a magnificent anticipation of the technique developed by French artists of the nineteenth century. His abiding tenet for success in art, founded upon Velasquez, was that the formal unity of a picture, its ultimate aesthetic value, must derive from the subjective view held by the painter, the structural harmonies being subtended by an angle of vision. Stevenson could, therefore, insist that 'the unity of a work of art should be organic and persuasive, like the blood in a man's veins, which is carried down to his toes',[45] and that a canvas should 'express a human outlook upon the world'. Reviewing *Velasquez*, MacColl condensed this into the technical rule that all 'impressionism', including that of Velasquez, results from the 'unity and order of impression gained by focusing the subject'. But for neither MacColl nor for Stevenson was mere 'focus' the sole source of unity, since visual attention is always controlled by feeling and those moments when, as Stevenson put it, the 'whole consciousness is absorbd in the eye'.[46]

In its commitment to the accessible pleasures of 'the human outlook' lay all the strength and the weaknesses of the New Criticism of the nineties. An appeal to Impressionism as the logical and pleasurable end of artistic evolution permeates MacColl's encyclopaedic *Nineteenth-Century Art*, written to accompany the fine art section of the Glasgow International Exhibition of 1901. Yet, for all its intellectual vigour, the survey concludes resignedly, with a note on 'the limits of painting'. These have nothing to do with space or depth, and are entirely concerned with the problems of rendering bright sources of light in their purity.[47]

And so, at the very turn of the century, MacColl found himself caught between his delight in the significant surface and his natural caution as to what it might be allowed to signify. Painting, he still maintained, revealed its subjects through its techniques. Courbet's 'realism', for example, is part of 'the hunger of the nineteenth century for the full visible beauty of an object'.[48] Monet was a scientific painter because 'what is sought as fresh beauty can be described as fresh fact';[49] yet even Manet had that hedonistic spirit so essential to the New Critical vision of art.

> Manet's mind is that joyful heedless mind of summer, beneath or above thought, the intense sensation of life with its lights and colours, coming and going in the head. Criticise his subject as insignificant and his views as superficial and you have said nothing to those who adore the radiant surface of the world and behold it in a glory.[50]

## 'THE CALLIGRAPHIC ACROBAT'

The sheer scale of MacColl's undertaking in *Nineteenth-Century Art* is a sign of the dangerous proficiency of the New Critics. Open-minded to a degree, written with a conscious sense of literary style that for all its excess is prompted by the belief that fine writing is a tribute to fine painting, MacColl's survey shows energetic enthusiasm about the past and the present but a kind of defeatism about the future. In 1901 he was ready, in fact, to call a halt to further experimentation. *Nineteenth-Century Art* is less complacent than it might have been but more resigned than it ought to have been.

For an alternative and much shorter guide to the critical dilemmas of the decade, his own in particular, there is the Beardsley memorial essay which MacColl wrote in 1898 for Serge Diaghilev's Symbolist magazine

*Le Monde Artiste*, published in St Petersburg.[51] This has a revealingly personal air about it, unashamed and probably justified, as MacColl had known Beardsley from the start of the artist's career and may have exerted some slight influence upon him through his essay on Greek vase painting drafted in Normandy in 1893. If Beardsley influenced MacColl in return, it was because he presented a formidable challenge to MacColl's hierarchies. Questions of 'mood' aside, Beardsley's medium, black and white illustration, should have meant permanent relegation to the inferior categories of 'decoration' and 'caricature'. MacColl's not entirely successful efforts to revise his system to allow for Beardsley reflect preferences that the New Criticism of the nineties never fully overcame.

MacColl begins with a retrospective. Nearly a quarter of a century had elapsed since the opening of the Grosvenor Gallery in 1877, when Burne-Jones caused such a sensation; years that had seen the dominating influence of Whistler, attacks on 'the literary' in support of realism and, most recently, excitement about the fantastical inventions of Shannon, Conder and Beardsley himself.

> With each little change of balance in the artistic centre of gravity, there is a disproportionate disturbance of doctrine. The modern Press aggravates such disturbances and the result is that the art of today, is overwhelmed with contempt and temporary oblivion.[52]

MacColl had experienced a good deal of press aggravation in his time, particularly at the hands of 'The Philistine', and his reaction had always been to insist that appreciation of art demanded some knowledge of the continuity of its history and practice. Of all the aspersions cast upon him in 1893, the most damning was the least well-judged. MacColl was never what 'The Philistine' accused him of being, 'a superior critic' professionally hostile to 'ordinary people'. He did profess, though, that understanding came slowly and needed 'a special endowment, assiduously cultivated'.

The Beardsley essay identifies the source of visual pleasure as the artist's nervous instinct, and reinvokes one of MacColl's earliest ideas about drawing: that it is a physical rhythm. Ignorant critics might dismiss Beardsley's execution as mere 'technique', but Beardsley has 'technical perfection'. Like a Japanese draughtsman, he makes us alive 'to the appeal of an action clearly, quickly, adroitly carried through'. Like Giotto with his 'O', he accomplishes a 'gymnastic performance', can 'do the trick with unfailing nerve and muscle'. Beardsley, says MacColl, was born a 'calligraphic acrobat'. His subjects came later. Pure arabesque was succeeded by 'significant arabesque', and then by 'half-realised forms with responsibilities to the logic of matter only at one or two expressive points'. He advanced to 'the grotesque' or 'caricature' when 'he drew hardly at all from nature; he elaborated witty remarks at her expense'. The 'mock world', this 'nowhere-in-particular world' was modern nonetheless because it gave 'the maximum of thrill, of nerve-disturbance, with a minimum of reason for it'. Beardsley did indeed die prematurely – his style was still ripening, getting ever closer to reality. The early work borrowed from the fantasies of Burne-Jones and Morris, from the later came observation: 'the maker of grotesque masks has turned to life and reality and found at its touch a new Hogarthian force.'

For an instinctive realist like MacColl the Beardsley essay made major concessions. It acknowledged that 'decoration' could cunningly allude to forms without representing them, and it respected the artist's satirical or 'decadent' intentions. That, however, was as far as MacColl was prepared to go. As he half-admitted, the innocent pleasures of appearance would always exercise their prior claim upon him. He recalled in the Beardsley essay a recent time when the favourite doctrine among critics had been that

> a man should paint only what was actually before his eyes in exercise of the imagination called for in painting. Painting accordingly ran to portrait, landscape, and scenes observed in the street, on the beach, at the theatre, under picturesque illumination.[53]

MacColl was obviously aware that he was being nostalgic here, which suggests that he at any rate had not been permanently blinded by the 'picturesque illumination' of the early nineties. It is just as obvious that he still had no wish to go beneath the surface. Degas, Sickert and Steer would remain his touchstones: the poets of the visible world, of street and theatre and beach.

In the nineties the beach was conventionalized pastoral. Light and expanse, sea and sand liberated the holidaymakers – and turned them into happy cyphers, as MacColl's famous phrase about Steer's 'Boulogne Sands', with its people 'flaunting themselves like flags', may well imply. 'To the dwellers in the town', remarked an essayist in *The Art Journal*, 'there is an inexpressible charm in being near the sea, in hearing the waves break with rhythmical sound over sand and shingle – in dreaming and allowing the mind to wander in a sort of floating reverie, whilst the body, under the influence of the ambient air, is wrapt in a languor which is thoroughly in harmony with the state of the mind.'[54] Imaginative art drew upon life's real dreams. George Moore said that the colour of another seaside painting by Steer, 'Children Paddling', was 'the optimism of painting ... what the drug is to the opium eater ... delicious, happy opium blue, blue of oblivion'.[55]

Paradoxically, an alternative source for pastoral reverie was the city – generally seen through the transforming gauze of twilight. Wilde went so far as to proclaim that while 'a policeman ... was not, under ordinary circumstances, a thing of beauty or a joy forever', he had once seen one 'in a mist on the Thames Embankment, lit up with dusky light ... Michael Angelesque in appearance'.[56] In the nineties, everyone writing about London echoed Whistler's rhapsody from his 'Ten O'Clock': 'When the evening mist clothes the riverside with poetry, as with a veil ... fairyland is before us.'[57] None quite matched its sublime imperturbability. 'The factory of brick and slate, pointing its tall fingers to the sulphurous break in the leaden London sky, seems to me not only beautiful but sensational,'[58] declared Sickert. When Whistler's 'Nocturnes' were exhibited in London in April 1892 they seemed to have acquired infernal tints. MacColl became quite fervid: 'Lamp-posts and railway lights that are read as topaz and emerald ... gardens of fiery flowers and fountains'.[59] Moore turned vatic: 'The vast blue and golden caravanserie, where the jaded and the hungry and the heavy-hearted lay down their burdens, and the contemplative freed from the deceptive reality of the day understand humbly and pathetically the casualness of our habitation.'[60] MacColl still thought that the 'Nocturnes' were 'recognizable' and 'poetic', but only 'because their blue and gold patchwork' had been 'redeemed out of a familiar squalor'.[61]

Whistler had painted London at rest, in its crespuscular pauses when the dying of the light softened and distanced the imminent world. Impressionists, even French ones like Pissarro and Monet, were to prolong the mood. One voice remained apart from New Critics and 'Philistines' alike, refused even to attempt to grow lyrical over misty treatments of 'the familiar squalor'. 'We cannot,' William Morris stormed as early as 1889, 'look upon the world merely as if it were an Impressionist picture, or be pleasantly satisfied with some ruinous piece of picturesque which is but the envelope for dullness and famine.' Impressionists who delight in the wreath of steam that floats from the funnel of a locomotive ignore the defiling coal that produced it. Yet whatever we see 'has some share of that sickness in it'.[62]

As an artist, Morris never engaged with contemporary subjects:

better, he thought, to set about transforming the world in reality with a tactic that coupled political activity with the making of ideal objects. This set him quite apart from the New Critics. Implicit in MacColl's criticism was the idea that the world could be changed with a lively eye and an active mind; whereas for Morris, the artistic imagination must penetrate the world with its alternative vision. Morris wanted a lyrical art that would vindicate the pleasurable labour that had gone into its making, and had no time for the supposedly realistic art that could disguise the realities of work. MacColl, on the other hand, tended to suppress the intellectual and moral effort demanded when artist saw subject and spectator saw picture. Artists had only their 'nervous organization', their 'poetic imagination', and their capacity for gesture; onlookers had only their 'special endowment, assiduously cultivated'. In effect the artists became disembodied: a retinal image, the trace of a hand; while the onlookers were confined to their training and to the evidence of their eyes. And, for as long as their subjects had to be pre-established facts, then artists would run the risk of becoming an arm of a conventionalized idea of the public. Treatment might rule, but subjects must still be familiar – to the extent, 'The Philistine' and the New Critics were at one.

# 3

# 'PRUDES ON THE PROWL'
## The view from the Empire Promenade

*Algernon*: Well, we might trot round to the Empire at ten?
*Jack*:     Oh, no! I can't bear looking at things.

Oscar Wilde, *The Importance of Being Earnest*

## AMATEURS AND PROFESSIONALS

As far as the papers were concerned, the main talking-point of the winter of 1894 was the state of the London music-hall. The *Daily Telegraph* started it all off but the other papers soon joined in, commenting and criticizing. Unlike some of the controversial 'topics' that filled the correspondence columns during the nineties, this one was firmly grounded in day-to-day events.

At the start of the decade the halls had undergone a process of rapid expansion as the shabby, suburban establishments, with their 'chairmen', their rough and ready 'turns' and their local clientele were challenged by the big West End theatres, the most celebrated being the two in Leicester Square: the Alhambra (rebuilt in 1882) and the Empire (a music-halls since 1887). These offered 'two shows a night' variety bills,

THE EMPIRE PROMENADE.

lavish dance spectacles and – less widely advertised – attractive venues for prostitutes. Both theatres were enormously successful, and their popularity brought disquiet even to those who were enthusiastic about the kind of stage entertainment they provided. There were many vested interests and continual battles about proprietorial power. The halls became too big a business not to carry a municipal significance and, like other kinds of popular diversion (including newspapers), they could be seen as the cause as well as the product of social instability.

So it was hardly surprising that when the *Telegraph* printed a letter warning that the halls were about to unleash a moral epidemic on the West End, the response should have been hot and noisy. The letter, signed 'Englishman', appeared under the heading 'Prudes on the Prowl' on 13 October and it spread over a column and a half. According to 'Englishman', it was time to stand up and be counted.

> The danger is this – that by holding our hands, restraining our influence, and silencing our voices, we shall help to destroy a good half-century's work in refining and purifying the amusements of the people, we shall turn the dread current of poisonous vice into our own domestic channels, we shall add to the nameless horrors of abandoned sexuality, and we shall drive to the despair of secret drink and loathesome death the poor, hunted, men-ruined outcasts of the city, who are trying with greater success than in any city of the world to behave decorously in public, and to preserve the last rag and vestige of their lost and stolen shame.

The piety of this rhetoric might well suggest that 'Englishman' was among the crusaders, on the same side as well-known 'Prudes' like W. A. Coote of the National Vigilance Association, and the well-known social reformer, Mrs Ormiston Chant of the Britishwoman's Temperance Association. Quite the reverse. 'Englishman's' argument was that any attempt to clean up the halls would be retrogressive, driving the women back on the streets: a feasible point of view, though one suspects a discrepancy between the moral pretensions and the worldly knowledge.

The music-hall did tend to put people in ambiguous positions of that kind. In the course of the 'Prudes' affair, it was members of the middle-class who championed proletarian tastes, employers who swore fidelity to their workers, men who supported certain female rights, a vicar who came to the aid of ballet girls,[1] and, in the case of Mrs Chant herself, a philanthropic woman who was spurned by her fallen sisters.[2] In a similar confusion of roles some of the most fervent admirers of music-hall 'turns' were elsewhere advocates of sombre 'problem plays': 'Ibsenites' even. In the nineties, the music-hall was a disorientating

place. You could see society changing before your very eyes; but the
longer you looked the less certain you became about where you were
looking from. It was a vertiginous atmosphere that was to make the life
of the halls an irresistible theme for artists and writers.

Although they offered carnival release, the halls were still beholden to
political authority, by virtue of the licensing laws alone – a vulnerability
that W. A. Coote and Mrs Ormiston Chant knew just how to exploit.
Three days before 'Englishman's' diatribe in the *Telegraph*, both
campaigners had been forcefully present when the Licensing Committee
of the London County Council met to consider applications for renewal.
Coote opposed the application from the Palace Theatre of Varieties,
Shaftesbury Avenue, on the grounds that it was featuring an
entertainment known as 'The Living Pictures' which was 'detrimental to
the best interests and moral well-being of the performers and
spectators'. Mrs Chant objected to the renewal of a licence for the
Empire, because of what she described as impropriety on the stage and
disorderliness in the auditorium. She was particularly concerned about
the Promenades, those areas of the theatre open to the public at large
and affording distant views of the stage where, for an admission price
of five shillings, people could relax during the shows and take
refreshments. Along the Empire Promenade she had seen 'young
women ... more or less painted, and gorgeously dressed' who 'accosted
young gentlemen'; while on the stage itself, ballets were being
performed whose 'chief object appeared ... to be to show the limbs of
the female performers'. An ally of Mrs Chant's testified that in a single
evening at the Empire he had counted 180 women 'of objectionable
character'.

George Edwardes, manager of the Empire, who was accompanied by
his lawyer, replied that anyone was free to go to the Promenade as long
as they behaved themselves when they were there. Moreover, because
the Empire always had full houses, 'any reflection upon the
entertainment was equally a reflection upon the spectator.' As for the
display of female limbs, the 'skirts of the *premières danseuses* are exactly
the same all over Europe ... There are the trunks which are invariably
covered with tulle, and finally there are the tights.'[3]

In the event, the Palace was granted its licence on the condition that it
would exercise greater caution over its 'Living Pictures', but the Empire
was told that its licence would only be renewed if alcoholic drinks were
no longer allowed in the auditorium and if the Promenade was
abolished. This was a more controversial request than anyone could have

envisaged, prompting the outburst from 'Englishman' and the subsequent 'Prudes' fracas in the papers. The *Telegraph* alone published 170
letters in a single week. Many were from pseudonymous correspondents:
'A Living Picture' ('Is it not better to have the women indoors rather
than out of doors?'); 'A Woman Who Has Not Yet Been Spoken To'
('As regards the music halls. I have visited them several times with my
sons, and have found them decorously dull'); 'A Publican and Sinner'
('The story of these prowling prudes is as old as that memorable one of
the Pharisee and the Publican'); 'A Benighted Foreigner' ('The "modern
drama" deals with far more risky subjects ... than anything heard on the
music-halls'); 'Another Englishman' ('The Empire affords me what I
want ... I can smoke my cigar in comfort and get just what a tired man
wants – relaxation and comfort'); and 'A Soiled Dove' ('It seems to me
that people imagine we lead this revolting life for our own pleasure ...
have they known what it is like to be starving, ill and disheartened?').
Others signed only their initials, like a regular visitor to the Empire,
'W.L.S.C.', who spoke on behalf of 'the average Englishman', and was not
shocked half so much by the goings-on there as by the 'spectacle of this
elderly woman dressed in "her prettiest frock" vainly endeavouring to
get herself "accosted"'.[4]

Meanwhile the directors of the Empire announced that if they were to
do away with the Promenade they would be forced to close the theatre
altogether, bringing unemployment to the 647 people who worked there
and hardship to a further 3,000 who were indirectly involved. Mrs Chant
countered that as the Empire paid a 75 per cent dividend on its shares,
threats of closure sounded very much like a rich man's bluff. The
workers were less sanguine. Many union meetings were held,
culminating in a corporate Sunday event at the Prince of Wales theatre
attended by members of the Theatrical and Music-hall Operatives, the
Amalgamated Society of Painters, the Theatrical Choristers Association,
the London Trades Council, the Amalgamated Society of Railway
Servants and representatives of the ballet dancers, scene-shifters and
cab-drivers. The performers' association, the Grand Order of Water
Rats, and Stewart Headlam's charitable Church and Stage Guild, also
made their protests against the withholding of the Empire's licence.[5]

Throughout October, up and down the country, Mrs Chant made
speeches and gave interviews in which she insisted that she did not wish
to close down the halls but merely to reform them. In mounting her
protest she had hoped to draw attention to exploitation and to 'clear
certain of the music-halls of the unclean features which debar decent

folks from attending and enjoying the performances'. For instance,

> I don't object to tights as such. I know that when you dance very vigorously
> you must not be impeded by clinging petticoats about your ankles, or even
> about the knees. If need be, I think I could devise a costume which would give
> this freeness and yet clothe the limbs, though I'm not one of those who think
> it is a shame to have legs.[6]

*Mrs Ormiston Chant.*

Some of the letters to the *Telegraph* warned that Mrs Chant might be
a particularly dangerous species of New Woman. It was reported that
the women's Pioneer Club had only narrowly passed a motion that 'the
attitude of some advanced women towards men' might be 'calculated to
ignore the best interests of the sex'.[7]

On the evening of Friday 26 October George Edwardes, having
unsuccessfully taken his case to the higher authority of the LCC itself,
addressed a packed house from the stage of his own theatre. After
announcing its closure he presented his entire company – carpenters,
scene-shifters and *corps de ballet* – and led the audience in a rendition of
'Rule Britannia'.

The Empire now dark, Edwardes moved to the courts, where the case
acquired considerable legal subtlety. Less complicated was what took
place on the night of Saturday 3 November, when Edwardes reopened
the Empire after carrying out the minimum of alterations by simply
portioning off the Promenade. At the close of the evening's

entertainment a group of aristocratic young men, Winston Churchill among them, made a sudden foray and destroyed the makeshift partition with sticks and umbrellas. This, it was agreed, advanced no one's cause, but the case of the Empire Promenade dragged on until even the papers grew weary of it.[8] It had been passionate enough while it lasted, and there were few interested parties who had not had their say. Politics was everywhere involved, for while Mrs Chant was far more astute than the opposition allowed, her critics were rather more cautious than they could afford to admit.

Here was no ordinary prude, but an articulate middle-class woman who, despite her arrogance in assuming that working people should be protected from themselves, obviously had a genuine concern for their economic as well as their moral welfare. Mrs Chant certainly obliged her critics to adopt a more complacent tone than was reasonably warranted

*A music-hall proprietor.*

by the plain facts of the case. Shaw, for one, whose public argument against Mrs Chant was characteristically mischievous. 'You can't have a better example of democracy than the Empire case,' he averred. 'Here is Mrs Chant, who is not more powerful than anyone else, and she flounces in and floors the whole County Council. The anti-Chants took up a stupid attitude, and became abusive, whereas they only had to work up their own side to the same extent, and with equal honesty and dignity, in

order to have precisely the same chance of carrying the day.'⁹ Although
he later used her as a model for the heroine of *Candida* (and Headlam as
a basis for her husband, the Reverend Morell),¹⁰ in 1894 he ingeniously
exploited Mrs Chant's discovery that the Empire prostitutes could earn
comparatively large sums of money. If this were true, he said, it was
in direct contrast to the poverty of most working-class women and
provided entirely sensible grounds for embracing the profession. Shaw's
enthusiasm for the halls was fairly limited, and his reasoning in this
instance is similar to the underlying thesis of his play *Mrs Warren's
Profession*, written in 1893: everyday society abuses women, therefore
prostitution is both symptom and escape. If society were to change
overall, bringing economic equality between ordinary women and
women like Mrs Chant, then the relatively minor problem of
prostitution would disappear. Meanwhile the intelligence of those who
practise it is to be respected.¹¹

Shaw's matter-of-fact tone may have been intended to shock but his
personal difficulty in allowing for the feelings of the women he claimed
to speak for was presumably unconscious. Many of the male arguments
against Mrs Chant's 'puritanism' relied equally heavily upon evasive
tactics. Arthur Symons's statement, for instance, made in a letter to the
*Pall Mall Gazette*, that in comparison with the Continental halls, where
prostitution was actually encouraged, and even the dancers openly
solicited the audience, the Empire was the 'most genuinely artistic and
the most absolutely unobjectionable that I know'.¹²

Symons protested too much. Though he could truthfully claim to have
made 'a special study of musical entertainments of every kind', his boast
of expertise undoubtedly jarred with his plea of innocence. He tried to
cover himself by asserting professional status. 'I have visited the Empire
on average about once a week for the last year or two in my function as
critic for several newspapers,' he told the *Pall Mall Gazette*, 'and I must
say that whenever I've had occasion to stand in the Promenade I have
never in a single instance been accosted by a woman.'

This was to play upon a technicality, because it was a convention of
the Empire that women never approached potential customers but
simply placed themselves at conspicious points. Symons knew full well
that the halls were the scene of sexual encounter, a secret he kept badly
by endlessly celebrating his own assignations in poems and essays.
Sometimes he argued that reforming the halls would make no difference
to the problem of prostitution: 'Is not human nature human nature, and
are not the streets the streets, and is not Piccadilly as convenient a

rendez-vous as the Empire?'[13] Sometimes, almost in the same breath, he would turn quite evangelical. The repressive legislation advocated by Mrs Chant would merely delay 'that permanent improvement which can be obtained only by influencing men and women to desire and aim at the elimination of animality and the development of the fair humanities that make life worth really living'.

Symons's writing on the halls often veers between these two poles: tolerance of natural proclivities and admiration for artistic expertise. A similar ambivalence is reproduced in the way that he presents himself as both participant and observer. Writing as a professional journalist he liked to describe himself as an 'amateur', intending the word in its precise or French sense of an unfettered devotee. He praised an act because it gave 'a new sensation to even the most hardened amateur of acrobatics',[14] and claimed that 'to the amateur of what is more artificial in the art of illusion there is nothing so interesting as a stage rehearsal'.[15] In this special sense the 'amateurs' of the music-hall included, along with Symons himself, Beerbohm, Shaw and the theatre critic A. B. Walkley, but not Thomas Hardy, who responded with a blunt dismissal. 'The dancing girls are nearly all skeletons,' he remarked after a visit to the Empire in 1892. 'One can see drawn lines and puckers in their young flesh. They should be penned and fattened for a month to round out their beauty.'[16] Nor, for that matter, should the poet John Davidson be counted an 'amateur', despite his authorship of a volume called *In A Music-Hall*. Davidson's use of the halls is mainly satiric: the true 'amateur', though highly knowledgeable, could always have his enthusiasm reawakened. He remained, in his way, an innocent.

Indeed the very professionalism of the halls was one of the things that most fascinated the 'amateur'. Mrs Chant had unquestionably demonstrated that sex as well as art was sold there, directly through prostitution and vicariously through performance, and there was more to it than that. She had also, if inadvertently, ruffled a central myth, the disarming principle that, as Symons famously put it: 'In a music-hall the audience is a part of the performance.'[17]

## MIRRORS AND PROMENADES

One of Mrs Chant's arguments was that because the stage of the Empire could be ignored from the Promenade, then the Promenade must serve some function unconnected with the performance – which it did. The 'amateurs', united in their opposition to her campaign, were also fascinated by the marginal location of the Promenade which, though clearly separated from the audience area, nevertheless offered them *frissons* that they considered to be a part of the Empire experience. After all, though they went to the music-halls looking for all that was vibrant in contemporary life, for what Symons called 'novelties', they were aware that the entertainment could be almost too revealing. The traditional theatrical process whereby the stage 'mirrors' its audience was reinvigorated by the kind of show that the new halls provided, even to the point where the 'amateur' began to sense a reversal of roles: the performance coming to look like a ghostly embodiment of his life, his life beginning to feel like a performance. The best known instance is Arthur Symons's poem 'Prologue', with its concluding stanza:

> My life is like a music-hall,
>   Where, in the impotence of rage,
> Chained by enchantment to my stall,
>   I see myself upon the stage
> Dance to amuse a music-hall.[18]

The Empire, however, was so structured that it offered not one but two relationships: the metaphorical mirror of the performance was actually reversed and replaced in the Promenade, where the walls were embellished by huge expanses of glass. Provided by a management anxious to persuade the customers of the glamour and scale of its enterprise, these mirrors were so plentiful and so dominating that they could easily reinforce a mood of introspection in an already self-conscious 'amateur'. If he turned from looking at the stage he was surrounded by reflections of himself. In his listless poem 'At the Empire', Theodore Wratislaw allows the two areas, stage and Promenade, to coalesce in a single mind, uniting spectator and performer. The poem begins in the Promenade, where it is the prostitutes and their customers who are performing 'the changeless programme':

> The low and soft luxurious promenade,
> Electric-light, pile-carpet, the device
> Of gilded mirrors that repeat you thrice;
> The crowd that lounges, strolls from yard to yard;
>
> The calm and brilliant Circes who retard
> Your passage with the skirts and rouge that spice
> The changeless programme of insipid vice,
> And stun you with a languid strange regard...[19]

In the second part the poet turns to the stage, which takes on the same qualities of 'insipid vice' and illusion, and rediscovers a double bind so characteristic of the nineties. A diversion initially promising relief from the tedium of ordinary life quickly turns out to be a chimera:

> Ah! what are these, the perfume and the glow,
> The ballet that coruscates down below,
> The glittering songstress and the comic stars,
>
> Ah! what are these, although we sit withdrawn
> Above our sparkling tumblers and cigars,
> To us so like to perish with a yawn?

The capacity to be stunningly bored was one of the prime qualifications of the nineties' poet that went with a certain indulgent self-regard and a fixation with entrancing iridescent surfaces. The music-hall satisfied these 'decadent' desires and the 'amateurs' actually competed among themselves in their possessive attitudes to the Empire. Wratislaw accused Symons of being lukewarm in its defence, but soberly wrote to the *Pall Mall Gazette* to 'corroborate him in saying that I never have been accosted in that Promenade by women'.[20]

As a regular critic of the halls Symons, unlike Wratislaw, had a professional obligation to pronounce on the subject. In any case, he enjoyed his job. Returning to the Empire after a gap in 1893, he was delighted by the welcome he received.

It was 'the reappearance of Mr. Arthur Symons in his favourite corner', to vary slightly the phraseology of the play-bills ... I expected a good reception, and I was not disappointed. Five minutes after the curtain had gone up, I heard my name, very audibly pronounced, on the stage; and from then to the end, I had all I could do to catch people's eyes, several at once, like a juggler.[21]

A pleasure in being spotted from the stage, a furtive affinity that made the spectator feel like 'a juggler', became a major element in the erotic excitement that Symons found at the halls. Consequently he always took great care where he sat. At the Empire it was a box stall, at five shillings, cheaper than the 7s. 6d. stalls, though unreserved. At the Alhambra, there was a front-row seat 'always at my disposal, how thoroughly I appreciated its privileges, how regularly I occupied it'.[22]

Yet the delight in being a regular fitting was countered by a nauseous sexual mood that recurs throughout his music-hall poems.

*The Alhambra chorus, 1893.*

The glittering ballet curves and winds
    Bewildering broideries of heat;
    I feel the weariness of feet,
And how the footlights' mirror blinds
The aching eyeballs soaked with heat.

Here in the stalls I sit and sigh
    For the renewal of the sea;
    I hear the cool waves calling me,
Where wave to cool wave makes reply
On the Mediterranean sea.[23]

There were times, though, when Symons succeeded in prolonging his vicarious sexual pleasure by retiring to the Promenade. 'It amuses me,' he confessed in 1893 in the *Sketch*, 'sometimes to sit at the back of the Promenade, and undistracted by my somewhat too agreeably distracting surroundings, to follow by the sound of the music every movement of the ballet on the stage, which I see only in my mind's eye.'[24] As it happened the ballet in question, 'Round the Town', was a particularly apt source for this fantasy, because it actually contained, along with a scene set outside the Empire, a number of dances imitating favourite stars like Lottie Collins, creator of 'Tara-de-boom-de-ay'. Symons had become so familiar with the Empire dancers that he had only to imagine their idiosyncrasies to be enthralled once again – 'that odd little jerk' of one, 'the soft hair of that Italian girl who smiles so prettily', the conventional bow of another, 'so personal, so winning'. Seated in the Promenade, he could carry out in his imagination what normally took place in the stalls: 'In my mind's eye I look from face to face along the two lines resting, perhaps on a particular oval, out of which two great, serious eyes smile strangely.' 'I see it all,' he wrote, 'and I see it as in a mirror, with something new and strange in its enticing artificiality.'

Symons was pursuing a torrid romance with one of the ballet girls at this time so, in a sense, his personal fantasy was real.[25] When not in the stalls or in the Promenade Symons was either backstage or haunting the stage door. Each position offered its own opportunities for fleeting impressions, instantly transformed into prose:

The most magical glimpse I ever caught of a ballet was from the road in front, from the other side of the road, one night when two doors were suddenly thrown open just as I was passing. In the moment's interval before the doors closed again, I saw, in that odd, unexpected way, over the heads of the audience, far off in a sort of blue mist, the whole stage, its brilliant crowd drawn up in the last pose, just as the curtain was beginning to descend. It stamped itself in my brain, an impression caught just at the perfect moment, by some rare felicity of chance.[26]

Symons became quite famous for these effects. So much so that sitting in a Paris café in 1897, with a theatre *entr'acte* bell ringing, the crowd clamouring for their *bocks*, Aubrey Beardsley confessed to a correspondent that unless he took serious care, he too would 'drop into a Symonsy mood'.[27]

It was more remarkable perhaps that Symons should have been confident that those who read his music-hall pieces in the daily papers should have appreciated his circumstances. But in the nineties the Empire, including its Promenade, was part of the London landscape and, despite the protestations of Mrs Chant, so it was to remain. Everybody knew what went on there, and 'Where have I seen you before?', reputed to be the opening gambit along the Promenade, became quite a catchphrase.[28] Not everyone approved of the levity. Shaw thought that 'witty things can be said by witty people about prostitution, as about any other subject; but prostitution is not a merry subject in itself – rather the reverse.'[29]

And if Mrs Chant lost her immediate battle, time was ultimately on her side. Max Beerbohm, who had been a true 'amateur' in his time, ogling 'The Mimetic Marvel', Cissie Loftus, at the Tivoli at the start of the decade, returned to the Empire with a friend from abroad in 1899.

> We bought two seats. As we passed, on our way to them, into the far-famed Promenade, I asked my friend to walk slowly and observe carefully the throng's demeanour. Everything was the same as it ever had been. The same glare, and the same music; the same congestion of silk hats and swallow-tails, pressed against the barrier of the circle, watching the ballet; the same slow and serried procession of silk hats and swallow-tails, billicocks and racing-coats, moodily revolving along the space between the ballet gazers and the long row of large-hatted ladies, who, bolt upright on the crimson settees against the wall, conversed with one another in undertone; the same old absence, in fact, of any gaiety, of any semblance of gaiety, of any wish or effort to contrive any little hollow semblance of gaiety.

Glamour's absence was all too painfully confirmed by the glimpsed presence in a mirror.

> As we threaded our way out, the Promenade was still glittering with its habitual gloom. I noticed in the distance two young men who seemed more gloomy than the rest; my brain, I suppose, was a trifle dulled by the whole evening, for it was not until I came quite close to them that I recognised my

friend and myself in a mirror. As we went out the mutes were still pouring in. Souls on the way to purgatory would have looked more cheerful.[30]

## 'A MINE OF SUGGESTIVENESS'

When the 'amateurs' described a visit to a place of popular entertainment as if it had been a dangerous foray into the unknown, they were acceding to a self-conscious atmosphere that continued to cling to the big halls even as they matured into London landmarks. Besides the erotic enticement there was the fascination of cultural uncertainty. Was it possible for class loyalties to endure in Leicester Square, or was this the commercial debasement of an authentic tradition? Might the nineties be witnessing the triumphant birth of a new and democratic kind of art?

The 'amateurs' had difficulty in committing themselves to a final evaluation. Even those painters who were instinctively attracted to the halls often adopted a shifting point of view. Walter Sickert, the greatest celebrant of the older establishments, brought further complexity to Symons's precept that at a music-hall 'the audience is a part of the performance' by posing questions about the composition of that audience through the medium of his painting.

For example, when Sickert submitted 'Gatti's, Hungerford' to the New English Art Club in 1888, one member declared that it was 'tawdry, vulgar and the sentiment of the lowest music-hall', and hoped that it was not 'a true reflection of the painter's mind'. He seems to have been assuming that the indefinite shape of a woman in the stalls was in fact that of a prostitute. Was the picture then 'a true reflection' of Sickert's mind, or was it rather a true representation of a social reality? Or was it both? Sickert did not record his intentions, but some people certainly thought they saw a prostitute in his picture.[31] Prostitutes were visually ambiguous – quite literally so. In general, though, Sickert's own ambiguous restraint set him well apart from his less distinguished contemporaries and imitators, who allowed themselves to serve an official ideology and whose art was often determined by political demands for clarity and symmetry.

In 1891 *Harper's Magazine* published an article on the halls by Frederick Anstey.[32] Illustrated by Joseph Pennell, the piece was based on researches that the two men had carried out in collaboration with the theatre critic William Archer. Picture and text alike were probably influenced by current events in municipal politics. Though the 'Prudes' scandal was still four years off, Mrs Chant and her allies, in particular a councillor named McDougall, were already putting pressure on the LCC to tighten up its policy on the halls, and the phlegmatic tone of Anstey's article certainly reads as if it were intended to temper any moral disquiet. In common with other Victorian investigating journalists he presumed (and consequently discovered) a fixed distance between himself and his field of enquiry. His article approaches the daily diversions of Londoners as if they are bizarre but harmless customs practised in some unexplored colonial pocket.

The alienation went both ways. Anstey's party may have passed unnoticed in the West End, but their enquiries took them to the smaller halls as well, and, in Hoxton, where they chose to seat themselves in a box, they were immediately spotted as interlopers. A murmur – 'McDougall!' – went through the house, making their visit, according to Pennell's wife, 'the most successful turn of the evening'.[33] In fact the Hoxton audience had nothing to fear from Anstey but condescension. His tour of the halls led him to the smooth conclusion that:

> After all, people who are critical in the matter of amusement do not go to music halls, which are chiefly patronized by men who can enjoy nothing without the aid of tobacco, and women who dislike any entertainment which entails the slightest mental exertion.[34]

And in much the same way, Pennell's illustrations patronized their subject pictorially, opting for frontal assault, for an undemanding compositional balance and a centralized focus. What Pennell presumably had in mind was to convey a feeling of total impartiality that neither romanticized the halls nor denied their hold over their audience.

The result, inevitably, was anaesthetic. A favourite device was simply to reproduce the postures of performers on stage in the outlines of employees in the auditorium and then again in the silhouettes of customers, as if nothing sparked between them. In 'The Chairman at Gatti's', the considerable bulk of the chairman – impassive stare, hands in pockets – implies the attitude of a headless performer behind him: while in 'A Lion Comique at the Oxford' the shadowy profile of the comedian is elucidated by the more detailed reverse profiles of the pianist in centre foreground and of several members of the audience. Receding rows of bowler hats create an unambiguous perspective. In 'A Serio-Comique Song and Dance Artiste at "the Middlesex"', a distorted diamond shape opens up an uninterrupted vista of the performer who, as so often in Pennell's work, responds with arms extended in a gesture

'*The Chairman at Gatti's*'.

'*A Lion Comique at the Oxford*'.

'*A Serio-Comique Song and Dance Artiste at the Middlesex*'.

of expressive self-display. There's neither vitality nor mystery here: distant outlines are always normalized by the homely countenances of the more proximate figures. Take away the pipes, the bottles and the glasses, and the audience could almost be a congregation, with the sluggish expressions on their faces suggesting an undemanding sermon rather than a comic monologue or a sexual song and dance. Thus did Pennell's pictures match Anstey's text: nothing to condemn because nothing seriously to question.

Pennell's exemplary audiences are seen from a hypothetical (and often unlikely) position that ranges them in an orderly perspective. In addition, in order to reinforce the music-hall as an essentially unified occasion, he had had to reduce the startling contrasts of illumination that artists (including himself) generally commented upon, lighting his audiences with a sourceless clarity only slightly less intense than that given by the footlights.

The inherent propaganda of these pictures may not have been fully apparent even to Pennell at the time. A few years later he found their anodyne quality extremely useful. In February 1895, soon after the 'Prudes' affair, he accepted another journalistic commission involving the halls. An LCC election was imminent and the Liberal *Daily Chronicle* set about campaigning on behalf of the Progressives, a party based on the Radical wing of the Liberals, with a set of illustrated articles on 'New London'.[35] These were to deal with various aspects of life in the capital – parks and so on, concluding with theatres and music-halls. The intention was to show, through a sequence of pictures by admired artists, that political radicalism, modern art and contemporary newspaper techniques were harmonious partners in a new spirit at work in the metropolis. Pennell, responsible for commissioning the pictures, delivered a series – including work by Burne-Jones, William Morris and Walter Crane – that marked an important stage in the history of modern illustration.

Working to a deadline, Pennell suffered a serious setback when the *Chronicle* objected to two of his submissions: a dangerously unclad dancer by Beardsley and a music-hall sketch by Sickert.[36] Luckily he was able to turn to his own stock of unused drawings from the Anstey piece, so that the final 'New London' article was accompanied by his 'Music in the Hall: the Lion Comique'. Despite the compromise, picture and text were again ideally suited. Referring back to the unfortunate events at the Empire the previous autumn the text proclaimed, naturally enough, that the Licensing Committee had behaved with unimpeachable good sense

*'Music in the Hall: the Lion Comique'.*

and that no one, not even the management, had really suffered from the restrictions imposed. Charges that the committee was composed of moral busybodies were quite unjustified:

> The generally-accepted view is that the Licensing Committee are engaged every night in trotting round music-halls, seeking to find some indecency in song or dance. And when they are not engaged in this work themselves, that they keep an army of inspectors, who are engaged in the same novel errand. There is not a word of truth in these statements.[37]

Pennell's illustration supports the contention that the halls could be trusted to be self-regulating, and that surveillance was not only unusual but unnecessary. The 'Lion Comique', topper askew, arms outstretched, offers himself in all his innocent pathos to an audience which stares back with academic intent and, despite the token drinks in front of them, obvious sobriety. Only one woman is clearly visible, and she looks at the comedian with the same concentration as a pipe-smoking, bowler-hatted man by her side.

This is the art of the people as anyone, as Mrs Chant even, might have applauded it. The Progressives did badly in the 1895 LCC election, but they could hardly blame Pennell, who had done his best to represent the music-hall as an essentially innocuous if empty-headed diversion that the well-meaning activities of the Progressives could only improve. And the contrast with Sickert lies exactly here, for Sickert, despite his political sympathies, always remained hesitant about portraying the people whose art he enthusiastically pictured.

Despite his lesser talent, Pennell was an early admirer of Sickert, and praised his music-hall study 'The Old Bedford' for its clever use of mirror images and its 'feeling of reflected light'.[38] In fact it seems certain that it was with Sickert's work specifically in mind that Pennell had set out with Anstey and Archer on their rounds in 1891, particularly as his panoramic view of the Alhambra is so very similar to Sickert's 'Oxford Music-Hall'. But the 'Oxford' was an extremely unusual picture for Sickert because it showed the whole spectacle – architecture, audience and performer – from a distant position, presumably at the very back of the theatre. The Impressionist critic R. A. M. Stevenson described it as 'painted very much from "chic"', regretting the absence of an individual angle of vision. He also said that it failed 'to give a sufficient variety of definition, a subtle magic of nuance, or the convincing quaintness of true light'.[39] It was really quite logical that the very picture that Pennell came closest to copying should be the one least liked by an experienced critic who always set greatest store by 'the human outlook'.

The most prevalent principle among the New Critics was, of course, that treatment must have priority over subject – strictly speaking, the music-halls could not be allowed to provide evidence of social shifts but only a supply of purely visual effects. The painter made no judgements, he did not 'go to the music-hall in the spirit of the County Council', as the painter–critic Charles Furze put it in 1892:

> He does not expect to improve his taste in music or be elevated by the words of the songs, but finding in the scene a mine of suggestiveness, he is content to take it as the pretext for a picture.[40]

A fashionable opinion that even D. S. MacColl couldn't leave quite there.

> Mr Furze takes back all that he gave away in a single word 'suggestive'. The County Councillor he condemns for finding one kind of suggestiveness in the ballet, but he himself finds another. Suggestiveness of what? Of feeling, surely – of emotion, of ideas.[41]

Which did not advance matters very far. Ideas of what? None of the New Critics was prepared to say, intoning merely that Sickert did to the

halls what Whistler had done to warehouses: turned them into 'fairyland'. Stevenson liked Sickert's rendering of 'the dim, warm depths of
theatrical illumination in which there is little true shadow, but
everything seems flushed with a low light and rippling all over with soft
reflections'.[42] George Moore marvelled at the way 'Little Dot
Hetherington at the Bedford' caught 'the lighting, the sense of space,
and the limits of that space',[43] and MacColl admired 'the fascination of
stage lighting, and the accidents of stage colour'.[44] But later MacColl
confessed that he was not always happy with Sickert's lack of detail, and
he made some disparaging comparisons with Degas. He felt that there
were times when the figures on stage became simply 'centres of reflected
light', and he was troubled by Sickert's disrespect for 'design'.[45]

Not that Sickert himself would have put matters any other way. A
defensive critic of his own work who well knew the value of polemic, he
was generally quick to say that he painted the halls because of the beauty
'created by the coincidence of a number of fortuitous elements of form
and colour'. But the paintings suggest more than that, because aesthetic
chance is always fired by human encounter. And that much even Sickert
would very occasionally admit.

> A graceful girl leaning forward from the stage, to accentuate the refrain of
> one of the sentimental ballads so dear to the frequenters of the halls, evoked a
> spontaneous movement of sympathy and attention in an audience whose
> sombre tones threw into a more brilliant relief the animated movement of
> the singer, bathed as she was in a ray of green limelight from the centre of
> the roof, and from below in the yellow radiance of the footlights.[46]

Sickert was attracted not by 'fairyland' but by 'the hectic mysteries of
stage illumination'.[47] Most 'amateurs' haunted the West End as well as
the suburbs; Sickert stayed on the outskirts, finding its proletarian
'mystery' quite challenging enough.

Every bit as aware as Arthur Symons (though for rather different
reasons) of the temptation to consider oneself the only member of the
audience who really counts, Sickert excused himself from his own
pictures. In his discreetly tender 'Little Dot Hetherington', painted
between 1888 and 1889, the subject points up into a spotlight, teasing
the gallery with the fancy that she can see them as they can see her. The
painter is protected from that illusion because he merely catches her
reflection in a mirror. This should leave him free to concentrate on the
audience who, faces turned to the stage, are all unconscious of his gaze
from the rear. Ironically, by keeping his unobtrusive place, the artist is

unable to reveal anything much more than a few intent faces among a string of undemonstrative hats. Elsewhere Sickert habitually depicted audiences whose haunting expressions, pale, rapt, indistinct, give little away. While the loose pattern of their faces hints at some collective identity, still, like birds on a wire, they never quite cohere into a group.

Sickert's reticence was anything but self-defeating. It confessed the essential problem about the halls everywhere, new as well as old. Whatever brought audience and artistes in contact was not to be easily explained, and the complexity of his pictorial arrangements reflects his own disinclination either to sentimentalize or judge prematurely.

Faithful observation was the quality that Sickert supremely valued in the painting of urban life. This did not preclude involvement. His early studies of the halls capture the ordinariness of exceptional artists while

*'Little Dot Hetherington at the Bedford Music Hall'.*

respecting the individuality of the supposedly ordinary audience. And, unlike Pennell, he refused to squeeze them together into a false unity. In 1898 he left England for Dieppe. When he returned to London in 1905 and again painted the halls, his attention was more firmly divided between performer and audience. His attempts at surveying the music-hall in its troubling entirety were now over and all that remained – it was to occupy the rest of his life – was to chronicle the apotheosis and the slow decline of the halls with studies that sometimes concentrated upon buildings, sometimes upon performers, and sometimes upon audiences, but rarely all three at once.

It was often said, and not only by Symons, that the halls destroyed distinctions, but clearly the habit of attendance fed upon the 'amateurs'' uncertainty about themselves. So much so that it was easy to rely on the halls for the stimulus that made their kind of evasive art possible – evasions ultimately related to class, for the most puzzling novelty of the halls in the nineties was that absolutely everybody was interested in them.

## 'POSES PLASTIQUES'

Margins and tangents, the oblique and never the direct, such were the purlieus of the true 'amateur', the man who went to the halls to lose himself in atmospheric reverie and to discover himself in fluorescent movement, who took his pleasures vicariously by observing what other people enjoyed. A particularly diverting example of popular entertainment were the 'Living Pictures'[48] which caused so much stir in October 1894, when Lady Henry Somerset and W. A. Coote of the National Vigilance Association, allies of Mrs Ormiston Chant, challenged the renewal of a licence to the Palace Theatre of Varieties in Shaftesbury Avenue on the grounds of indecency.

At the Palace, the 'Living Pictures' were quite literally that – recreations on the stage of well-known works by respected artists, achieved by substituting living models for the painted figure. In fact, 'Living Pictures' and 'Living Sculptures' had long been a slightly risqué theatrical attraction, and it's hard to say whether the fuss they caused in 1894 came about because the Palace had overstepped some implicit border of the permissible or whether it was simply because they had come to the attention of prominent persons. During the LCC hearings much was made of William Archer's surprised observation in *The*

*World* that it was 'now possible to present on the stage of a duly licensed place of entertainment, before an audience of both sexes and all classes, the living female body unobscured by a single stitch of drapery'.[49] Three *tableaux* were particularly commented upon: 'Ariadne', which showed a naked woman on the back of a lion; 'The Naiad', a woman lying on a mound slightly on her left side, with the neck, stomach, thighs and legs partly exposed, and a thin piece of gauze, by no means sufficient to conceal it, thrown slantingly across the body; 'The Polar Star', a practically nude woman standing on a pedestal, her arms well extended above her head, holding an electric lamp. A fourth *tableau*, 'The Moorish Bath', also drew comment, though it had already been withdrawn by the management for reasons that remain unclear.

For a short time the painful postures of the 'Pictures', which suggested less than they possessed but far more than they could decently display, came to stand for one aspect of what the halls could offer. Inevitably they reinvigorated the old topic of the 'naked' versus the 'nude'. Coote commented that even if the models were wearing 'an extra cuticle of flesh-coloured tights', it was 'purely an affair of inference and in one sense a matter of observation',[50] while the artist Henry Holiday, a convinced dress reformer, thought that 'we should welcome any occasions that may offer for seeing the human figure accompanied by none but beautiful associations'.[51] In general, the 'Pictures' stimulated much happy male banter of this order. Was the female figure, strategically draped in fleshlike muslin, her outline smoothed, stiffened and redistributed by applications of plaster of Paris, more erotic or less erotic than, on the one hand, a woman who was truly naked or, on the other, a woman who was fully and provocatively attired?

When Shaw eventually went to see them in April 1895, it was, or so he said, as a result of a statement made by Coote that they were 'the ideal form of indecency'.[52] That unfortunate piece of phrasing prompted a volley of Shavian logic: the appeal of indecency depends on privacy, and is therefore incompatible with theatrical show; art does not always idealize its subjects, so that even if the 'Living Pictures' qualified as art, their moral purity would not be guaranteed; and so on. Coote's own attempted paradox, that because they offered no moral inspiration then there was no 'life in the "Living Pictures"', was quickly trumped. For Shaw, it was precisely because the 'pictures' were 'living' that they were more natural than art, and therefore healthier and less erotic than much that was held to be art, and than many of the clothed women – petticoat dancers, for example – who were regularly seen on the London stage.

Beardsley shows a dancer in a costume which suggests precisely what it is
intended to conceal. The outline achieves phallic potential while the train
floats into the shape of a breast or nipple. Drifting fig-leaves trace what lies
beneath. Beardsley was master of this kind of perceptual game and frequently
teased the spectator by planting a prurient observer within the frame. When
the picture appeared in a lavish volume called The London Garland in 1895 it
was known as 'At a Distance' to match the title of a voyeuristic poem about a
music-hall star printed alongside it:

> And sometimes through St James's trees
>    You drive, a goddess of the light;
> And I can see you, when I please,
>    Behind the level lamps at night.
>
> Where from some corner I can stare
>    Across that line of yellow fire,
> And feed upon your face and hair –
>    The pain of exquisite desire.

Separation of the sexual from the natural was the price that Shaw, a puritan of a different order, had to pay in order to distinguish himself from members of the National Vigilance Association. Not that he considered the 'Living Pictures' scandal to be anything more than an opportunity for moral meddling. Arthur Symons, equally amused, opted for the possibilities of aesthetic mayhem: 'A picture, for the most part, is an imitation of life, and a living picture is life imitating an imitation of itself, which seems a little roundabout.'[53] 'Living Pictures' Symons thought to be directly opposed to sculpture because the women, held fast by corsets and plaster, took on that very rigidity that good sculpture struggled to transcend. They were at best an aesthetic curiosity, rather like a juggling act. This was Symons the connoisseur of artistic paradox rather than Symons the philosopher of sex, but on one issue he was more frank.

> If the female figure is supposed to be indecent, why is not the male figure indecent also? Why is it that the very 'purest' of women have never yet, to my knowledge, objected to the semi-nudity in which every kind of athlete is seen, indoors and out of doors, wherever a manly sport or a gymnastic exercise is engaged in?[54]

Was it, he wondered, because women had no sexual feelings? Shaw, too, had asked why women were not debased by the sight of male athletes.[55] Neither chose to confront the point made by Mrs Chant herself that the issue of nudity on stage would never have arisen if men had been involved, because 'men would refuse to exhibit their bodies nightly in this way'.[56]

Lady Henry Somerset thought that the girls who posed for the 'Living Pictures' were corrupted not by their nudity but because they were being looked at and were not ashamed. Symons had a careful reply to that.

> A girl who is accustomed to the stage thinks no more about the eyes of the audience and the cut of her costume than you and I, when we are walking along the street, think about the swift, imperceptible criticism of the indistinguishable crowd. Or, if she thinks of the matter at all, it is as a friend of mine thought when she said to me the other day: 'I sometimes wish I had a better figure; I never think about anything else.'[57]

This authoritative and obviously well-researched statement is no more to be trusted than Symons's testimony that he had never been accosted in the Empire Promenade. It simply extends his favourite thought that he alone among the 'indistinguishable crowd' has been spotted by a dancer on the stage, that his gaze has been acknowledged, and that a girl

*The chorus rehearses at the Alhambra.*

is continuing to display her illumined body for his sole benefit. For, whatever Symons and his fellow 'amateurs' might sometimes publicly profess, dance in the nineties undoubtedly had its libidinous side, and the 'Living Pictures', static and figurative where dance was fluid and abstract, only vulgarized sensual suggestions that were more subtly and satisfactorily expressed in movement.

In the nineties, dance was controversial. Literary historians have documented the rise of the dancer as Symbolist ideal or, famously, the 'Romantic Image': Yeats's 'Unity of Being' traced back via Symons and Mallarmé to the exploits of Loie Fuller, all coloured lights and flowing draperies.[58] This is the dancer as an image of perfection, and correspondingly inhuman, magnificently sterile: but she belongs more to poetry than to the tough exploitative environments complained of by Mrs Chant and her friends. Not only was the art of dance practised in a coarse and dangerous place, selective history has ignored the wide variety of styles available. Like her fellow artistes – jugglers, acrobats, comedians – the dancer held no clear status in the world of art. For the 'amateur', then, there were choices to be made, preferences to be expressed, criteria to be established. Not all dance was ballet, and in England even ballet was not yet the elevated form of expression it was to become.

It would be wrong to make too much of Max Beerbohm's weary protest in 1906 that 'there is no essential reason why ballet should not, like opera, have words'[59] (there were, and are, several reasons, all of them obvious), but it is a sign of a certain English resistance to Symbolist assimilation of the dance. Beerbohm's other complaint, that ballet 'ought to be a representation of life, it ought to awaken a sense of reality – a fantastic sense of reality' – was probably provoked by the claims increasingly put forward by Symons that dance was a superbly artificial and therefore pure form of expression. Back in the early nineties, however, even Symons had spent time puzzling over the relationship of dance to representation and to dramatic illusion.

In the context of the halls, with their dizzying 'variety', the answers were not so immediately forthcoming as the later history of Symbolist poetry might suggest. The Symons who was eager to subject dance to an aesthetic enquiry vied with the Symons who was willing prey to its charms. It was with his own divided self in mind that he posed a dichotomy between those whose involvement was 'concrete' (an interest in dancers) and those for whom it was 'abstract' (an interest in dancing).[60] As a highly professional 'amateur', Symons belonged in both camps simultaneously, and his earlier writing on the dance is fired by conflicting principles.

Like his master Baudelaire, Symons determinedly pursued the doctrine of the greater the artifice the greater the truth. Ballet 'is so entirely and beautifully artificial, so essentially and excellently conventional, that it can gain nothing by trying to become what it never can and never should be, a picture of real life'.[61] Alternatively, 'I like a ballet to have as much of the fantastic, unreal and impossible as it can be got to contain.'[62] But dance was also an art of the body, of straining muscle and recalcitrant flesh, a fundamental truth that Symons discovered when he attended rehearsals and saw the dancers at work, their faces pale and tired, their clothes dull and worn. 'In this fantastic return to nature', he confessed, marvelling, 'I found the last charm of the artificial.'[63]

Somewhere in the mysterious interplay of skill and shape, in the way form sprang from labour, lay dance's secret. What linked all the dancers that Symons saw and enjoyed – the solo ballerinas with the *corps de ballet*, skirt-dancers with novelty dancers, can-can dancers, serpentine dancers, belly dancers and gypsy dancers – was the female body, though the blatancy of the evidence varied greatly.

Some of the dancing to be seen in the halls was unashamed: skirt-dancing most obviously, which was designed to reveal a swelling expanse of petticoat as the kicks went ever higher. In Symons's all too 'suggestive' word, this kind of dancing was more 'pungent' than 'sterile'. According to Shaw, also bluntly to the point, the audience for such dancers was 'really gloating over their variegated underclothing ... silken censers of *odor di femmina* which is the real staple of five-sixths of our theatrical commerce'.[64] Shaw dismissed the skirt-dancer because she wasn't even required to perform intricate movements with her feet, let alone use her whole body in an integrated harmony. For Symons, though, it was precisely because she did one thing only, but did it supremely well, that the skirt-dancer was so interesting a subject. Skirt-dancers and high kickers might only be 'novelties', but in the new aesthetic of the halls novelty was an essential ingredient. Symons had studied the French stars – La Goulue and Nini Patte en l'Air – on their home ground, the Moulin Rouge, where he had learnt to appreciate the technical control that went into their abandoned effects. When Nini appeared in London in 1894, he wrote:

Her effects are all conscious, deliberately extravagant for a purpose, and extravagant according to a method; she never loses for an instant that perfect command over herself.[65]

Symons was continually discovering this combination of extravagance and control in unlikely places. An American visitor to the Alhambra, 'Cyrene', so impressed him that he told her, at a private demonstration, that she outkicked even the French. Cyrene, 'very simple, natural and delightful ... an expression of nervous expectancy on her pretty, serious, piquant face',

specialized in a dance which was joyous and spontaneous and triumphant, which did the incredible with ease, which did the splits and the high kick with modesty, which captivated the eye and distracted the intelligence at once. The extravagance of the thing was never vulgar, its intricate agility was never incorrect, there was genuine grace in the wildest moment of caprice, there was real science in the pointing of the foot in its most fantastic flights above the head.[66]

*Cyrene.*

Dance inspired Symons's most agitated writing. Jennie Joyce, an imitator of Loie Fuller, was 'like a great white, silky bat ... a beautiful living corkscrew';[67] Marie Leyton 'a figure that seemed suddenly to burst into flame... What at the first moment had looked like ropes of pearls blossomed magically into globes of electric light – shifting, scintillating snakes of many colours.'[68] Sometimes, though, he was doubtful about lighting effects which, while admirably modern, got in the way of the dancing. So carried away was he by Leyton that Symons suggested that real snakes might have been even better, turning her into a Medusa designed by Simeon Solomon. Given Symons's penchant for sexual hyperbole, this may have been a serious proposition.

The 'amateur' set about his study of dance conscious of the French Symbolist notion that dancing, because it was a natural activity raised to an almost supernatural level, was the expression of an ideal. Even Shaw, not normally associated with the art, enthused over

> the perfect dancer along whose limbs the rhythmic stream flows unbroken to the very tips of the fingers and roots of the hair, whose head moves beautifully, whose nape and wrists make the music visible, who can flex the spine of each vertebra more certainly than an ordinary person can flex his finger at each joint, and who is the personification of skill, grace, strength and health.[69]

Beerbohm's petulance throws this orthodoxy into sharp relief. In a swipe at the Symbolist adoration of the dancer's thinking body, he vilified the ballerina as an essentially unnatural creature who systematically destroyed the symmetry of her normal physique. 'Such power of thought as she may once have had was long since absorbed into her toes. She does not know that she is ridiculous. Her fixed smile is no assumption to hide an aching heart.'[70] It was too late: the Symbolist dancer was already set on her journey into literature.

While dancers still fell seductively short of aesthetic purity, the 'amateurs' were very much aware that creative goals were being airily realized elsewhere on the music-hall bill. Acrobats are hardly ever evoked in the poetry of the nineties, but they were consistently appreciated in the journalism, and almost always as exponents of a high endeavour. They stood head and shoulders above singers, comedians and even dancers, because they had totally mastered (in acrobatics there are no half-measures) an art that served no mimetic function, told no story and, despite the 'daring young man on the flying trapeze' of contemporary song who pleased all the girls, posed no sexual challenge.

The 'amateurs' responded with unalloyed delight. To the theatre critic
A. B. Walkley, who knew his Pater, acrobats were 'expounding in action the
philosophy of the *joie de vivre* ... muscular Cyrenaics, illustrating the
principles of a sane hedonism by the development of the flexor
muscles'.[71] Wilde, too, recognized the aesthetic lessons to be gained from
other people's physical skills. 'The acrobat,' he allowed, 'is an artist.'

> The mere fact that he never speaks to the audience shows how well he
> appreciates the great truth that the aim of art is not to reveal personality but
> to please. The clown may be blatant, but the acrobat is always beautiful. He is
> an interesting combination of Greek sculpture and the spangles of the
> modern costumier. He has even had his niche in the novels of our age ... *Les
> frères Zemganno* is the apotheosis of the acrobat.[72]

This was a book that Symons also knew well: he had studied the
Goncourts' circus novel alongside Gautier's tributes to Debureau, the
great French mime. Acrobatics, Symons above all was thoroughly aware,
was a serious discipline whose history and achievements demanded all
'the diligence, the enthusiastic diligence of the *dilettante*'.[73]

'If Pindar were living it is about the acrobats that he would write his
odes,'[74] declared Symons, though he wrote no poems on the subject
himself, confining his admiration to prose. The trained body of the
acrobat was a 'poem in flesh and blood', whose wordless perfection kept
it for ever suspended as an unattainable ideal. Through the study of
acrobatics, though, the 'amateur' could be led to a deeper understanding
of the physicality involved in other kinds of art. Speed for one thing: the
thrilling discrepancy between the execution and the comprehension of
an act. 'It is impossible', wrote Symons, 'to reflect, in the space of time
between two somersaults, on the exact nature of the movements which
have just passed before our eyes.'[75] Shaw marvelled at the acrobat's
'complete physical self-possession, his ambidextrous grace, his power of
making several deliberate movements in the space of a pang of terror –
as when, for example, he will coolly alter the disposition of his body at a
given moment, whilst he is falling headlong through the air: all these
accomplishments of his really exist.'[76] Those amazing movements were
undeniably real, they had actually happened. Often incredible, acrobatics
are never impossible. Beerbohm cited a 'thoughtful critic' who had
pointed out that the skill of the acrobat, while 'seeming to defy the laws
of gravity, owes its success to the completeness of its obedience to
them.'[77]

The study of acrobats left a trail of aesthetic paradoxes. There was the realization that the spasmodic sense of danger felt by the spectator depended upon the fine equilibrium of the performer. Moreoever, as Symons insisted, 'What looks difficult is really easy, and what looks easy is really difficult,'[78] so that acrobatics were an example of art concealing art, as well as of art displaying art. According to Symons, the intelligence of the poet Mallarmé, as revealed in his conversation, 'moved ... with the half-apologetic negligence of the perfect acrobat'.[79] In another sense, though, acrobats were unique, because they took not just imagined but real risks. By stretching the spectator's belief in what he saw, they extended his knowledge of the world he inhabited.

It followed that appreciation of acrobats benefited from a scientific approach, especially when their feats involved some distortion of the body that shifted the line between grace and deformity. The capacity to admire contortion was a mark of the true 'amateur', requiring him to demonstrate his sensitivity to the natural along with his openness to the abnormal, his wide-eyed amazement with his cool-headed analysis. That, at any rate, was how Symons rationalized his interest in performers like Eugenie Petrescue, the girl who walked on her hands. Wilde was so taken with Petrescue, whom he saw perform at the Moulin Rouge in Paris, that he sent her his card and planned to ask her to dance the part of Salome in his play. He wanted her 'to dance on her hands, as in Flaubert's story'.[80] Symons delighted in Petrescue because she united 'opposite qualities: hand-walking requiring firmness of the arms and shoulders, and india-rubber movements requiring looseness of the joints and elasticity of the muscles'.[81] What especially impressed Symons was that the girl had been trained by her father, a Roumanian scientist who had investigated and developed her unusual qualities.

The Petrescue phenomenon was an example of science contributing to art. At first horrified by this 'new incredible animal', Symons soon learned to look at her as a 'marvel' rather than a 'monstrosity', a 'human work of art' with all the 'originality of an invention'. Yet while Petrescue had inspired a distinguished German scientist to contribute a learned article to the *Zeitschrift für Ethnologie* (an article Symons diligently read), she also reminded him of 'Japanese grotesques, kakemono or carving'.

One of the great delights of visiting the halls was that the 'amateur' was for ever discovering prodigies who nevertheless embodied essential laws. The Rowe brothers, for example, who performed contortions on the trapeze: one of them was an instinctive acrobat, who had shown his

*Eugenie Petrescue.*

abilities in childhood, the other had had to be carefully trained. The result, however, was the same: a mastery of style, a 'certain grace in the abnormal'. Watching the Rowe brothers at the Alhambra, 'human eels ... with the light shimmering on their spangled, sinuous tights', Symons 'could fancy that one of those eighteenth-century Japanese carvings had come to life, or that a page from one of the priceless albums which I have seen at the Goncourts had escaped from that quiet study, to act itself out on a stage here in London'.[82]

Totally absorbed in his skill, representative of nothing but himself, the acrobat was popular, proficient and pure. And it was precisely because he harmonized intention and act, mind with body, that his performance seemed so miraculous to the concerned spectators in the stalls. Only the greatest artists came anywhere near it. D. S. MacColl was paying Beardsley the ultimate compliment when he wrote that his drawings had 'the appeal of an action cleanly, quickly, adroitly carried through'.[83] Beardsley executed feats that could 'be followed with a strain of excitement comparable to that with which we follow the juggler or tight-rope dancer'. He was, in short, a 'calligraphic acrobat'.

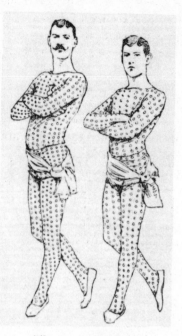

*The Rowe Brothers.*

## 'THE NEW ART OF THE VARIETY STAGE'

A. B. Walkley, writing in 1895, described the 'Evolution of the Music-Hall' as being on Spencerian lines, moving from the homogeneous to the heterogeneous, its progress ever threatened by a contrary 'degradation'. The determining moment had been the Theatres Act of 1843, which had offered the embryonic halls the choice between becoming regular theatres, ruled by the Lord Chamberlain and deprived of their licence to serve drinks, or remaining as taverns but unable to stage full-length plays. The result: 'specialization of function' and the emergence of the 'music-hall proper', with its 'variety entertainment' – ballet, acrobatics, juggling.[84]

Walkley was being ironical, parodying the cruder sociological methods of his time, but the neo-Darwinist model usefully allowed him to stand apart from the phenomenon he was describing. Symons expressed a rather similar view that the halls would become more heterogeneous,[85] and it was commonplace to observe how serious actors could learn from music-hall techniques. George Moore did so frequently, while John Gray eulogized popular performers in a lecture on 'The Modern Actor'.[86] Even Henry Irving was interested in the topic.[87]

In many ways traditional, yet with their electric light, thick carpets and profusion of gilt, dazzlingly modern, projecting the values of emotional sincerity but in a blatantly commercial setting, the new halls had an unpredictable future. Nothing did more to upset Symons's disarming principle that 'in a music-hall the audience is a part of the performance' than the realities of profit, which the 'amateurs' saw as an interesting but complicated and possibly destructive artistic challenge. The new halls could pay large salaries, and successful performers enjoyed personal lives that were at a far remove from their own origins and from most of their admiring audience. The standard apologia may have stressed unique ambitions and hard work along with residual roots. This still left the 'amateurs' free to praise individual performers while reserving judgement about the changing context in which they now worked, or to acknowledge that 'variety' was an accurate sign of the times while confessing to a sense of loss. They could even see 'variety' as an ideal to be cherished.

Belonging nowhere in particular themselves, the 'amateurs' thought that they were peculiarly well equipped to assess the authenticity of the performances they observed. When he visited the Britannia, Hoxton, in 1898, Shaw perceived a strong sense of class solidarity that bound audience to performer: 'They are jealous *for* the dignity of the artist, not derisively covetous of his (or her) degradation.'[88] Beerbohm also made a point of regretting the demise of the older, more intimate environments which, like Shaw, but rather more condescendingly, he identified with the decline of working-class communities.[89] As a younger man, though, Beerbohm had eagerly indulged his own taste for glamour with his trips to the Tivoli. As for Symons, he was as fond of the seedy Metropolitan in the Edgware Road as he was of the Alhambra and the Empire, remarking that 'To the discriminating amateur, each music-hall has its *cachet*, as definitely as each music-hall artist worthy of the name.'[90]

All were curious about what happened when artistes moved from the outskirts to the centre. Would they have to jettison the capacity for direct communication that had originally marked them out, or would improved facilities and larger, more varied audiences breed altogether new skills? The 'amateurs' particularly wondered about performers who relied on words: comedians and monologuists, the 'lions comiques' and 'serio-comics', whose acts were the staple of class-based entertainment. Every

time a Cockney 'lion comique', attempting to pass himself off as a West
End socialite, failed to live up to the aspirations of his top hat and tails, a
symbolic blow could be said to have been struck on behalf of proletarian
integrity. Similarly, the songs of the 'serios' may have been sentimental,
but the emotion they engendered was undoubtedly corporate and
generally local.

*Katie Lawrence: a Serio.*

In the end the 'amateurs' decided that class relationships were of less
importance than dramatic expertise. This came about partly in response
to changing comic styles – exemplified by Arthur Roberts, Albert
Chevalier and Dan Leno – that replaced the exposure of class
pretensions with distinctive personalities and individual pathos. The
'amateurs' welcomed this development, not just because they had no
personal commitment to the notion of working-class resilience, but
because they were primarily men of the theatre, who didn't expect to
admire performers for the 'authenticity' of their origins so much as for

their acting power. The world they knew best was the 'legitimate' stage where, even then, great stars like Irving and Terry, Bernhardt and Duse were admired for their capacity to radiate a unique aura against a background of moral melodrama.

In this respect alone, their standards were rather different from those of modern academic writers on the halls who see mainly the debasing effects of 'mass entertainment'.[91] By contrast, the 'amateurs' of the nineties felt a vitality that had much to offer the conventional theatre. Their main criterion was 'individuality', conceived as an innate quality that inspired performers to make their own experiences of life relevant to a variegated audience. Direct expression allowed music-hall artistes to transcend their origins without, as in a dramatic role, concealing their true identity. Symons aired the topic in a piece on Arthur Roberts in 1893:

> The contest and the contrast between the music-hall and the legitimate drama is largely concerned with one question. The former not merely permits, but demands all the individuality of which an actor is possessed. The latter requires that the most individual of actors shall sink his individuality in his part, shall subordinate himself to fit the framework which has been prepared for him; in a word, shall be a single instrument in an orchestra, a single voice in a chorus. Mr Irving, who is a man of genius, may be justly blamed, from a certain standpoint for the brilliant obtrusion of personality into all the characters which he represents; and Mr Beerbohm Tree, who is a man of talent, might, on the same showing, be exalted to the skies because his personality is unimportant, and he can assume the appearance of any character. In Mr Albert Chevalier one sees what the music-hall can do for the Artist of Individuality. In abandoning the legitimate drama for the variety stage Mr Chevalier passed from the chorus to the principal role. He 'found himself' as the phrase is. With Mr Arthur Roberts the case was just the reverse, at first sight. A clever and amusing music-hall singer, he has become, since the change of profession, the finest comic actor we have. Well, how is this accounted for? Simply by the fact that he has brought from the music-hall the method of the music-hall, that he has grafted a new sort of comedy on the old-fashioned comedy of the stage, that he has persisted in being himself – a character in a play certainly, but first and foremost, Arthur Roberts ... the new art of the variety stage.[92]

The 'individuality' of the performer had its ideological partner in the 'individualism' of democratic or liberal politics. If 'individualism' was the creed of the future, then what could be more representative of present aspirations than the energetic 'individuality' of favourite entertainers? A shared concern with modern ideals would eventually bring together

*The Costers' Laureate, Mr Albert Chevalier.*

Arthur Symons and Mrs Ormiston Chant, both of whom professed particular admiration for the 'Cockney coster' Albert Chevalier. Mrs Chant patronizingly described him as a singer who had expressed

> the finest sentiments in the human heart; who had voiced themes that had been there, but before were not voiced, and had done so in a language understood of the people … [which] might be the means of introducing into lives a tenderness and a sentiment not hitherto displayed.[93]

Symons explicitly connected Chevalier's 'tenderness', 'pathos' and 'wonderful dramatic power' with his mixed race. Not for Symons the doubt that because Chevalier came from French and Italian stock he might be disqualified from representing the life of a Cockney.[94] Quite the contrary: Chevalier's achievement was to have created a theatrical type that reflected the cosmopolitan realities of modern London. Nor were these the pieties of intellectuals alone. In the nineties managers and performers, not to mention audiences, came to endorse them almost without thinking, as the complex pattern of twentieth-century popular entertainment was set in motion.

The 'amateurs' were, above all, aware that the new halls, like the New Journalism, carried lessons for established artistic practice. Like the newspapers, the halls enclosed a dizzy round of ever-changing items within a finite time and space; their audiences were disparate, and would become more so; and they purported to allow for the free expression of individual talent. The comparison was made quite specifically by Max Beerbohm: 'As the penny weekly magazines are to literature, so are the music-halls to drama: snippets there, "turns" here …' But the energy that sprang from all this 'variety' could be overwhelming, sometimes alienating: 'catching your attention for one thing and switching it on to another before you know where you are'.[95] At a music-hall, rather as in a newspaper, modern life was on bewildering offer.

# 4

# 'OUR DARK PLACES'
## Poetry and reform

The horror of prison life is the contrast between the
grotesqueness of *one's aspect and the tragedy in one's soul.*

Oscar Wilde in 1897 to Leonard Smithers,
publisher of *The Ballad of Reading Gaol*

'THE HORROR OF PRISON LIFE'

The professed aim of the New Journalism was enlightenment; sometimes a shocking glare had to come first. It was with its public responsibilities in mind, its journalistic resources in action, that the *Daily Chronicle* dispatched, late in 1893, a select group to illuminate the condition of the nation's prisons, publishing its findings in January 1894.[1]

Some sixteen years earlier, in 1878, a governmental policy of centralization had transferred administrative power from local magistrates to the Prison Commissioners in Whitehall, working under the chairmanship of Sir Edmund du Cane.[2] The *Daily Chronicle* team, much aware of the harmful effects this legislation had had upon everyday life within the prisons themselves, was determined that public concern should at last be aroused. Consequently, they entitled their articles 'Our Dark Places', signing them, with conscious irony, 'Our Special Commissioner'. In fact, they had been put together by three men, two of them experts in the field: H. W. Massingham, at this time a leader-writer on the *Chronicle*;[3] the Reverend W. D. Morrison, a regular contributor to the paper on penal subjects as well as chaplain at Wandsworth Prison;[4] and John Burns, trades union leader, member of the Independent Labour Party and MP for Battersea.[5]

The point of 'Our Dark Places' was to bear human witness to statistics which already demonstrated that Sir Edmund's regime, with its military discipline and its reliance upon solitary confinement, had led not only to an increase in recidivism but to a growing number of cases of madness and suicide. In the event, empirical research exposed how thoroughly ignorant prison staff were of modern ideas. 'I question', wrote 'Our Special Commissioner', 'whether a single reform of the smallest consequence has been introduced since 1878 – a period covered, be it noted, by the work of men like Lombroso, Ferri, and the American prison reformers, and by a series of experiments not less important perhaps than those which were responsible for *The Origin of Species*.'[6] This was a pointed reference to 'criminal anthropology', a science pioneered by an Italian professor, Cesare Lombroso, who had published the first volume of his *L'Uomo Delinquente* in 1876.

'Criminal anthropology' tried to categorize criminals according to their physical traits: height, shape and size of skull, susceptibility to certain diseases such as epilepsy. This research suggested to Lombroso that there were direct links between criminal conduct and certain bodily factors, and that these could be hereditary. But because it was basically evolutionist in assumption, 'criminal anthropology' also allowed, with varying degrees of emphasis, for the determining effects of environment. Most followers of Lombroso concluded that the criminal was a complex product of both inheritance and environment and that his condition could best be understood as a particular form of insanity. When it came to implementing the law, weighing questions of moral responsibility, of punishment, of incarceration and of possible rehabilitation, all relevant factors should be taken into account.

Though 'Our Dark Places' did not labour the 'anthropological' aspect, it clearly helped to determine the writers' approach to the subject. After all, within the prisons, signs of an official unwillingness to try to understand the criminal nature were everywhere in sight. First, though, it was necessary to penetrate the 'heavy, castellated, frowning blocks of masonry' that made up the prison's façade.

Within, when you have passed the double outer gates and been locked out and locked in all of them in succession, you find yourself in a central hall out of which run high, cage-like galleries, divided into tiers and landings, with a

*'Holloway Prison', from* Secrets of the Prison-House *by Arthur Griffiths, 1894.*

row of small low cells on either side. In some cases wire netting is stretched above the lowest tier to prevent prisoners throwing themselves over the higher landings in one of those frenzies of rage or despair of which every prison record has its traces. Every cell is like every other. It glistens with whitewash, and its polished floor is so clean that you could dine off it. Its furniture consists of the plank bed, with its mattress and blankets neatly rolled together in a corner, a wooden stool, a set of tin pannikins, a little table for reading, and two or three books – the inevitable Bible, prayer and hymn books or devotional manual leading off. There is a single window high up, barred, and letting in no sight even of the small, mean world of the prison yard.[7]

Prisons were places without perspective, texture or colour, where a heavy silence was interrupted only by the all too predictable sounds of controlled movement. No wonder the inhabitants – many of them already biologically inadequate – could be seen to be further dehumanized by sensory deprivation.

Here you come across a prisoner with his face to the wall, like a dunce in a village school, simply waiting an order in the sharp warder's voice. That is one of the small and needless humiliations of prison life, which in the end

*'Prisoners at exercise', from* Secrets of the Prison-House.

*'Wormwood Scrubs', from* Secrets of the Prison-House.

turn criminals into machines, without initiative or self-respect. When you enter a cell its occupant rises, salutes, glances at you in a shy animal way, and so stands till you disappear. In the exercise ground you have a dreary counterfeit of life and movement. Round and round goes the melancholy drab-yellow crowd on in concentric rings of stone – the *cirque effaré*, as Verlaine calls it. The stronger men take the outer and longer rounds, the weaklings and the older prisoners the inner and shorter ones. No man speaks to his brother, and no man approaches his fellow within a distance of some feet.[8]

'Our Special Commissioner' may have been wholly humanitarian in his aims, but he nevertheless felt the need, like most newspaper campaigners, to employ a professional rhetoric that would adjust the focal distance between his readers and the world they were reading about. And in this case the sharply detailed 'realism', although conventional in writings about prisons, served as a much-needed induction. For most readers, quite unaccustomed to such things, looking into prisons was indeed like peering into darkness.

'The ponderous iron gates, that hide more human misery than any other corner the civilized world contains, rarely open to receive a critical visitor,' the *Chronicle*'s 'Commissioner' chastised. 'More might go if more knew or cared. But few know or care. The great machine rolls obscurely on, cumbrous, pitiless, obsolete, unchanged.'[9] It was an appeal

*Convicts at Labour, from* Secrets of the Prison-House.

partly for charity, partly for understanding, mainly for enquiry. Briskly
ignoring potential confusions between cause and effect, frankly evading
the charge of circularity, the *Chronicle* had no difficulty in identifying
most of the prisoners, through physique alone, as a separate kind: 'poor,
attenuated, flaccid, pale from want of fresh air, with sloping shoulders,
narrow of chest, the eyes expressionless'.[10] More than that: appearance
could still provide evidence of true character, because some faces could –
quite literally – be 'read'. 'You see young – often charming and beautiful –
faces among the grown men – rare flowers sprinkled among the mass of
weeds.'[11] You might discern, for instance, 'a strong well-set-up boy with
a face on which all sorts of good qualities were legibly written ... sent to
prison simply because he had been found in the streets at night and had
nowhere to lay his head'.[12]

In a prison all human life was present, condemned in law through
conduct, birth or chance. Accordingly, 'Our Dark Places' ended with a
number of demands based on both modern 'anthropological' discovery
and ageless moral principle. A Royal Commission was needed which
would, among other things, establish a school 'for the study of the
pathology of crime'. Power must be returned from the central government to local authorities, there must be separate prisons for juvenile
offenders and an overall increase in the number of prison staff.

Even before the series had ended the response was underway. The
*Chronicle* published some twenty-five letters from the 'immense mass' it
claimed to have received. Many of those printed were from workers

within the prison system, including such senior men as the 'Principal Medical Officer' at Wormwood Scrubs; other letters were from MPs. It is almost certain that the inquiry carried out for the Government in 1894 by the Departmental Committee on Prisons was inspired by 'Our Dark Places'. As this committee was responsible in turn for the Prisons Act of 1898, which went some way to improve conditions, it can truly be said that this was one of the occasions when investigative journalism did produce concrete reforms.

The theoretical grounds upon which the reforms were based remained obscure. When the Departmental Committee produced its report it pointedly avoided any detailed consideration of the pathological origins of criminal behaviour, maintaining that

> Criminal anthropology as a science is in its embryo stage, and while scientific and more particularly medical observation and experience are of the most essential value in guiding opinion on the whole subject, it would be a loss of time to search for a perfect system in learned but conflicting theories, when so much can be done by the recognition of the plain fact that the great majority of prisoners are ordinary men and women amenable more or less, to all those influences which affect persons outside.[13]

That brief disclaimer should probably be interpreted as a bureaucratic ploy: a message for those who had ears to hear, tacit acknowledgement of the growing importance of 'criminal anthropology' without as yet the appropriate action. Still, it did at least recognize that future methods would have to be more scientific and that even now punishment could no longer be viewed as the sole purpose of confinement.

In the nineties significant changes took place in the way people thought about crime, its causes as well as its cures. Reform was in the air, and the *Chronicle* made its contribution. So did a poem by one of the paper's most devoted, if quizzical readers. *The Ballad of Reading Gaol* commemorates two prison lives: that of its hero, a guardsman soon to be executed for having murdered his unfaithful wife, and that of its author. Either way the subject-matter was real enough.

## 'THE GROTESQUENESS OF ONE'S ASPECT'

'The criminal classes are so close to us that even the policeman can see them,' wrote Oscar Wilde in *A Few Maxims for the Instruction of the Over-Educated*. 'They are so far away from us that only the poet can understand them.'[14] Few of the over-educated managed to see the problem of the criminal quite that plainly, and soon after his own imprisonment even Wilde tried to learn something about contemporary criminology, ordering, from his cell in Reading Gaol, works either written or edited by the Reverend Morrison. Signs of this reading are to be found in the extraordinary letter of self-justification that Wilde wrote to Lord Alfred Douglas, later known as *De Profundis* and, less overtly, in *The Ballad of Reading Gaol*.

It was in every respect a little late in the day. Progressive opinion had for some time been worried about the state of the prisons. Amongst the most committed – radicals like Edward Carpenter and Peter Kropotkin, social scientists like Havelock Ellis – the main intellectual sticking-point was rehabilitation, because it meant returning the criminal to a society which they largely disapproved of. The question was further aggravated when 'criminal anthropology' told them that illegal activities were often a form of inherited behaviour not far removed from congenital madness.

Unfettered by the conservative leanings of the Departmental Committee, they therefore insisted that prisons could only be reformed alongside simultaneous improvements in the outside world. Edward Carpenter,[15] for example, founded his criminology, like his sexual theory (he was, within the legal and social constraints of the time, a campaigning homosexual), on a doctrine of organic development or 'exfoliation'.[16] For Carpenter, 'function precedes organization' but 'desire precedes function'. Inevitably, in a capitalist or 'mechanical' society, where function is honoured above desire, the man who prematurely follows his desires might appear like a criminal, might actually become one. Whilst Carpenter quite openly admitted to the utopianism of his protests against the maltreatment of criminals, he was able to trace his ideal back to 'the healthy body' itself: the 'living unity' which was 'the most perfect society conceivable',[17] where each part operated according to an innate energy irrespective of the function that it would serve in the whole. Wilde greatly admired Carpenter's *Civilization, Cause and Cure* of 1889, which he eventually read in Paris in 1900;[18] while, in a reciprocal tribute, equally belated, Carpenter's specific treatment of the criminal, *Prisons, Police and Punishment* (1905), made much of Wilde's *Ballad*.[19]

The anarchist Peter Kropotkin,[20] whom Wilde hailed in *De Profundis* as 'a man with the soul of that beautiful white Christ that seems to be coming out of Russia',[21] went even further than Carpenter in his diatribes against the prison system. Kropotkin had himself spent time in prison before coming to England, and in a series of books and tracts he insisted that all forms of incarceration were intolerable, a systematic destruction of the human capacity to develop.

The right to 'develop' being absolute, Kropotkin found in 'criminal anthropology' only a deepening of contradiction. He replied to Lombroso's biological classifications with hard logic – 'We cannot consider society as entitled to exterminate all people having defective structure of the brain ... all idiots do not become assassins'[22] – and he saw through to the moral muddle behind the orthodox view that society had the right to punish the criminals it admitted to having produced.

Kropotkin's overall confidence derived from his trust in the individual 'will', an inherent human quality which, as he stressed in his anarchist writings, would, if left unrestricted, allow a natural balance between altruism and egoism. What distinguished him from other reformers, even from Carpenter, was his conviction that all social organization demoralized the will, so that prison was simply the most shameless, the most blatantly self-negating form of political control. If indeed, as Kropotkin put it, humanity was 'one great family, no member of which can be injured without the injury being felt by a wide circle of his fellows, and ultimately by the whole of society',[23] then the business of defining the anomaly was obviously futile.

Carpenter and Kropotkin were agreed that concepts of the criminal were inseparable from prevailing social ideologies. In that respect at least their views were not far removed from one line of argument put forward by Havelock Ellis,[24] whose *The Criminal*, first published in 1890 but later revised, can stand as a representative textbook of advanced opinion. *The Criminal* is almost totally divided between an overall optimism based on social reform and a Lombrosian attempt to classify criminals according to medical records. No sooner has he insisted that legal 'crime' and moral 'vice' must not be confused than Ellis is equating them himself:

> They both spring from the same root. The criminal is simply a person who is, by his organization, directly anti-social; the vicious person is not directly anti-social, but he is indirectly so ... They are both anti-social because they are both more or less unfitted from harmonious social order, both from organic reasons, more or less lazy.[25]

While doubting the importance of the 'morbid' or 'insane' element in criminal behaviour – an over-emphasis that he explicitly associated with the influence of Lombroso – Ellis did nevertheless concede that the 'morally insane' and the 'instinctive criminal' 'overlapped to a very large extent'. His difficulty in maintaining distinctions resulted from his habit of explaining everything in terms of social function. Given the negative function of crime (as Ellis understood it) all categories of criminal conduct inevitably tended to merge back into one.

In spite of their many differences, the advanced reformers of the nineties were all seeking to redefine the criminal as someone whose illegal impulses, whether the product of 'heredity' or 'environment', were in some sense intelligible, and even, on occasion, legitimate. Apparent deviants had to be understood within the context of a social ideal: Carpenter's 'a healthy body', Kropotkin's 'one great family', Ellis's model of 'harmonious social order'. In the course of the decade the progressive wing reached a point where the injustice of justice could best be explained as a transitional inefficiency or malfunction of the social system as a whole. This insight by no means relieved all the difficulties. In some ways, modern ideas perpetuated an ancient principle whereby the degree of punishment was determined by the degree of responsibility, but they also prompted a further thought, which might turn out to be either sinister or constructive: the exceptional man might need to be exceptionally treated. And, then again, what should be done with that other kind of offender, the criminal who was, in effect, everyman? How to reform the norm?

Such moral conundrums can hardly have been foremost in their minds when 'Our Special Commissioner' and his friends had researched 'Our Dark Places' for the *Daily Chronicle* back in 1893. 'Criminal anthropology' was obviously important, but within the limited space of a newspaper investigation there was no particular pressure to consider its implications further. Their goal had been comparatively simple: demonstrate, from direct experience and with convincingly realistic detail, that the prisons were inhumanly run, and humane reform would surely follow.

## 'THE TRAGEDY IN ONE'S SOUL'

By the time he was released from Reading Gaol in May 1897 Wilde had, naturally enough, developed a strong personal interest in prison reform.[26] He immediately decided to offer the *Daily Chronicle* an article about his experiences[27] and, according to Richard Ellmann, planned eventually to write three essays, 'of which two were to describe prison, and the third, as foreshadowed in *De Profundis*, to deal with Christ as

*The Contrast' from George Griffith, 'Sidelights on Criminal Life,'* Pearson's Magazine, *January 1902. The criminal on the left betrays his moral decline with slumped shoulders, shifty gaze and hands in pockets. Once inside the prison signs of reform are apparently there for all to see: the upright posture on the right speaks of what already lies within. Compare Wilde in* De Profundis: *'Our very dress makes us grotesque. We are zanies of sorrow. We are clowns whose hearts are broken'.*

the precursor of the romantic movement in art'.[28] On the 27th the paper published his letter protesting at the treatment of children in prison, in which he remarked, apropos the Du Cane policy, that 'wherever there is centralization there is stupidity'.[29] In March 1898 he sent another letter to 'the one paper in England that has taken interest in this important question', listing the additional and unacknowledged punishments of hunger, insomnia and disease that every prisoner underwent.[30] Yet when the *Chronicle* had given *The Ballad of Reading Gaol* an enthusiastic review the previous month, Wilde (who at one point had wanted the paper to print his poem, and had thought that John Burns or T. P. O'Connor might contribute a preface) felt that his intentions had been misunderstood.[31] 'The *Chronicle* meant well,' he conceded, but 'there is more in the poem than a pamphlet on prison reform.'[32]

The *Chronicle* had described *The Ballad* as an 'indictment against our common dealing with the criminal' which told 'with a poet's brevity and power what we have persistently maintained about the evils of our prison system'.[33] Recognition indeed, though Wilde, by his own instinctive literary criteria, had every reason to feel dissatisfied. For one thing he had, before his own downfall, and even after it, come to think of criminals as antinomian heroes rather than simply as suffering victims. This was a gradual but unwavering conviction. When he had visited a penitentiary in Nebraska in 1882 he had commented upon the bestial faces of the prisoners as revealed in their photographs. 'I should hate to see a criminal with a noble face,' he had remarked.[34] In his maturity, though, Wilde came to see criminals as being like the best kind of writer, contemptuous of the stultifying mores of the bourgeoisie: a high estimation that set him firmly apart from those of his contemporaries who were primarily interested in criminals in order to reform them, and who were attracted to the idea that what separated offenders from society was some kind of initial biological flaw. Wilde certainly knew and preferred Baudelaire's view that 'crime, the taste for which the human animal draws from the womb of his mother, is natural in its origins.'[35] 'Laughter,' wrote Wilde, continuing another Baudelairean association, 'is the primaeval attitude towards life – a mode of approach that survives only in artists and criminals.'[36]

In his own writings protagonists took to crime because it satisfied their imaginative needs. This was as true of the historical figures he favoured as of the fictional characters he invented. He had written with respectful approval about Thomas Chatterton, the forger and, in 'Pen, Pencil and Poison', about Thomas Wainewright, the author and murderer.[37] He liked the idea that literary invention was a form of criminality but turned it into a double paradox by presenting literature's one true crime – plagiarism – as if it were a kind of moral virtue. Eventually, in *The Importance of Being Earnest*, he constructed a character, Ernest Worthing, who metaphorically 'murders' his own creation, brother Jack, in order that he might conform to the rules of society. When poets are dishonest it's a measure of their integrity; when other men tell the truth it's a sign of their short-sightedness: that had been the message of 'The Decay of Lying', and almost everything else that Wilde had to say on the subject of art.

As well as to criminal writers, Wilde was drawn to political criminals, particularly as they appeared in literature. Like others of his generation he saw in contemporary Russia signs of a new kind of criminal who appeared to link an aristocratic style with democratic ideals. *Vera*, the play he wrote soon after leaving Oxford, may well have been prompted by a reading of Turgenev's *Fathers and Sons*, with its definitive Nihilist hero, Bazarov. Wilde was equally at home with the starker view offered by Turgenev's compatriot Dostoevsky and, in an anonymous review of *Crime and Punishment*, he identified Raskolnikov as someone who 'has fled the society of men; has brooded over many social questions; has written an article in a social paper on crime, in which he declares that crime, though it is punishable in ordinary men and women, is permitted to extraordinary beings.'[38]

At the end of 'The Soul of Man Under Socialism' (1891), his most coherent social statement, he brought together Nihilist heroism and the kind of anarchist socialism then in vogue among certain London intellectuals. 'A Nihilist who rejects all authority because he knows authority to be evil and welcomes all pain, because through that he realizes his personality' was, Wilde had decided, 'a real Christian'.[39]

The concept of the 'political criminal' was quite widely mooted in the early nineties – even Lombroso allowed the possibility[40] – and Wilde was nothing if not *au fait* with current ideas. His interest in criminals, however catholic, always excluded the purely pathological. Nor, like Miss Prism in *The Importance of Being Earnest*, was he in favour of 'this modern mania for turning bad people into good people at a moment's notice'.[41] 'Never attempt to reform a man. Men never repent,' he told an interviewer a year before he was arrested,[42] clearly implying that reform without repentance was either not worth having or a contradiction in terms. As for criminals whose activities could be explained by environmental determinism or whose motivations could be glimpsed by statistical tables and sociological research, these fell badly short of his romantic imaginings. He had no interest in the kind of criminal famously discovered by Lombroso and later much publicized by Max Nordau's *Degeneration*, and he was particularly antipathetic to the theory that artists were also criminals because they were in some sense or another 'insane'. Wilde did know, however, that in the mid-nineties this was the coming idea, and so, for instance, in a desperate petition to the Home Secretary written from Reading Gaol in July 1896, he allowed himself to explain his situation through an appeal to the very pathology that had marked him out as a dangerous case:

Such offences are forms of sexual madness and are recognized as such not merely by modern pathological science but by much modern legislation ... on the ground that they are diseases to be cured by a physician, rather than crimes to be punished by a judge. In the works of eminent men of science such as Lombroso and Max Nordau, to take merely two instances out of many, this is specially insisted on with reference to the intimate connection between madness and the literary and artistic temperament.[43]

On his release he was free to mock the spurious diagnosis he had formerly espoused: 'The fact that I am ... a pathological problem in the eyes of German scientists is only interesting to German scientists.'[44] Wilde's concept of the criminal as society's exemplary outcast was the reverse image of the more prevalent notion that the criminal was society's tell-tale symptom. To say that the radicals wanted to reform the criminal by reforming society, but that Wilde wanted to reform society while preserving its visionary outsiders is also correct, if insufficient. In *The Ballad*, at any rate, Wilde would endeavour to make criminals of his readers, to express a universal truth about human nature through the tragic paradox that not just some, but all men 'kill the thing they love'. 'All limitations, external or internal, are prison-walls, and life is a limitation,' he wrote to the ex-prisoner Cunninghame Graham.[45] With such a comprehensive vision as that in his mind, no wonder he felt frustrated when *The Ballad* was praised merely for its advocacy of prison reform.

Even as he was composing the poem Wilde knew that there would be problems. In August 1897 he wrote from France to Laurence Housman:

I am occupied in finishing a poem, terribly realistic for me, and drawn from actual experience – a sort of denial of my own philosophy of art in many ways. I hope it is good, but every night I hear cocks crowing in Berneval, so I am afraid I may have denied myself and would weep bitterly, if I had not wept away all my tears.[46]

And he voiced similar doubts to Robert Ross a month or so later, when he confessed:

The poem suffers under the difficulty of a divided aim in style. Some is realistic, some is romantic: some poetry, some propaganda. I feel it keenly, but as a whole I think the production interesting: that it is interesting from more points of view than one is artistically to be regretted.[47]

When his poem finally appeared, all Wilde's fears were at once confirmed by the critical response. There were few reviewers – apart from his particular friends – who failed to remark on an unresolved conflict between realistic propaganda and romantic abstraction, Arthur Symons setting the terms for an enduring consensus with his complaint that the poem 'is partly a plea on behalf of prison reform; and so far as it is written with that aim, it is not art'.[48]

Nearly forty years later W. B. Yeats made much the same objection. When he compiled *The Oxford Book of Modern Verse*, he had no qualms about omitting whole stanzas from the poem, including the celebrated refrain: 'I plucked out even famous lines because, effective in themselves, put into *The Ballad* they become artificial, trivial, arbitrary: a work of art can have but one subject.'[49] Yeats, we might note, then took the opportunity to quote in his introduction some of the 'effective' lines he had cut from the text.

It was the combination of 'realism' and 'reform' that caused, and has continued to cause, the trouble among literary people: ballads that were unequivocally about execution were perfectly acceptable. Wilde's poem belongs to a tradition that includes, for example, Kipling's 'Danny Deever' and a poem in Housman's *A Shropshire Lad* (1896) about another hanging:

> There sleeps in Shrewsbury jail:
> Or wakes, as may betide,
> A better lad, if things went right,
> Than most that sleep outside.

*A Shropshire Lad* appeared when Wilde was in gaol. Robert Ross is said to have learned some of the poems by heart and to have recited them to Wilde on his prison visits.[50] But Housman's was one, only one, of several poetic moods that Wilde was seeking, and Wilde's poem was to be subjected to a harsher critical test than Housman ever had to endure.

Naturally on the defensive, Wilde typically reacted to his critics (who were often only making points similar to those that he had already admitted in private) by protesting at their very right to comment. Their supposedly detached reading, he complained, merely reproduced the principles of judicial authority and moral alienation that his poem set out to dissolve. Answering an anonymous review in the *Academy*, which concluded that Thomas Hood's *The Dream of Eugene Aram* was finer than *The Ballad* because Hood was 'superior to morbidity and hysteria',[51] Wilde conceded, with appropriately heavy irony, that here was 'a heavy judicial charge'. He went on to protest: 'People don't understand that criticism is prejudice because to understand one must love and to love one must have passion. It is only the unimaginative who are ever fair.'[52] The point was to assert the power of his poem to transform 'morbidity and hysteria' through its expression of what he had elsewhere called 'the mystery of love'.

It was because Wilde was so fiercely ambitious that the fissures within his poem ran so deep. In a way, the formal divisions are a tribute to his intellectual integrity. Dissatisfied by the simple expedient of turning the criminal into a mistreated casualty, which might have been the method of 'anthropology' or 'reform', veering sometimes towards the idea of sacrifice but unable to find an innocent specimen, Wilde had ended up writing a poem that repeatedly tried to free the condemned man by identifying authority with its object, reaching in its refrain for a trope that would go far beyond the reformatory impulses that even authority was slowly beginning to apply to itself.

The result is an unsettled and unsettling poem in which present mercy is threatened by ultimate forgiveness, yet heartless justice meshes with original sin ('Strange it was to think that he/Had such a debt to pay').[53] If in the prison world innocence cannot guarantee martyrdom ('For none can tell to what red Hell/His sightless soul may stray'), then neither is guilt proved by suffering. Sometimes the condemned man is apart from those who 'watched with gaze of dull amaze'; sometimes to share in the pain is to share in the offence: 'Alas! It is a fearful thing/To feel another's guilt.' This pull between sympathy and distance only induces numbness ('Though I was a soul in pain/My pain I could not feel'); while sympathy itself is but the partner of terror in a gathering of ghosts. 'It is sweet to dance to violins/When love and life are fair' turns, via 'the slouch and swing' of 'the Fools' parade' into, first, 'the formal pace and loathesome grace' with which 'the phantoms kept their trust', then 'the pirouettes of marionettes'. Terror reduces the sympathetic imagination to a puppet theatre, a nightmare vision that grimly confirms a common neo-Darwinist metaphor for an unknowable determinism overruling human consciousness. The poet multiplies his ghastly *danses macabres*, his images of the mind's inability to stand apart from its own processes and what they create.

This is the condition of hellish solipsism, the failure to distinguish between self and surroundings, which prison conditions bring about. The only thing men have in common is the solitary confinement of their minds. Those – Chaplain, Governor or Doctor – who would pretend that the law of the land is God's law are not merely blind to the principle that the way in which laws are implemented determines the justice that they might embody, but lack the terrible imagination which renders all justice an illusion. The prisoners who do see this, among them the poet, see little else.

It should hardly come as a surprise that there is hesitation over the indictment. 'And so he had to die', 'For each man kills': the connectives are weak, unconvincing. Even the ballad injunction, 'By each let this be heard', is initially robbed by the 'each' of its appeal to community.[54] Before 'each' has finally become 'all', the poem has already pronounced its elegaic ending: 'In silence let him lie'. Sacrificial language accumulates in the closing stanzas, it is true, but the final references are to Christ in Judgement, divine intervention a very distant compensation when, all the while, the remote vision of redemption has been accompanied by the insistent empirical rhetoric of a prison reformer, noting the 'hangman with his gardener's gloves', the 'white-washed wall', the 'three-planked bed', the 'slippery asphalte', the 'quicklime on their boots'.

Wilde's poem was also 'realistic' in other simple senses. Records of the guardsman's trial support Wilde's presentation of his situation. The defence counsel had managed to convince the Judge that 'the prisoner was fondly attached to his wife' and that 'the marriage was the result of a pure love for one another',[55] so Wilde was certainly entitled to refer in his poem to 'the poor dead woman whom he loved', though it was not exactly the case that she was 'murdered in her bed'. That the condemned man 'often said that he was glad/The hangman's hands were near' was true, however, and it was later recorded that the guardsman died in a spirit of Christian repentance.[56] Wilde was as much taken by the man's appearance as by his fate. *The Ballad* insists that his 'step seemed light and gay', endorsing an observation made at the actual trial: 'He walked out of the dock with a firm and light step and with a smile on his face.' Here, physically, was the criminal with the 'noble face' who Wilde had once dreaded seeing, but had later come to believe in as a symbolic portent.

When his publisher, Leonard Smithers, worried that there might be a risk of libel, Wilde protested that he was 'describing a general scene with general types',[57] which was evasive. He did admit, though, that he had 'libelled' the warders, since 'they were – most of them – as good as possible to me. But to poetry all must be sacrificed, even warders.'[58] Some confusion between 'realism' and 'poetry' was clearly inevitable, though for Wilde the mixture was a lasting source of pain.

Realism was like a concession to his oppressors – to the 'actual experience' that he believed sullied the purity of art, curtailed the freedom of the artist. It was as if the realistic style, albeit in the service of reform, menaced him with a return to the place from which he had just been released, an extended punishment. After all, he had always maintained that art must refuse to respect the demands of its time if it were to retain its independence, even if he had also allowed that art might be prophetic of an improved society that would, as he put it in 'The Soul of Man', be like 'a thoroughly healthy organism'.[59] For Wilde, the 'tragedy in one's soul' that prison brought to light was both literal and universal, specific and continuous. Faced with the tragic paradox of human motivation, prison reform, however wholehearted, must always be a half-measure. Universal guilt, even when sexual in origin, had, like original sin, no earthly cure.

Many years later, long after Wilde's death, Lord Alfred Douglas pointed out that the inspiration for *The Ballad*'s refrain came from an exchange in Shakespeare's problem comedy *The Merchant of Venice*:

> *Bassanio*: Do all men kill the things they do not love?
> *Shylock*: Hates any man the thing he would not kill?

Douglas remarked that Wilde had 'inverted the meaning' but retained the 'music',[60] which is correct, but he failed to point out that Shakespeare's characters avoid the paradoxical admission that killing might be loving, that loving might be killing. Throughout Shakespeare, whenever justice is a real possibility, references to the convolutions of desire tend to be guarded. Only in tragedy, where justice is strikingly distant, does the paradox wound. Othello, for example, who progresses from 'That death's unnatural that kills for loving' to 'I kiss'd thee ere I kill'd thee. No way but this/Killing my self to die upon a kiss.' In tragedy, killing and loving compose an act of bonding, a kind of desperate blackmail that rebounds, turning the active party into his victim's victim whilst at the same time, by a vicious twist of moral logic, continuing to hold him responsible. However sententious its origins in *The Merchant*, Wilde's refrain, provocative yet forbidding, had retrieved an oracular trope, best suited to tragedy, from what in Shakespeare's comedy was mainly a rhetorical trap.

As a realistic document, on the side of reform, *The Ballad* is a protest against the limitations of the public view. As a poem it sets up a tragic confrontation within its readers, making them both accuser and accused. Interpreting its refrain as an expression of their own nature, they are obliged to earn their own sentence.

At least, that was probably the only justification that Wilde could decently have allowed himself. Douglas also reports that when asked for an explanation of 'All men kill the thing they love', Wilde answered: 'It's a mistake to ask a poet what he means by any obscure phrase in a poem because he may mean one thing or several things. The answer is that it means just what it says in the poem:'[61] an unsatisfactory reply that must stand for as long as 'the tragedy in one's soul' conflicts with 'the grotesqueness of one's aspect'. Or, putting it another way, for as long as the introspection of the poet is expected to go deeper than the well-meaning uncoverings of 'Our Special Commissioner'.

# 5

# 'TIRED OF LIFE'
## Letters, literature and the suicide craze

If I were not afraid my people might keep it out of the
newspapers, I should commit suicide tomorrow.

Max Beerbohm to Will Rothenstein,
October 1893

## 'HE DIED ARTICULATE'

In the summer of 1893 a carpet designer named Ernest Clark was briefly news. He won this status by announcing his forthcoming death in a letter to the *Daily Chronicle* – a letter which he knew would be received only when the event was over. Here, almost in full, is what appeared in the paper on 16 August under the heading 'Tired of Life':

SIR, – When you receive this I shall have put an end to my existence by the aid of a bullet. This act is thoroughly premeditated, being planned six months ago. My best and most serious thoughts have been given to it, and my sanity, if ever man was sane, can be acknowledged by the friends I have spent the last fortnight with.

I resolved long ago that life is a sequence of shams. That men have had to create utopias and heavens to make it bearable; and that all the wisest men have been disgusted with life as it is. Carlyle and Voltaire advise hard work, but only as an anaesthetic. The good Socialists look forward to society with brains and love, but there will always be the animal, in and out of us, to fight with. The apostles of sensuousness have always had an interest for me, but when seen from a distance their lives, from Rousseau to the great Frenchmen of today, are despicable. The religions give each man an entity after this life, but why not all other animals, insects, etc? which even they will say is absurd. Only the transcendental and aesthetic in life are worth our thought. Only a life following beauty and creating it approaches any degree of joyousness, but the ugliness and vile monotony in my life have crowded beauty out ...

Three weeks ago I bought a revolver. On going to spend my holiday in Cambridgeshire I left it at the cloak-room, Liverpool-street, until this evening. The last two weeks, the happiest days in my life, were spent with my only friend. We had George Meredith and Théophile Gautier for companions. We lived in the fields, sketching, reading to each other, with strolls and days on the Cam. My greatest agony all these months is the idea of causing grief to my darling, whose friendship is the most sacred thing life has given me. But rather this blow than render her life wretched with my gloom.

I consider this explanation due to my fellows, to those who care. I was not consulted when I became a sentient being. Having reached maturity I object to life. Will not have it. Hate and despise it. That there should be no doubt in my own mind have been at least three months with the certainty of my end before my eyes.

This is the only writing concerning my death.

– August 14th, 8.5 p.m., Liverpool-street Waiting Room.

ERNEST CLARK

*A cartoon from the* Pall Mall Gazette *of 25 August 1893.*

This is the traditional suicide note in an ingeniously modern variation. Like any other newspaper reader Clark knew that editors believed self-inflicted death to be newsworthy, so he could be confident of receiving attention; and by posting it when the act was irrevocably decided upon, he could be sure that the macabre experience of reading an explanatory letter from a dead hand would be available to a countless number. Reading it now, as a modern literary critic might, at a safe historical distance and as a symptomatic text, Clark's letter would seem to try to combine, in however crude a way, the 'disembodied' quality that Arthur Symons thought marked the authentic Decadent voice[1] with a lastingly realistic record of 'the ugliness and vile monotony' of his own particular travail. Since he was, as he boasted, a reader of Gautier and Meredith, and since he left behind him a short poem in French beginning 'La vie est brève', it is quite possible that this was indeed Clark's ambition.

'He died articulate', someone commented at the time, 'and his voice had just that faraway, sepulchral note which fascinates a certain class of ghoulish beings to whom death is a mystery and life is not.'[2] Not quite so in fact; the whole business of suicide was highly topical. On the 17th – the day after Clark's letter – the *Chronicle* created a single column out of eight separate reports of suicide attempts, while in its correspondence columns, the 'Tired of Life' exchange at once got underway. It was to last for over a week, to involve fifty-seven letters and a thoughtful leader written by W. D. Morrison, the penal reformer,[3] to spill over into other journals and, predictably, to provoke from rivals the accusation that the whole affair had been engineered by the *Chronicle* in the first place.[4]

Public interest in suicide was prompted by two slightly contradictory forces: the theory that it was on the increase, dramatically, and the suggestion that the suicidal individual was exceptionally sensitive to the world around him, as a Decadent hero might be; that he possessed the kind of 'swift, disastrous and suicidal energy of genius' that Symons attributed, typically, to the poet Ernest Dowson.[5] Although this present study is primarily concerned with the ways in which the topic of suicide became ensnared in the workings of certain literary texts (largely as a result of the kind of attention the subject was given in the papers), it is also about how certain lives, of which Edward Clark's was one, aspired in the manner of their ending to the lasting reverberations of literature.

Alongside Clark's letter, the *Chronicle* had printed an account of another suicide: that of a sixteen-year-old boy, thought by his family to be quite happy, who had suddenly hanged himself, leaving a note confessing that he had been miserable for months. In its editorial, the paper commented on both deaths and also recalled the recent 'Canterbury Suicides', when a young couple had carried out a death pact. At the inquest it emerged that they had decided on 12 May to kill themselves on 9 June and that the act had been meticulously carried out: 'Their hats, umbrellas and a walking-stick had been carefully laid aside and a bunch of wild roses tied with crepe placed upon them.'[6] Was premeditation, the *Chronicle* wondered, evidence of a balanced mind or was it rather the opposite?

The same question preoccupied many contributors to the subsequent 'Tired of Life' debate. Did Clark's letter prove him to be supremely rational – the master of his own fate – or pitifully weak, even to the point of insanity, driven by forces beyond his control? Furthermore, did his avowed intention – to escape the insufficiency of life – conceal an unacknowledged motive: to achieve notoriety?

The specific issue of Clark's state of mind coincided with a general unease about the issuing of verdicts at inquests. Ever since the early nineteenth century the formulae of 'unsound mind' or 'temporary insanity' had been commonly adopted by coroners, mainly to protect relatives of the deceased from anachronistic laws which held that suicides could be denied proper burial and have their estates seized after death. Even when the law had been changed, the legal fictions continued to be used, though long before the nineties there was concern that they prevented serious comprehension of acts of self-destruction. 'Unsound mind' and 'temporary insanity' begged questions that were extremely pertinent to nineteenth-century theories of behaviour, and particularly to the philosophical problem of 'intention'. The essential distinction between suicide and accidental death was that suicide clearly involved an intention – which could be either announced by the perpetrator or inferred by others (such as coroners) from various kinds of evidence, of which suicide notes were the most obvious.

The trouble with diplomatic verdicts of 'insanity' was that they deprived the suicide of any real understanding of an act that was intentional by definition. For example, there were some who argued that suicide could be a rationally intended decision when it was a protest against the modern world. This viewpoint was applied to Ernest Clark, much as he had applied it to himself.

Personally, I do not think such suicides as Ernest Clark are insane, in the conventional sense. They are intensely out of harmony with their surroundings. They are a kind of first fruits of the new spirit that is abroad – a spirit which will one day be the world's regeneration, but which is apt, as yet, to shrink from the world's brutality – so hideous is the contrast often between the dream and the reality .... He who increases the sense of the beautiful may increase morbid repugnance to ugliness.[7]

But there were others who said that suicide was an insane act precisely because it was a symptom of an unbalanced society.

I hold ... that mental aberration is in nearly every case the precursory accompaniment of suicide. As mental disease and insanity are frightfully upon the increase, we may expect a proportionate rise in the number of self-murders during the coming years. To discover and stay the causes of the predisposing disorder is the only remedy for suicidal tendencies.[8]

Either way, Clark was seen as the product of a diseased social organism. And, more frighteningly still, he could be identified as an unusually voluble victim in what threatened to become a national epidemic of suicidal mania. After all, as nearly everyone agreed, the signs were already there.

A species of craze of suicide is palpably on the verge of breaking out among us. The conditions of life are daily narrowing the relationship between the imagination and the will, with a too obvious consequence, namely the subjugation of the latter to the sensuous and mysterious potency of the former.[9]

The present dreadful epidemic of suicide amongst the more intellectual seems to point to some most lame and impotent conclusions in our logic. We have certainly fallen below the Pagans when a studious suicide deliberately (and more or less sanely) addresses a document to an editor in defence of self-slaughter, for though a few of the ancient world's brilliants did advocate self-effacement, the majority submitted that it was ever man's duty to struggle on in the conditions imposed by the gods. A scientific age has, however, proved that 'he who increases in knowledge increases in sorrow', and a commercial age has superadded that to fail in the race for wealth, renders unworthy of life. There is also a sadder dictum.

We have abolished Providence. Each man is to the full the architect of his own fortune, idolised if lucky, ostracised if otherwise.[10]

We cannot help noticing that a great increase in suicides is taking place amongst the better educated – in fact, amongst those whose ideals are placed on a more elevated plane – amongst those who are disappointed with the slow rate that progress towards a better state is taking place – a progress hindered by the ignorance and selfish pleasures of the many.[11]

Deliberate suicide is simply the ultimate expression of moribund individualism – of the competitive system of production and distribution ....
Within a comparatively brief period ten men of good culture, with whom I was more or less intimately acquainted, have committed suicide.[12]

While Clark's true 'intentions' remained unknowable, his act of provocation brought promptly to the surface the growing apprehensions of the letter-writing, newspaper-reading (and highly moralistic[13]) community in the early nineties. And their obsessional fears must in turn have been fuelled by the string of scientific studies of suicide that had appeared on the Continent in recent years, all of them apparently based upon statistics far more commanding than any yet gathered in England.[14]

But cultural moods and statistical discoveries can be strangely interdependent – or so they were in the late nineteenth century – and both made their contribution to an extremely gradual shift in public awareness which eventually replaced the belief that suicide was a personal decision involving grave moral issues with the more modern view that held it to be a socially determined act and, therefore, to a greater or lesser extent, beyond moral aspersion. The essential work was Henry Morselli's *Suicide: an Essay on Comparative Moral Statistics* (1879), which was translated into English in 1881. Morselli claimed to have irrefutable proof of a 'terrible increase in suicide' in 'almost all the civilised countries of Europe, and of the new world'.[15] His book was typical of the scientific social methods of the time in that it tried to grasp the causes of deviant behaviour by categorizing and quantifying the conditions under which it became manifest: by reconsidering official tables that charted suicide rates in relation to a wide spectrum of disparate circumstances, Morselli hoped to establish the factors that influenced suicidal acts. *Suicide* parallelled Lombroso's study of crime and Maudsley's researches into insanity and, like them, fed into the intellectual current that reached a strident and somewhat aberrant climax with Nordau's *Degeneration*.

The sense of panic that pervaded the coming of the *fin de siècle* was by no means unconnected with the way that statistical categories tended, in the hands of scientific enthusiasts like Morselli, to proliferate almost beyond control. The factors allowed for in *Suicide* ranged from 'Cosmic-Natural Influences' (the seasons, the weather) to 'Social Influences' (religion, culture, economic conditions – within nations and between them) to 'Influences Arising out of the Biological and Social Conditions of the Individual' (including madness and a peculiarly modern phenomenon, 'tedium vitae').

Admittedly, as evidence of his intellectual integrity, Morselli made a point of raising objections to his method – which he then invariably dismissed fairly briskly. Whilst conceding that it was impossible for statistics to say anything conclusive about personal motives, he maintained that they could nonetheless provide a basis for reasonable deduction. To the more serious charge that statistics could never get to the bottom of what made people want to kill themselves because failed suicide attempts generally escaped official notice, he replied that records of the successful ones provided enough evidence to be going on with. Nor did he accept the criticism that suicides, murders, accidental and even natural deaths could on occasion be quite indistinguishable from one another after the event.

It may now seem odd that Morsellian moral statisticians persisted with their supposedly scientific approach when the foundations of their method were so open to question. They appear to have done so for one overwhelming reason: they believed that their statistics, however approximate, proved that suicide was increasing at a regular rate, and that consequently there must be some determining factor or factors at work. This positivist conviction was so strong that it seems to have overruled the most obvious objection to the truth of statistics – which was that as the scope, frequency, quantity and type of statistical surveys increased, so the number of suicides on record would also tend to multiply.[16]

In any case statistics would only produce, at the very most, a 'normal' or 'average' suicide that bore little or no relation to any actual instance. But given the need to account for the steadily rising figures, generalized explanations were only too welcome. Hence the force of Morselli's fashionably deprecating conclusion: 'Suicide is an effect of the struggle for existence and of human selection, which works according to the laws of evolution among civilised people.'[17] This set the pessimistic tone for several English writers.

In *Suicide, its History, Literature, Jurisprudence, Causation, and Prevention* (1885) W. Wynn Westcott, Deputy Coroner for Central Middlesex, approached the subject by taking the 'Epidemic Suicide' and 'tedium vitae' as adjuncts to his basic theory that 'the suicide rate increases with the amount of education.'[18] No wonder that the suicides of the summer of 1893, some of them carried out by frustrated auto-didacts like Ernest Clark, seemed like grim evidence of a social prognostication. They inspired a further Morsellian work: S. A. K. Strahan's *Suicide and Insanity*, completed in October, which held that a suicide was someone who was 'unfit to live' but also argued that the recent plethora was 'due to two causes: first, because the increase of wealth has not beneficially affected the great mass of people; and second, because many of the people are deteriorating from city life, unhealthy occupations, and the wear and tear of modern life generally.'[19]

In the nineties, and for a long time to come, the causes of suicide formed a subject upon which many people had at least one opinion, and some people had several. Modern methods had disclosed the cost of modern life; but modern life was not necessarily held responsible for modern methods. So it was that the suicide had become the classic modern instance of any number of modern ailments – as Ernest Clark may have known all too well.

## 'DOING IT BEAUTIFULLY'

On the subject of suicide, metaphysical philosophers could be every bit as treacherous as moral statisticians. Arthur Schopenhauer was widely respected by intellectuals and writers in the nineties for his belief that all men were subject to the vagaries of an impersonal 'Will' that made daily life totally unpredictable and frequently unbearable. Yet Schopenhauer, though ranked the supreme 'pessimist' of the age, had no patience with the idea that suicide could be an apt response to a possibly pointless existence, counselling instead a kind of stoic, even Buddhist withdrawal. After all, as he put it in his major work, *The World as Will and Idea*:

> Far from being a denial of the will, suicide is a phenomenon of strong assertion of the will; for the essence of negation lies in this, that the joys of life are shunned, not its sorrows. The suicide wills life, and is only dissatisfied with the conditions under which it has presented itself to him.[20]

The same logical refutation informed Schopenhauer's essay 'On Suicide', which became widely available in English as one of the *Studies in Pessimism* translated in 1891.[21] Here he spoke out strongly against the attitudes of the Church and of the law, particularly in England, but stuck to his conviction that suicides were pitifully misguided people. They had abandoned their chance to achieve an elevated state of endurance, and as an inquiry into the meaning of life their experiment was self-contradictory because it destroyed 'the very consciousness that puts the question and awaits the answer'.[22] Schopenhauer was a paradoxical pessimist, disconcertingly lively and operating at a level of abstraction far removed from most English discourse, but his glamorous gloom compelled some notable writers to engage with him. In the early nineties the most flamboyant of these was Shaw, who co-opted a pessimistic philosophy for his own optimistic purposes; and Shaw, though he made no contribution to the 'Tired of Life' debate, certainly had a direct influence upon the opinions of someone who did: his friend, the dramatic critic William Archer.

A letter from Archer published in the *Chronicle* on 18 August presented, in an extreme form, the modern 'rational' case. Even the Bible, its argument ran, contained no injunctions against self-inflicted death, so in our present secular world it would surely, sooner or later, come to be seen as a wholly acceptable option.

> What we want – what our grandsons or great-grandsons will probably have – is a commodious and scientific lethal chamber which shall reduce to a minimum the *physical* terrors and inconveniences of suicide, both for the patient and for his family and friends. In a rational state of civilization, self-effacement should cost us no more physical 'screwing up of courage' than a visit to the barber's and much less than a visit to the dentist's.[23]

Complaints about the 'selfishness' of suicides were hardly ever valid because from a 'rational' viewpoint no one was indispensable. Archer was prepared to make only two concessions, both of them topical: first that 'there is a certain snobbery in suicide as in everything else. Some foolish young people get it into their heads that it is in itself rather a fine thing, as Hedda Gabler would say, to "do it beautifully"'; and secondly, that 'there are even people, who ... would kill themselves in order to get a sentimental letter into the newspapers.'

The provocation appeared in the *Chronicle* on the same day as the verdict on Clark's death ('Suicide ... whilst of unsound mind'), a letter from one of Clark's friends testifying to his remarkable sincerity, and reports of five more suicide attempts. It led to the intervention of Richard Le Gallienne, who noisily upheld the values of 'common sense, charged with a few sparks of common courage',[24] and to Morrison's editorial, which rejected Archer's proposal that suicide should be made easy but admitted that 'It is not the stoical idea of suicide but rather the laxative idea, if we may so phrase it, which nowadays gains hold of the imagination. Life is so complicated, so difficult to our many-sided outlook that we tend to grow "in love with easeful death".'[25]

As a contribution to a correspondence column Archer's letter bore the hallmark of ironical overstatement that identified its author as a professional, and it almost certainly represented a personal effort to reopen public discussion on a matter of private conviction. The real-life deaths of 1893 (which were quickly to earn the epithet 'Ibscene')[26] gave Archer a chance to rake up arguments left unresolved since 1891, when he had reviewed Shaw's *Quintessence of Ibsenism* with an open letter in the *New Review*.[27] At the time Shaw had refused Archer's invitation to reply in print, but he had written privately rejecting the charge that he had misconstrued Ibsen's intentions.[28] It had been an obtuse exchange, with both men taking pains to be as uncooperative as possible by continually misunderstanding the meaning of each other's key terms. The crux, though, was Schopenhauer, and arguments for and against the 'rationality' of suicide.

Throughout the *Quintessence* Shaw had adopted Schopenhauer's philosophy that life is controlled by a universal 'Will' which overrides all our supposedly 'rational' attempts to control it. This was a metaphysic that Shaw approved of in the main, but he enjoyed manipulating the ironies. The reality of existence, he said, was that whatever our reason tells us about its miseries, human life will continue nonetheless. That, for example, was why Hedda Gabler's attitude to suicide was so absurd. 'Doing it beautifully' was an aesthetically grotesque comment upon an intellectually empty gesture. Archer, too, thought that Hedda was wrong-headed, but only because she trivialized what could, in the right circumstances, be a wise course of action.

Both men made much of a pronouncement they attributed to Voltaire, that he 'could not see the necessity' for the continuance of life.[29] Shaw's point was that the absence of any apparent 'necessity' proved the existence of an exterior force which could, in Schopenhauerian terms, be called the 'Will'. Archer's reply was that the absence of any perceptible necessity obliged man to rely on his own judgement, call it the 'reason'. Shaw said that the 'reason' was merely a positive manifestation of 'Will'. Archer said that while it was true that the 'reason' fell short of absolute knowledge, it was all that men had to go on. Which was why Archer supported suicide as a rational act but at the same time admitted that one might question its appropriateness according to circumstances.

Shaw was the nineties' surreptitious metaphysician: a materialist and a relativist in his daily politics, who secreted his absolutes elsewhere, in unfathomable impulses for survival. Archer, undoubtedly Shaw's imaginative inferior, better understood the issues as many readers of the *Chronicle* saw them. Archer knew that in a godless and arbitrary universe, such as Schopenhauer envisaged, all moral absolutes would appear to be absent, and that human behaviour could only be evaluated 'rationally', that is to say, *adverbially*. Archer's 'reason' told him that the act of self-destruction could not only be carried out 'rationally' but 'fashionably', 'ambiguously', 'studiously', 'snobbishly' and 'stoically'. It could even be done, as in Hedda Gabler's ideal, though not in her life, 'beautifully'.

For another interested reader of Schopenhauer and regular student of newspapers, Thomas Hardy, there was a further possibility, which was to kill oneself 'obscurely', especially during an 'epidemic'.[30] *Jude the Obscure*, published as a book early in 1896 but composed between 1890 and 1894, incorporates the most sensational fictional suicide of the nineties along with the most easily overlooked. The first is that of Jude's young son 'Father Time', who hangs himself after murdering his even younger step-brother and step-sister. A reviewer called this a 'nauseous tragedy' that came close to 'regions of pure farce'.[31] It certainly comes with a suspiciously melodramatic patness, with incentives for suicide almost too overwhelming. Sue Bridehead, the boy's step-mother, hysterical with guilt, believes that Jude's actions were triggered by her confession that she was pregnant again. Jude looks for the sociological or philosophical, indeed Schopenhauerian, explanations and as usual cites intellectual authority.

> It was in his nature to do it. The doctor says there are such boys springing up amongst us – boys of a sort unknown in the last generation – the outcome of new views of life. They seem to see all its terrors before they are old enough to have staying power to resist them. He says it is the beginning of the coming universal wish not to live. He's an advanced man, the doctor.[32]

Neither Sue's nor Jude's explanation is conclusive, but neither can be discounted, nor do they exhaust all the possibilities. There is, after all, the fact of Father Time's own suicide note, 'Done because we are too menny', which suggests an unconscious Malthusianism.

The pressing need to explain the horrific suicide of an innocent child is reflected by the unstable narrative tone that surrounds the whole episode. Is this the blackest of comedies or the most sentimental of tragedies? Awkward questions disrupt the reader's habitual impulse to appropriate such incidents for reassurance – to rest with interpretation. They also reflect back upon the cultural period over which the novel was written, and the wave of speculation about the causes of suicide that engulfed the early nineties. That in itself is enough to make *Jude* an historical classic among suicide texts.

But Hardy was sufficiently sensitive, both fascinated and appalled, to balance the high visibility of Father Time's suicide with another, more clandestine act of self-destruction. When he first conceived his novel he had it in mind to have Jude kill himself outright. What he eventually produced was more devious: a challenge both to statistical methods and to the Schopenhaurian paradoxical metaphysics to which he was personally drawn. Quite early in the book Jude considers drowning himself, but recoils, telling himself that he is not a 'sufficiently dignified person for suicide'.[33] Such delusions of worthlessness keep him alive until, towards the end, battered by all that he has seen and felt, Jude sinks ever deeper into depression, unable to assert enough 'reason' to put paid to his life, too tired or drunk to appreciate whatever vestiges of the 'Will' might remain within him. By deliberately catching a fever, he grants himself a slow and miserable death that eludes all the categories: metaphysical, ethical or statistical.

It is nevertheless a social death, of a kind that a Darwinistic sociology could easily miss. Havelock Ellis was right to insist that *Jude the Obscure* was not simply 'a study of gross pathological degenerescence, a study of the hereditary evolution of criminality'.[34] It is much more solid than that: it is a fictional representation of the actual forms taken by social disillusion in the 1890s. The significance of Jude's behaviour, though invisible to the other characters in the novel, should not have been unfamiliar to Hardy's readers: his hapless idealism and his pathetic mimicry of supposedly intellectual superiors had been grimly foreshadowed by Ernest Clark and his type.[35] Like Jude, Clark had struggled to believe that 'only the transcendental and aesthetic in life are worth our thought'.

## 'AN EXTRAORDINARY COINCIDENCE'

No one will ever know for sure the scale of the increase in suicide in the late nineteenth century.[36] An epidemic now seems most unlikely, though there were certainly many who were convinced of it at the time, and some, writers and critics among them, who thought that the apparent outbreak had something to do with the power of modern communications. There were complaints that the *Chronicle* had been irresponsible even to print Clark's letter:

> Do you think it advisable to publish in a widely read daily paper such letters, which will fall into the hands of those in a similar position to that unfortunate young man, and may cause them to do likewise?[37]

Suicidal tendencies are not likely to be checked, but rather prompted by newspaper discussion, as it draws to the subject many who had better let the subject alone.[38]

And there were chidings from rival publications. 'What a pity it is', remonstrated the weekly *Speaker*, 'that any class of journalists amongst us should be ready to minister to the morbid instincts of these miserable beings, and in doing so to lure them on the road to destruction!'[39]

If papers were to stand by their own claim that they had an important social role they needed to take seriously the criticism that they could adversely influence individual conduct. In addition there was the fear, by the nineties already well established, that papers could create a climate of feeling without necessarily making editorial comment. Separate items coincidentally juxtaposed could have a cumulative effect. The *Spectator*, another weekly, noted in 1894 that 'there is hardly a single daily newspaper now which does not contain the record of some remarkable suicide, often of more than one'.[40]

Suicides were eminently reportable because reports of coroners' inquests were invariably compact and dramatic. This had been the case since the early nineteenth century.[41] But grouped together as in the nineties they increasingly tended to be, they all too easily implied a terrifying and incomprehensible concatenation of similar events: they became *related*. Having recorded eight different suicides as one continuous column on 18 August 1893, the *Chronicle* had gone on to give news of three more on the 19th, a further three on the 21st, and another four on the 22nd. That was during the Clark affair, but it was not exceptional for the nineties, nor was it a phenomenon confined to the English press. In 1895 the *Pall Mall Gazette* related that Swiss doctors had asked their newspapers to abstain from all suicide items. Suicides, the Swiss believed, 'are a species of epidemic, and often originate from a diseased love of fame'. If we 'pass the victim over in silence' or 'record to blame', then 'vanity and undue self-love will no longer furnish forth the alarming list of self-destroyers.'[42] The *Pall Mall* doubted that this was really true, pointing out that the suicidal impulse, like the sexual, was essentially private, and unlikely to be restrained by the knowledge that it would not be publicized.

'Epidemic' theories rested upon the principle of 'contagion' – the potential power of a successful suicide to influence the decisions of others who had the same tendency. And that raised the further worry, clearly expressed by Archer in his references to Hedda Gabler, that the morbidity of recent literature might be as influential as prurient newspaper attention.

As journalistic luck or coincidence would have it, the facts were prone to match the fears. On 2 April 1895, the *Pall Mall Gazette* printed three suicide cases on the same page. There was an account of the discovery of a male corpse on Hampstead Heath: 'the head was nearly severed from the body, and by his side was a bloodstained razor'; a report of a 'young man of respectable appearance' who had been seen leaping from Westminster Bridge; and a story with the heading, 'Death of the Real Mrs Ebbsmith. An Extraordinary Coincidence'. This told how the body of a fifty-year-old woman of private means, divorced wife of a solicitor called Joseph Ebbsmith, had recently been found in the Thames near Reading. She had drowned with two tickets for Pinero's current play, *The Notorious Mrs Ebbsmith*, on her person.

Although not quite as sensational as Pinero's earlier heroine Paula Tanqueray, who had in fact taken her own life, the fictional Mrs Ebbsmith was still a troubling character, a fallen woman torn between Christian principles and loyalty to her politician lover. The 'real Mrs Ebbsmith' had apparently read a personal message into the coincidence of the names. At the inquest, her brother testified that 'he had received a somewhat remarkable letter from his sister to the effect that she had had a dreadful week over *The Notorious Mrs Ebbsmith*, lashing herself into a fury about it; but she added that the play was a superb work of art, and she (the deceased) ought to feel flattered ...'

It was hardly unreasonable for the coroner, while recording an open verdict, to observe that the play must have 'preyed on her mind'.[43] Just as it was scarcely unforgivable for Shaw, no admirer of Pinero, to offer his flippant regret that it would take more than a single suicide to end the run of a meretricious play.[44]

Curiously, suicide was never a taboo subject for humour in the nineteenth century,[45] and the Clark affair produced quite a few jokes, or reminders of old jokes, like the famous self-penned epitaph, 'Born a man, died a grocer'. It may even be that Archer was trying for a comic tone when he spoke of a day when 'there should be an automatic electrocutor on every railway platform, and one need only stand on the foot-rest and put a penny in the slot'.[46] In any case only the more straight-faced correspondents like Le Gallienne professed to be unamused, preferring the mood of R. L. Stevenson's famous short story of 1882:

*The Suicide Club* which does not offend, because its whimsicality is kept under control by the deliberate regard for proportion which, above all, marks the true humourist. Mr Stevenson never affects anything throughout his *jeu d'esprit* but that death is anything but a solemn and awful mystery.[47]

In truth, the mood of Stevenson's story was incompatible with the changed atmosphere in the nineties, when interest in suicide was more empirical. Rumours of 'suicide clubs', of small groups of people who had agreed simultaneously to kill themselves, were now a source of much serious speculation. If authentic, they might provide real confirmation of the 'epidemic', of 'contagion', and of the morbid influences that individuals could have upon one another. Stevenson's story, though still popular in the nineties, is far removed from this macabrely scientific spirit of enquiry, for it contains no suggestion of a general malaise, and modern life is less to blame than old-fashioned profligacy.[48]

The hero of *The Suicide Club* is a Prince of Bohemia who amuses himself by wandering the world incognito. One night in London he comes upon an organization dedicated to helping people end their lives. Its members are men who are 'in the prime of life, with every show of intelligence and sensibility in their appearance, but with little promise of strength or the quality that makes success'. For the entrance fee of £40 demanded by the club's Mephistophelean president, they are linked with others of like mind, on the understanding that an arbitrary draw will ultimately decide who kills whom. In other words, this isn't really a 'suicide club' at all, but a criminal organization based on mutual murder and financial gain. Righteously shocked, the Prince can set out to identify the president on the untroubled assumption that all potential suicides deserve to be rescued from themselves.

That is some way from the blacker humour of the *fin de siècle*, which is authentically conveyed by several of the more sardonic responses to Ernest Clark and by books like M. P. Shiel's *Prince Zaleski* (1895). The opening sentence of *Prince Zaleski* pretends to an authority on the subject of suicide as preparation for the pseudo-scientific sophistication of its plot.

> To say that there are epidemics of suicide is to give expression to what is now a mere commonplace of knowledge. And so far are they from being of rare occurrence, that it has even been affirmed that every sensational case of *felo de se* published in the newspapers is sure to be followed by some others more obscure.[49]

Shiel's explanation is that suicide epidemics are in fact caused by modern medicine which, by keeping degenerate specimens unnaturally alive, obliges them to seek their own destruction. Left alone they might have died more easily and more promptly – Shiel's bleakly 'rational' irony.

If merely reading about suicide could be dangerous, what risks might not be run by those who chose to write about it? Just as there were cases like the disconcertingly 'real' Mrs Ebbsmith, so there seemed to be a lengthening roll-call of writers who had succumbed to the 'influence' of their own daily imaginings. They had become like characters in their own poems or stories. On that point the common wisdom was in unexpected agreement with Wilde's famous pronouncement that life imitates art.

The chilliest instance was that of Hubert Crackanthorpe, whose unexplained drowning in Paris in the autumn of 1896 was one of the first symbolic deaths.[50] His very name, as a wit once noted and soon regretted, could be made to rhyme with 'corpse'.[51] His fiction had always been notorious for its morbidity, and after his death it seemed to have incorporated disturbing premonitions of his own fate.

But according to Morselli's *Suicide*, Paris was 'the city in all the world where there are most victims to suicide'.[52] So if Crackanthorpe did throw himself into the Seine, he was in a way only conforming to a sociological norm – and to a tradition of watery deaths. Two great rivers run through nineteenth-century art and literature, creating a dark undertow of miserable associations. Appropriately enough, Ernest Dowson's poem in memory of Crackanthorpe, 'Vesperal', has the poet gazing at the Thames while mourning a novelist who died in the Seine.

> Strange grows the river on the sunless evenings!
> The river comforts me, grown spectral, vague and dumb:
> Long was the day; at last the consoling shadows come:
> *Sufficient for the day are the day's evil things!*[53]

Death wishes were something that nineties' writers, even the more buoyant ones, professed to know well, an intimacy they sometimes justified in terms of the moral and scientific tenor of the age. To the creative artist, suicides were sympathetic and, arguably, rational – though it certainly helped if the chosen location was recognizable, predictable even. In Crackanthorpe's story 'A Conflict of Egoisms' from his collection *Wreckage* (1893), a struggling author marries a middle-aged woman of eager but limited sensibility. Reluctant to reconcile his tortured habits of work with his new domestic responsibilities, and unable to share his solitary suffering with his wife, he soon drifts back into his previous existence of lonely wandering and black introspection.

He and his story meet their end on Chelsea Bridge:

> A long fall through the air – the water black, cold and slimy, the rush down
> his throat, the fight for breath, to sink down, down at once, and the yearning
> for the peace of death swept down through him.
>   Could he crawl through the iron-work? No, it was too small. And some
> one might see him. He must clamber over, quickly. As he looked round him
> to see if he were observed, his eyes fell on a heap of flints a few yards off,
> where the road was under repair. He went up to it, and stooping down,
> began, with the feeble slowness of an old man, to fill his pockets with the
> stones. Then he went back to the bridge edge, and gripping the stanchions,
> prepared to swing himself on to the top of them.

The suicidal impulse comes either too soon or too late, for it is precisely
at this moment of resolve that the hapless author is struck down by the
heart attack that forestalls and fulfils his intention.

> A blackness filled his eyes: a dull thud; his body dropped back on to the
> roadway – dead.[54]

Crackanthorpe's abrupt and monosyllabic finale poses the kind of
deterministic riddle that the nineties greatly relished, but the concluding
enigma of 'A Conflict of Egoisms' must have seemed unusually relevant
when the author was reported missing early in November 1896. Last
seen on the Quai Voltaire at a time when the Seine was unusually high,
he reappeared near the Pont d'Alma, an unrecognizable corpse, on
Christmas Eve.

Suicide was never proven and some of Crackanthorpe's friends found
it difficult to rest with the thought – even when they meditated upon the
interesting *ménage à quatre* that he had been running on the Avenue
Kléber: with his mistress (the sister of Le Gallienne), his wife and his
wife's French lover. Le Gallienne worried in public at the thought that
Crackanthorpe might have departed 'of his free will, without a word of
advice, without a wave of the hand'.[55] Less surprised was a memorialist
in *The Critic*:

> No young man, or old one for that matter, could write such morbid,
> loathsome stories as he wrote and have a sane mind. He was the most
> pronounced type of decadent ... there is, after all, a good deal of truth in some
> of Nordau's theories.[56]

Many of Crackanthorpe's last stories are little more than solipsistic
fragments, short prose poems and opaque paragraphs dimly lit by ennui.
'The pursuit of experience is the refuge of the unimaginative', runs the

sub-Wildean epitaph to his collection, *Vignettes: a Miniature Journal of Whim and Sentiment*, published shortly before his death.[57] Resistant to logical explanation, yet heavy with significance, his episodes of isolated despair invariably close on unanswered questions. Like coroners' reports, they cast long shadows.

## 'DYING IN PARIS'

As they strolled across the Pont des Arts in the early 1880s, only yards from what was to become the scene of Crackanthorpe's tragedy, the journalist Robert Sherard felt impelled to ask his friend Oscar Wilde whether he would go after a man whom he saw throwing himself into the river. 'I should consider it an act of gross impertinence to do so,' Wilde apparently replied. 'His suicide would be a perfectly thought-out act, the definite result of scientific process, with which I should have no right whatever to interfere.'[58] Nevertheless, Paris provided a unique setting for the contemplation of 'scientific process'.

Once dredged from the river, Hubert Crackanthorpe's body was, according to legal custom, taken to the Paris Morgue, where it was identified by his brothers on Christmas Day 1896 on the evidence of his jewellery and cufflinks. The brothers had a grim and unavoidable reason to attend the morgue. Most of those who went there did so with more elusive motives.

Morselli explained Paris's eminence as suicide capital of the world on the grounds that 'all the economical and political revolutions, all reforming habits, and the new channels of thought' first made themselves felt there.[59] By the nineties, the morgue had become one of Paris's monuments to its own myths: its status as the centre of progressive thought, along with its other claim to be the capital of indulgence, and what comes after indulgence. With its ever-changing display of *mementi mori* the morgue, in short, was on the itinerary.

All the English guide-books gave the basic information.[60] A small, squat edifice rebuilt in 1864, it stood at the southeast end of the Île de la Cité, strikingly close to Notre Dame. Bodies whose provenance was unknown were delivered by hand-cart and passed through to a central area where, behind a glass screen, they were displayed on marble slabs, kept cool by a constant flow of water. Here the process of identification took place. There were several adjoining rooms: an office where, after due formalities, the corpses were surrendered to relatives or other

NOTRE DAME      THE MORGUE      PONT ST. LOUIS AND HOTEL DE VILLE

'Eastern end of the Île de la Cité', from Old and New Paris, by H. Sutherland Edwards, 1894.

claimants; a magistrates' room where, on occasion, suspected murderers were said to be confronted with the remains of their victims; and a dissecting room that could be used for lectures. There were also facilities for freezing or, conversely, thawing. When corpses left the morgue they went either, if claimed, for funeral rites and interment in one of the city's cemeteries or, if unclaimed, to the *fosse commune* area at the Bagneux burial ground. According to the *Tit-bits Guide to Paris* of 1889, about a thousand bodies passed through the morgue each year and there were always two or three on view at any one time. Recent statistics showed that by far the greatest number had drowned, making it most likely (but not certain) that they were suicides.

Those who ran the morgue were quite aware of the sensational aspect of the institution, and they preserved a small collection of curiosities. Among them was a dried and shrivelled heart pierced with a coronal of nails. The story behind this object, which must have been frequently related, was that it had been found on a woman's grave, placed there by her lover who had presumably wished to express, either out of jealousy or devotion, the true extent of his passions. Even when it was discovered that the heart had in fact come from a sheep, horrific visions of an ultimate in self-destructive acts continued to attach to the would-be tell-tale organ.

As only a small proportion of the visitors to the morgue were there out of necessity, the English guide-books felt obliged to offer warnings. The spectacle of death, they were careful to stress, had a distinct element of class about it. The morgue was very much the haunt of 'the lower orders of Paris', of 'the dressmakers and factory girls' who went there in their dinner-hour. Naturally, the guide-books implied, their English readers were of a very different kind, but should they, too, find themselves driven by inquisitive impulses, they were warned to avoid entering the place 'unless the nerves are strong'.

What journalist could resist such a challenge? According to a contributor to the *Pall Mall Gazette* in 1894, him or herself unnamed, it was the anonymity of the corpses that allowed people to gawp in such open curiosity. The morgue, the writer testified, was the final resting-place of the dispossessed, one stage beyond those other dark places that the intrepid modern investigator had to penetrate.

When the door closed on me and I found myself in the interior of the Morgue, I felt I was in the most horrible place in the wide, wide world. It is worse than a prison, a hospital, or even a madhouse. Who has not heard of the horrors that fill these? Yet this is worse than either of them. God, in His mercy, may will that they have an exit on the world; here there is none. It is the end of all, a blind alley where misery, shame, and crime are swept together, where the defeated in the battle of life are driven by the stress of circumstances. I was behind the scenes of a stage where the most pathetic of all tragedies are presented to the public. The audience is that ever-changing gaping crowd, which I had just left in order to come into the wings and watch the play thus closely for a moment. The actors are the corpses. They are pushed forward to the front of the stage to give the cue to a drama of real life, the mystery of which is often no sooner unravelled than it is forgotten, even if the audience, and the larger public it represents, keep up their interest in a piece that they know can have but one dénouement when they see the principal actor laying cold and lifeless before them. The cue given, the action set going, the corpses disappear and their places are taken by others of the ghastly company. Then the curtain rolls up on some fresh drama. Failures are as frequent on this stage as on that other where less tragic plots are developed. The subject is generally so threadbare. Drink, dishonesty, shame, is the burthen of the story; and the revolver or the river seem such natural ways of escape from the world's disfavour that the audience is satisfied with the spectacle and cares nothing for the plot.[61]

That passage reads like sincerity but at the same time is obviously sensational, the combination of elements that the morgue classically engendered. For the attractions of the place were by no means confined to journalists. More cautious writers also succumbed to its unique pull. A surprising number of thoroughly middle-class and quite well-established novelists and poets made the pilgrimage – a fact which either negates the snobbery of the guide-books, or confesses to the genuine morbidity of the literary mind at the time. By the nineties it was something of a tradition to test one's responses there: and there were distinguished precedents, the most notable being Robert Browning, whose poem 'Apparent Failures' had been inspired by a visit in 1857.[62] Thomas Hardy dropped in on his honeymoon in 1874, when his wife observed that it was 'not *offensive* but repulsive';[63] George Gissing, in Paris in 1886, merely said that it was 'at once very horrible and very simple'.[64] Arthur Symons recorded his 1894 visit in a poem that turned his own favourite theatrical motif, the space between the stage and the wings, into a grim cosmic irony:

> I am afraid of death to-day,
> For I have seen the dead
> Where, in the Morgue, they lie in bed,
> And one dead man was laughing as he lay.

And that still laughter seemed to tell,
With its inaudible breath,
Of some ridiculous subterfuge of death,
Some afterthought of heaven or hell,

The last and lost mystery,
Which, being known, had bred
Such cynic laughter in the dead,
A laughter that outlived mortality,

Ah, mortal to mere mortal breath,
This ultimate farce of things:
To have heard the laughter from the wings,
The coulisses of the comedy of death![65]

Wilde, who looked in during his Parisian exile of the late nineties, also responded in character, remaining, at least by comparison with Symons, studiedly unperturbed. The morgue, he maintained, was 'a dignified place'; he could not understand why some people objected to visiting it.

There is nothing horrible in death. Death is solemn. Now waxworks are horrible, if you like. I remember ... going to the Morgue after seeing a brilliant function – all colour and music – at Notre Dame. A woman of the lowest class was on one of the slabs. She was having her day. All Paris might look at her gravely. She was no longer despised.[66]

This was to treat the morgue not just as a grisly theatre (as both Symons and the *Pall Mall* reporter had done) but also as a gallery displaying 'still life' or, more accurately, *nature morte*. Aesthetes like Wilde seem, above all others, to have gone there searching for the *frisson* of impersonality. Wilde was prepared to shock luncheon tables with 'a discourse about morgues in different capitals',[67] while Pater's prose reverie 'The Child in the House' cites the Paris Morgue, along with a particular cemetery in Munich where bodies were exposed before burial, as one of those places where a certain kind of refined and impressionable temperament might exercise its *penchant* for gazing on dead faces and brooding on the fragile boundaries between life and art and death.[68]

The degree of self-indulgence that the Aesthetic cult of dead bodies encouraged among its camp followers is further, if unwittingly, suggested in the memoirs of a retired actress published in 1896. She recalls how, after a visit to the studio of an untalented sculptor, one of her friends suggested an excursion to the morgue, 'as a means of driving from our minds the hideous creations we had seen'. Not a shudder is shown. 'We gladly assented,' she wrote, 'and indeed the three or four figures were far more beautiful with the calm majesty of death upon them, than any of the representations of life we had seen in the studio.'[69] Shaw, who reviewed the book, regarded this passage as conclusive proof of the actress's sterility of vision.[70] As he had already made clear during the great music-hall scandals two years earlier, a moving body meant infinitely more to him than any statuesque pose. To seek inspiration in the final immobility of death was simply too much.

As Canon Chasuble observes in Wilde's *The Importance of Being Earnest*, a desire to be buried in Paris 'hardly points to any very serious state of mind at the last'.[71] In 1900 Wilde died there himself, but in pathetically reduced circumstances which rumour soon made lurid with tales of a hideous and suppurating carcass, as if the decadence of the soul had finally caught up with the body.[72] The Hôtel d'Alsace was Wilde's penultimate resort. Already, in 1898, he had written to Frank Harris, 'The morgue yawns for me.'[73] In the event he only narrowly avoided playing out the melodramatic scenario of finally achieving dignity on a 'zinc bed'. His friends were told by the undertaker that the fact that he was living under an assumed name made removal there a distinct possibility. 'Dying in Paris', remarked Robert Ross, who was in charge of things, 'is really a very difficult and expensive luxury for a foreigner.'[74] Wilde's final journey took years and criss-crossed the city – from his funeral at the Church of Saint Germain des Prés, to what was always intended to be a temporary grave at Bagneux, eventually, in 1909, to Père Lachaise.

Before signing the death certificate, the French doctor had required assurance that Wilde had not committed suicide or murder. Neither was remotely in his character, though he had once remarked, turning to a metaphor which came rather easily to him and to his contemporaries, that 'the artistic life is a long and lovely suicide'.[75]

There may be some comfort in remembering that Wilde also invented the most amusing Parisian death of the nineties. The timely demise of Jack (Ernest) Worthing's imaginary brother, also called 'Ernest', is perhaps closer to fratricide than to suicide, though there's a hint in the play text that when Jack recounts the fabricated death of his fabricated sibling, he implies, almost, that it was self-induced, self-announced. 'He died abroad; in Paris, in fact. I had a telegram last night', reports Jack to the assembled company, 'from the manager of the Grand Hotel.' It is on record that when the actor George Alexander, who originally played Jack, delivered this line he seemed, but for a second, to be on the brink of saying that the telegram had come from 'Ernest' himself. Only at the very last moment did he succeed in righting himself, avoiding a disastrous solecism. As it turns out 'Ernest' is deprived of suicidal heroics and condemned to die of 'a severe chill'.[76] Because he is the fictional creation of a fictional character there is no real need for an inquest. Had he been altogether Wilde's there might well have been, and Wilde might well have provided it.


## TEXTUAL INQUESTS

One can but sadly smile with pity and contempt at the wretched creature who climbs Fish Hill, pays threepence for the privilege of mounting the monument, and then hurls himself over the railings, to the not inconsiderable inconvenience of passers-by below. He makes a sensation, and there at once is an end to the dignity of the act; it becomes, like all sensations, merely vulgar. And in that fact is comprised much of the disrepute into which suicide has fallen; for it is well-nigh impossible to avoid a sensation. The penny newspaper system forbids it. No matter how circumspect and cautious is the self-exterminator, the reporter is always near him, and, instead of respecting the wishes of him who would pass away in silence, straightway, for a paltry price, publishes the deed to the daughters of the Philistines and other readers of daily papers. A self-found death may in itself and the manner of its attainment be poetical and beautiful, but recorded in a paragraph, it is nothing but food for morbidity .... It would be pleasant and encouraging beyond measure to take up a news-sheet without finding the tale of badly-conceived and worse-executed self-murder; and it is really unnecessary.

'The Suicide's Guide', *Court and Society Review*, 4 May 1887

On the pages of newspapers the suicide paragraphs lay like memorial tablets, the printed verdicts like unconvincing epitaphs. Arranged *en bloc*, they naturally suggested epidemic; read separately they could almost be condensed versions of some shocking modern novel. Effects preceded cause; heroism was proved only by despair; and like any character in any fiction, the protagonist in a successful suicide bid was unavailable for cross-examination. And then again, much as in some novel or story designed mainly to intrigue, events would never be fully accounted for, even when the surrounding emotional and moral complexities demanded explanation. The majority of inquests may have concluded with the tired formula 'of an unsound mind'; but that this was

# REYNOLDS'S NEWSPAPER.

### Government of the People, by the People, for the People.

LONDON, SUNDAY, SEPTEMBER 8, 1895.

## THE SUICIDE SEASON.

### ACTRESS, DOCTOR, AND LOVERS.

#### LONDON ACTRESS'S SUICIDE.

It is reported that a London actress—a member of the company that went to South Africa to play the "Gaiety Girl," under the management of Mr. Luscombe Searelle—has committed suicide.

The young lady's name was Miss Daisy Melville, the daughter of most respectable parents, living in London. The affair is still wrapped in mystery, for no details have yet arrived to throw any light on the motive of the poor girl's action. The last letter received by her mother gave no signs of any unhappiness or coming trouble. On the contrary, she wrote that she was "just the same as ever she was," and that she had been the recipient of many kindnesses and presents. Miss Melville was only eighteen years of age, attractive in appearance, and of engaging manner.

#### LOVERS' TRAGIC FATE.

"Suicide during temporary insanity" was the verdict delivered by a Coroner's jury at Eye, Suffolk, on Friday night when they heard of the circumstances under which Frederick Rogers, a man of thirty-two, and Edith Elgood, a girl of twenty-one, met their deaths. The two had been engaged for the past month. Rogers, who was in no regular employment, had been turned out of a club at Diss, and this had preyed on his mind, a great deal. His father had locked the door against him because he brought home his sweetheart after everyone had retired. The Father of the girl said he had always treated her kindly. On Thursday he found the following written in chalk on his door: "You will find me and my Fred in the pond up the field. You are the cause of all this.—From your broken-hearted daughter." The bodies were recovered from the pond afterwards. The girl was enciente.

#### SUICIDE OF A DOCTOR.

Dr. Hodges, a medical man with a large practice at Leicester, formerly house surgeon at the infirmary and a specialist in eye diseases, committed suicide yesterday by hanging himself from a bannister in his house with the cord of his dressing-gown. He had suffered from nervous depression for some months, and returned from a holiday last week little or no better for the change.

#### UNPLEASANT WORDS.

Edith Mary Small, aged twenty-two, the daughter of a well-known Chester gentleman, committed suicide on Friday by drowning herself in the River Dee. She had an appointment to meet a gentleman, and, according to his statement, unpleasant words followed. Miss Small ran away from him and jumped into the river. He attempted to save her, but was unsuccessful. The gentleman is a married man, and the affair has created a great sensation. The body has not yet been recovered.

#### THE VESTRY WORKER'S SUICIDE.

At the inquest yesterday on Alfred Maton, road sweeper, employed by the Marylebone Vestry, who took poison after telling the people at home that he "had got the sack." It was said that he was a sensitive man, and took things to heart. A verdict of "Suicide whilst of unsound mind" was returned. Mr. White, the superintendent, said deceased was not dismissed, but only suspended for a few days for abusive language.

#### TIRED OF LIFE.

Yesterday Mr. Baxter held an inquest at the Vestry Hall, St. George's East, concerning the death of James Bostock, aged forty-two years, a lighterman, late of 55, Red Lion-street, Wapping. George Bostock, a brother, proved finding a large piece of crude opium and a knife lying on the deceased's box, with some little pieces of opium cut off. On the mantelshelf was a piece of paper bearing the following words:—

Dear George Bostock,—Take charge of my goods that are in this room. Good-bye. God bless you. Look after my cats and dogs. Bad luck to Home Rule. I cannot get any employment. I am tired of life.

JAMES BOSTOCK.

Dr. Anthony stated that death was due to the combined effects of opium poisoning and excessive drinking. Deceased had been out of work for a month. A verdict of "Suicide while of unsound mind" was returned.

#### SHE TRIED SUICIDE.

At Dover, on Friday, a woman named Laura Godfrey, giving an address at Islington, London, made a determined attempt at suicide in the police cell, whilst awaiting being on a charge of drunkenness. She was found unconscious, with a rope, made of strips torn from her dress, round her neck.

#### AN ATTEMPT ON HIS LIFE.

Taken to Bridewell for being drunk in Fleet-street, W. Felgate, a porter, hacked at his throat with a penknife. He became very violent and had to be taken to the infirmary strapped on an ambulance. At the Mansion House he was fined 5s. and had to pay the damage to the ambulance.

#### WHAT FOREIGN COMPETITION DOES.

At the inquest on Francis Jackson, watchmaker, of Macclesfield-terrace, City-road, who was said that he was a steady man, but had been depressed by slackness of work—he had not earned 1s. since Christmas.

Robert Worthington, watchmaker, said deceased was better known in Clerkenwell as Frankson. He adopted that name because he was a runaway apprentice from Coventry. For several years past deceased, in common with other watchmakers in Clerkenwell, had suffered greatly because of the sale, as English-made watches, of inferior Swiss and American watches which bore the names of presumably respectable shopkeepers. The merchandise Marks Act was passed to prevent this kind of fraud, but a fatal defect of the Act was that no machinery was provided to enforce it. There were no inspectors to see that it was enforced. The Watchmakers' Protection Association had instituted prosecutions which were invariably successful, but now their funds were exhausted. If trade does not mend, more Clerkenwell watchmakers will commit suicide.

The jury returned a verdict of "Suicide while of unsound mind."

#### RELIGIOUS MANIA.

A young lady named Hurley, belonging to a well-known family in Rochester, arose from her bed and, going down to the River Medway, threw herself into the water. A man named B arne, who was passing on his way to work, jumped in and rescued her. The would-be suicide was, it is alleged, suffering from religious mania, and had been for some time under medical treatment.

#### SUICIDE AT AN INFIRMARY.

A man jumped out of a lavatory window at Bethnal Green Infirmary on Friday night and was killed. This is the second suicide which has happened recently at the institution.

known to be intended to forestall speculation served only, as in the case of Ernest Clark, to fuel it.

Moreover, there is textual evidence to support the theory that in the nineties other writers as well as Hardy were very much aware of the fictional dimensions of these newspaper reports, and that their imaginary suicides capitalized upon the structure of hypothesis that encased the real-life victims. The results make teasing reading for, just as at a real inquest, the more succinct and confident the verdict provided, the less accurate it is likely to be: a particularly useful resource for someone who wishes to expose the innocent credulity of his readers.

Precisely this function is served by the paragraph from the *St James's Gazette* which announces the death of Septimus R. Podgers in Wilde's short story 'Lord Arthur Savile's Crime'. Reproduced virtually as a facsimile and headed 'Suicide of a Chiromantist', it reads:

> Yesterday morning, at seven o'clock, the body of Mr Septimus R. Podgers, the eminent chiromantist, was washed on shore at Greenwich, just in front of the Ship Hotel. The unfortunate gentleman had been missing for some days, and considerable anxiety for his safety had been felt in chiromantic circles. It is supposed that he committed suicide under the influence of a temporary mental derangement, caused by overwork, and a verdict to that effect was returned this afternoon by the coroner's jury. Mr Podgers had just completed an elaborate treatise on the subject of the Human Hand, that will shortly be published, when it will no doubt attract much attention. The deceased was sixty-five years of age, and does not seem to have left any relations.[77]

But this verdict, as every reader knows, is not quite accurate: Podgers' death is the climax of a circuitous episode.

At the beginning of the story Lord Arthur is warned by Podgers, a society fortune-teller, that he is destined to commit murder. Feeling that he cannot go ahead with his plans to marry the lovely Sybil Merton with this hanging over him, he sets out to assuage Podgers' prophecy by pre-empting it himself. Two attempts to dispose of elderly and for the most part expendable relations with potentially lethal devices come to nothing. At last, though, Lord Arthur is wonderfully provided with a solution when he encounters the very man Podgers near Cleopatra's Needle in the early hours, and neatly tips him into the river. The news that Podgers' murder has been taken for suicide is therefore more than good; for Lord Arthur, it's life-saving. It guarantees that his crime will remain undetected whilst leaving him free to marry the woman he loves. His desperate evenings searching the columns of the *Pall Mall*, the *St James's*, the *Globe* and the *Echo* for accounts of his relations' dramatic demises are now over. Lord Arthur has mastered Destiny.

He had, it might be added, been fortunate in the time and place: 2 a.m. on the Thames Embankment, the sleeping city all around them, as if 'silver and shadow had fashioned the world anew'. Lord Arthur had encountered fate where fate was famously to be found: by the river at night. For Whistler, an occasion for romance and poetry; for too many others, the *locus classicus* of self-determined death. Lord Arthur never stops to ask himself why Podgers, who is certainly no artist or poet, might be there at that moment, nor does Wilde's narrator ask the question on his behalf. Readers with a taste for morbid irony might, however, wish to consider the most likely explanation.

Podgers is a pessimist and, with his dubious personal habits and his faith in pre-destination, would make a perfect candidate for suicide. If Lord Arthur had not taken over at the crucial point, might Podgers not have gone ahead and drowned himself? Which would not have solved Lord Arthur's problem at all. Although he is not, as we are reminded by Wilde, Lord Hamlet, Lord Arthur must make a lethal decision. And the coroner's inaccurate conclusion that Septimus R. Podgers had committed suicide may be a luckily conventional reading of a situation which Lord Arthur, to his own undoubted advantage, had himself entirely failed to read.

Inquests were supposed to make events intelligible, and the newspapers in which they were reported were supposed to make their verdicts widely known. Wilde's story exploits the hazards by embedding a brief report from the *St James's* within a narrative that complicates and disrupts its conclusions. It is a device he was to use again in *The Picture of Dorian Gray*, a novel shot through with self-inflicted deaths. When the young actress Sybil Vane, whom Dorian has rebuffed, swallows poison, he is at first overcome by a feeling that he has in effect murdered her, 'as surely as if I had cut her little throat with a knife'. Sybil's death is noted in the *Standard* and the *Globe*, and eventually an inquest is reported in the *St James's*.

INQUEST ON AN ACTRESS. — An inquest was held this morning at the Bell Tavern, Hoxton Road, by Mr Danby, the District Coroner, on the body of Sybil Vane, a young actress recently engaged at the Royal Theatre, Holborn. A verdict of death by misadventure was returned. Considerable sympathy was expressed for the mother of the deceased, who was greatly affected during the giving of her own evidence, and that of Dr Birrell, who had made the post-mortem examination of the deceased.[78]

There's an unwitting truth in that 'verdict of death by misadventure'. Yet in *Dorian Gray* all deaths are presented, in characteristic Wildean fashion, by lies that hint at honesty. There's the unexplained history of Dorian's 'great friend', a 'wretched boy in the Guards who committed suicide'; when Dorian murders the terminally depressed Basil Hallward, he tells his friend Alan Campbell that it was suicide; and when Campbell shoots himself in his laboratory, having carried out unspeakable acts on Dorian's behalf, he does so in order to keep Dorian's secret. No one dies innocently and no one dies openly. All die according to a romantic standard. Lord Henry Wotton, a romantic of a peculiarly modern kind and no idealist, speculates that Hallward died a version of the classic Parisian death, fantasizing that he fell into the Seine from an omnibus for reasons that will be for ever unknown; that the conductor hushed up some extraordinary scandal, leaving Lord Henry to indulge all the poetically morbid possibilities of a male Ophelia: 'I see him lying now on his back under those dull-green waters with the heavy barges floating over him, and long weeds catching in his hair.'[79]

But the most haunting questions of all come with the death of the novel's hero. Like Jude Fawley's, it is secret, yet known to every reader. When Dorian slashes the image that tells the truth about his life, he destroys his very being. It may be impossible to judge the intentionality, the rationality of that famous act. Was Dorian's death a willed decision or an accidental result? Wilde leaves the verdict open, obliging literary critics to write their own coroner's reports on the death of Dorian Gray.

# 6

# 'ASTOUNDING DISCLOSURES'
## The era of the interview
## and the end of anonymity

If a journalist is run over by a four-wheeler in the Strand, an
incident I regret to say I have never witnessed, it suggests
nothing to me from a dramatic point of view. Perhaps I am
wrong; but the artist must have his limitations.

Oscar Wilde, 1895 interview

## THE PRICE OF A NAME

So optimistic was the mood of the press at the start of the decade that
the Institute of Journalists, whose membership numbered over three
thousand, made their annual Congress of September 1893 an
international affair, inviting as guest of honour the controversial French
novelist Emile Zola. For an author whose works had been banned in
England only a few years before,[1] the welcome Zola received must have
seemed quite overwhelming. He was given honorary membership of the
Athenaeum, the Savage and the Garrick, taken to the Alhambra music-
hall and lodged in a suite at the Savoy. There, surrounded by bouquets
(including one from Oscar Wilde, who had within recent memory
criticized his novels for their 'dreary vices and drearier virtues'), Zola
could gaze out on the Thames and into the fog that he, along with other
Frenchmen, assumed to be the most interesting aesthetic experience the
English capital had to offer. Zola went so far as to regret not being able
to stay until November, when he understood 'you never see the sun from
one week's end to the other', and he generously acknowledged Turner as
the father of French Impressionism.[2]

Throughout his stay, Zola worked hard to match the boundless
hospitality of his hosts with the expansiveness of his own
pronouncements. Speaking at the Crystal Palace, after the opening
banquet but before the firework display which would paint his portrait
in coloured flames, he looked forward to a time of equality when the
'brotherhood of writers' would constitute 'the kingdom of human
intelligence, of fine arts and letters, of universal humanity', and all
categories of literature would finally merge. 'Why', asked the famous
Naturalist, 'should there be realists or idealists, why Positivists or
Symbolists?'[3]

In 1893 literature was in the news. At a dinner given for Zola by the
Authors' Club, the absence of Thomas Hardy permitted a free-ranging
discussion of the recent and scandalous *Tess of the d'Urbervilles*. Later
that evening, over the *bombe Théodora*, conversation turned to Sarah
Bernhardt, and how the odds were against her ever wanting to play
Thérèse Raquin. Replying to yet another toast, the well-known
abstainer again expressed gratitude for his reception in London as 'un
homme de lettres', but contrasted it with the hostile judgements his
novels sometimes still suffered. The coda passed largely unnoticed, so
few of his literary audience being able to follow French.

THE ILLUSTRATED LONDON NEWS, SEPT. 30, 1893

*M. Zola reading a paper before the Institute of Journalists in the Hall of Lincoln's Inn.*

*The Institute of Journalists at the Guildhall.*

It was also in his own language that Zola addressed the full Congress of Journalists, but on that occasion printed translations were to hand so that everyone could respond. His audience was, in any case, anxious to engage with his ideas about the relationship that the English press held to English life and, in particular, to hear him on the subject of 'Anonymity'. As Zola stressed in his speech, he believed the English tradition of unsigned articles to be a mark of a national respect for impersonal authority. The French, who valued individuality above all things, set greater store by signatures and produced an endless stream of ephemeral polemics. They took the same approach to literary criticism. Signed criticism, said Zola, 'enters into the domain of literary production, ceases to be the trite item of information which deals with the appearance of a book in much the same way as a street accident'. In contrast the English readership was 'perfectly contented so long as it sees in print every morning its own ideas, the ideas it expected to see'. For Zola, the 'unity' of the typical English newspaper was largely due to the fact that most contributions were unsigned. This he regarded as a precondition for systematic production and consistency in format:

> All have the same voice, the same talent, so long as they are unknown. There remains only the joint production, that compact mass of ideas, of all sorts of information, that makes one of your newspapers a veritable daily encyclopaedia. Unity engenders power, and thus one clearly perceives the mechanism of those formidable machines, founded upon the revenue of a vast system of advertisements, like factories in full swing, feeding with the pabulum they have chosen for the various sections of the nation.[4]

Zola had, possibly without knowing it, touched upon an already sensitive nerve. English journalists were hotly aware that authorial status had to be the basis for professional advancement and 'respectability'. How, unless their personal efforts were publicly acknowledged, could they expect to be decently rewarded? The liberal ideologues of the New Journalism, which had tried to introduce signed articles from the start, had gone further. It was the individuality of the parts, they said, that guaranteed what Zola called the encyclopaedic 'unity' of the whole. Then again, how else, unless there was a signed attribution, could the journalist's work be judged for what it was, a piece of crafted writing, or for what it might perhaps become, 'literature'?

Open discussion of the anonymity question brought together several concerns that were already running parallel. The modern journalist asked to be recognized as a prized employee, an essential team-member, a reliable source of information and a practised author. It was hard to see how the addition of signatures might satisfy all these ambitions at once, but Zola's enthusiasm was appreciated, even if his overall feelings about the English press were not.

All those present at the 1893 Congress knew that the industry was going through a crucial phase. There was talk of the contribution that technological developments were already making in the area of illustration and, in a long address on 'The Future of the Newspaper', the President of the Institute himself anticipated a time when a daily paper would be delivered to every household like the daily milk. The recent increase in titles and in circulation was not, he said, the result of the spread of education or of democratic aspirations so much as the improved quality of the modern paper. It was now incumbent upon journalists to encourage the trend by developing new styles of writing: 'The public are beginning to prefer literary to mechanical form', and as the daily paper became more and more of a 'daily magazine', so journalists would have to learn to write on an ever-increasing variety of subjects. All the more disturbing, then, were such lapses in taste as 'a tendency ... to what have been called "snippets", to paragraphs relating to persons and to interviewing. Some would say that this is a tendency to a lessening of the call upon the mental powers, and to a gratification of the idle curiosity of the reader.' Interviewing might be justifiable on two counts – 'first, that it helps to the individuality of the newspaper, and, second, that it supplies a more or less dramatic form' – but one had to be wary of the excesses of America, where 'the interviewer forces himself upon unwilling subjects, and so constitutes himself a bore and a nuisance'.[5]

As the pomp and muddle of Zola's visit displays, cultural idiosyncrasies could be highlighted in a cosmopolitan exchange of ideas, even as the spread of mass communications was apparently dissolving international differences. This was only one of several confusing processes in which journalism was implicated. The future looked imminent in 1893, but it was coming into focus with its values in reverse. Journalists already saw that their professional status would advance mainly according to the power that their employers granted them; that, for instance, the value of an interview could be measured by the force of the questions as much as by the veracity of the answers; that originality could be endorsed by a signature and truth by a literary style. But while journalists were saying that they were writers, what writer would ever want to be thought a journalist?

Two contrasting campaigns in the nineties – the journalist's right to a name and the imaginative author's right to privacy – indicate significant changes in the social practice of writing. The journalists were eventually allowed to sign what they had written, which made them personally liable for the veracity of its contents. At that very moment writers of fiction were being asked to supply, usually in an 'interview', coherent justifications of their own work. They were torn. They wanted aura, but they needed readers. Healthy hatred of editors and deadlines couldn't entirely suppress the pull of the papers.

There was a more obviously ideological aspect, too. Zola's vision may have been premature, but it invoked a distant ideal of social unity in which all voices would be one and one voice would do for all. In the twentieth century, that dream, like its antidote, was to take on sinister resonances. Even by the time of the Moderns, the capitalist press had become an unquestioned enemy and the self-respecting writer had learned to keep himself at a distance from the papers. (Who would want to be at one with a reader who was content with the dailies?) In the nineties, writers were merely apprehensive at the idea of Utopia, and they debated the prospect within themselves.

### SPEAKING FOR ONESELF

When the *New Review* conducted a symposium on the anonymity issue in 1889, Shaw declared himself 'roughly and practically speaking' in favour of signatures because he wrote with a greater sense of responsibility when he knew that a piece would appear under his own name.[6] He liked the personal credit as well and, in a slightly contradictory aside, he recalled the recent past when he, Archer and Wilde, distinguished stylists all, were anonymously reviewing for the *Pall Mall Gazette* and were sometimes accused of having written each other's pieces. In such cases the style was obviously not the man.

Shaw followed the convention of distinguishing between journalism's two functions, the reporting of facts and the expression of opinion; but he then made a further separation, between expressions of editorial (or proprietorial) and personal views. Although he was, in general, contemptuous of anyone who wrote in the third person, he gave the impression of being unembarrassed by editorial demands. With a rough practicality obviously intended to overshoot the mark, he suggested that 'when the editor means the article but doesn't write it, and a professional journalist writes it but doesn't mean it, it could be signed Buckle *inv.*: Brown (or Robinson) *scrip.*' If, however, Shaw happened to write an article in favour of socialism (which, of course, he well might), he would naturally sign it 'Bernard Shaw *inv. et scrip.*'

This was typically brazen. It wasn't that Shaw ever expressed opinions that he didn't in some way hold, but he did tend to over-simplify the problems he and other journalists had to face. He was, after all, as much a product of modern literary practice as anyone else. As a 'New Journalist' he was able to record innovations – the New English Art Club, Impressionism, Ibsenism – as they occurred, and in an appropriate manner. His own critical output grew along with the number of new titles needing his kind of opinionated versatility. Sometimes he wrote pseudonymously (the unmistakable blast of 'Corno di Bassetto', music critic of the *Star*), sometimes under his own name; sometimes even anonymously, often on subjects close to his heart, as if they might benefit from an air of generality. In the ten years between 1885 and 1895, when he became theatre critic of the weekly *Saturday Review*, Shaw contributed about 160 items, signed and unsigned, to the *Pall Mall Gazette*, over 200 to the *Star*, and over 300 to the *World*. In the single year of 1889 he made 144 contributions to periodicals of one kind or another: in May, there were seventeen items, in June nineteen; on a single day, 1 May, he had articles in three different journals; on another, 7 June, the *Star* alone carried four separate notices, all by Shaw.[7]

The output may have been relentless; in content it was studiously provocative. The secret of a successful 'New Journalist' lay, according to Shaw himself, in the ability to make 'a vast body of readers conscious of his personality and anxious to hear his opinion'. Clement Scott, for example, the theatre critic of the *Daily Telegraph*, who habitually held positions quite opposed to those of Shaw, had seized on the opportunities offered by the modern papers to create a new type of 'sympathetic critic'.

> The excellence of Mr Scott's criticisms lies in their integrity as expressions of the warmest personal feeling and nothing else. They are alive: their admiration is sincere and moving; their resentment is angry and genuine. He may be sometimes maudlin on the one hand, sometimes unjust, unreasonable, violent, and even ridiculous on the other; but he has never lost an inch of ground by that.[8]

This was to damn with praising feints – a classic Shavian form of attack. In 1895, when Shaw wrongly identified an anonymous piece as being by Scott, he found himself having to apologize. He did so with elegance, excusing himself on the flattering but unyielding grounds that a man with such a uniquely imitable style as Scott was duty bound to sign everything he wrote.[9]

Shaw always said that he reserved his greatest hostility for journalists who trivialized their profession by following or 'reflecting' public opinion rather than by leading it. This was the basis of his attack on Max Nordau – a journalistic Judas:

> Imagine a rehash not only of the newspaper criticisms of this period, but of all its little parasitic paragraphs of small-talk and scandal, from the long-forgotten jibes against Oscar Wilde's momentary attempt to bring knee breeches into fashion years ago, to the latest scurrilities about 'the New Woman'. Imagine the general staleness and occasional putrescence of this mess disguised by a dressing of the terminology invented by Krafft-Ebing, Lombroso, and all the latest specialists in madness and crime, to describe the artistic faculties and propensities as they operate in the insane. Imagine all this done by a man who is a vigorous and capable journalist, shrewd enough to see that there is a good opening for a big reactionary book .... He appeals to the prodigious extension of the quantity of business a single man can transact through the modern machinery of social intercourse: the railway, the telegraph and telephone, the post, and so forth.[10]

When these articles were reprinted in 1908 under the title *The Sanity of Art*, Shaw prefaced them with a short manifesto summarizing what had by then become his standard position: that 'the highest literature is journalism'. As good journalists belong to the present, so should good artists. A final twist of mock humility implied that artistic work would, in the real long run, be as timebound as journalism.

The argument for journalism was to be directed against all comers, most notably against Henry James, but with a forthrightness not always borne out by Shaw's own conduct. The image of the writer as journalist was offered in response to a modern world in which, according to Shaw, again in 1895,

> The hugeness and complexity of modern civilizations and the development of our consciousness of them by means of the press, have the double effect of discrediting comprehensive philosophies by revealing more facts than the ablest man can generalize, and at the same time intensifying the urgency of social reforms sufficiently to set even the poetic faculty in action on their behalf.[11]

That came in an essay on 'The Problem Play', which was devoted to the proposition that social questions would eventually become so overwhelming that writers would have to deal with them first before getting on with more creative work. The playwright would, in other words, be a newspaper reader like everyone else. He would devour 'everything with a keen appetite – fiction, science, gossip, politics, technical processes, sport, everything';[12] and feel the need to have his say.

Because they were initially designed to maintain his own usefulness as a journalist/writer, Shaw's theories allowed him to keep some distance from his audience: his own 'problem plays' were public debates conducted by a private man, who erected his own targets, and made monologue out of dialogue. Shaw needed to be in control. Style, preferably branded with a signature, was one way; but guarded privacy was the other. In the course of the nineties he developed strategies for dealing with the wanton press to which he belonged. He was to rely on them for the rest of his life. Asked to give an interview, he would simply supply the would-be interrogator with a prepared set of statements.

Alternatively he would create a fictional interviewer and an only slightly less imaginary interviewee, a stand-in called 'Mr Bernard Shaw', and have them meet in a one-sided scenario. The purpose of the make-believe was first of all to ensure that Shaw's opinions were presented in the form, and at the length, that he thought they deserved. So, for instance, on 31 October 1893, the *St James's Gazette* and the *Pall Mall Gazette* both published long, detailed and remarkably different 'interviews' on the subject of the Fabian manifesto, 'To your tents, oh Israel!', which had just been published in the *Fortnightly*. In both, the 'representative' of the paper feeds Shaw with brief questions to which he receives extended answers. In the *St James's* he concludes that Fabian proposals would at least make politics more interesting: 'from that point of view, at any rate, a journalist may well wish you success.'

The comic possibilities of ventriloquism could be taken much further. Sometimes Shaw invented a hapless '*Star* man' who had the professional luck and personal misfortune to run up against 'Bernard Shaw' at his most opinionated. A review of George Moore's play, *The Strike at Arlingford* (1893), half-admits the deceit with a nudging third-person narration that opens with an elaborate caricature of 'Shaw' sketched by Shaw.

A *Star* man, crossing Regent's Park the other day when the mercury was bursting out at the top of the thermometer, looked enviously at the toilworn working men who lay simmering on the sward, prone or supine, or curled up sideways like cats, taking their siesta. The *Star* man had learnt at his mother's knee that no gentleman would think of lying down in the park in this vulgar manner; and he was passing on with becoming dignity when one of the prostrate ones, attired in a modest suit of bright cinammon colour, a revolutionary red tie, a sombrero, and a pair of boots, each of which was a platform in itself, rolled over and revealed the well-known red beard of Bernard Shaw. In a moment, the *Star* man threw his social position to the winds and flung himself down by the basking sage of the Fabian Society.[13]

The piece ends with a nod towards the mutual benefits that keep writers and journalists talking to each other.

'May I ask whether you have given all these particulars to any other representative of the press?'
'Not that I recollect. You are the first to pay the compliment of expressing any curiosity.'
The *Star* man sprang to his feet, and made for Stonecutter Street with the news without another word.

An even more theatrical fancy, written to publicize the opening of Shaw's *Arms and the Man* in 1894, has 'the extra special *Star* man' pursuing Shaw to the Avenue Theatre. Here his perfectly sensible questions are met with entirely unjustified impatience from a dummy playwright who tells him, in the course of an extended puff for the new play, that he is more interested in improving the journalist's mind than in 'talking about his own works'. Driven by Shaw's violence to hide beneath a chair, told that he is wasting valuable time, the '*Star* man' finally exits when 'the face of the Fabian suddenly turned a frightful greenish purple as he snatched up a length of iron gaspipe'. The interview is over:

The *Star* man, already flying for his life along the Embankment, heard no more. He signifies his intention of raising his terms for future interviews with the author of *Arms and the Man*.[14]

Taken to this level of ingenuity, pretend interviewing not only brought publicity but allowed Shaw to indulge his intimacy with the medium itself. On one occasion he had the 'journalist' ask 'Shaw' to check the transcript of their conversation, which 'Shaw' duly did. '

It also allowed the playwright to adopt a comic mask which, though not identical with what it concealed, wasn't entirely distinguishable either. And if this language of masks and of puppets sounds familiar, there could be a reason. For it cannot have been entirely by accident that when 'our representative' swooped on Shaw in the *Pall Mall Gazette* on 21 March 1895, less than a fortnight before the hearing of Wilde's case against the Marquess of Queensberry, he should have discovered that his target lived in 'a pleasant sitting-room, where were many photographs and some charming old blue china in an antique cabinet', and noted '*Shirley* and *Jane Eyre*, standing cheek by jowl in a small bookcase with a play of Mr Wilde's'.[15] These are glancing jokes for the literate, not unworthy of Wilde himself. Shaw's inventions, like Wilde's, depend greatly on a mixture of inside knowledge and self-directed irony. It was as if he had to protect himself from undue exposure to those among whom, as a socialist, he belonged, and to whom, as a didactic journalist, he was committed. To honestly admit error, to allow for mistakes or the unexpected, was to risk being caught napping in the future, and would leave his readers leaderless. On the other hand, what degree of trust should those readers have placed in a writer who could only trust himself?

## 'SOMETHING FOR EVERYONE'

In the nineties many authors professed their mistrust of the papers but none came close to Henry James in his continual attempts to define the literary vocation as contempt for journalism. James himself had virtually given up regular newspaper work in 1879, and after that supplied only carefully prepared essays to the monthlies, concentrating his energies on novels, stories and, for a time, plays.

Everything he said on the subject suggests that he came to loathe the daily press, seeing it as prime agent in the creation of a frenetic, superficial, exploitative modern environment. James even seems to have blamed the kind of reading that journalism provided, and the variety of temptations and demands that it placed upon serious writers, for his own periods of commercial failure. Essentially he thought of all modern papers as following the example of American scandal sheets, and what he claimed to fear was the reduction of knowledge and understanding into personal gossip.

The modes of modern communication were so thoroughly alien to James's self-image that they eventually became a subject of almost compulsive interest. An initial embarrassment in the face of the New Journalism was prolonged by a deep and oddly responsive curiosity about what it had to offer. So much so that James's own fiction became a double-sided account of his obsession. Again and again, in novel and short story, journalists play a distinctive and quite irrepressible role.

Sometimes they are what James liked to call *ficelles*, subsidiary characters whose function is to offset the main agents of the plot; even so, they tend to hog the limelight.

Henrietta Stackpole, in *Portrait of a Lady*, published in 1881 when James had been resident in London for about five years, is a significant prototype. Nearly thirty years later, in the preface to his collected edition, he was still going out of his way to put her in her place. We have of her, he said, 'indubitably too much'; since she is 'but wheels to the coach'.[16] Embarrassed and irritated by her popularity with his readers, he bemoaned the absence of responsible criticism that might have been drawn to the novel's major themes rather than to its minor characters. In an act of revenge against his own creation he disowned her as the momentary indiscretion of an immature writer.

In fact, Henrietta is considerably more than the comic figure that James chose to remember, and her status in the novel belies her moral power. Even in 1908 he was unable to edit her out of his text. As a responsible contributor to the New York paper *The Interviewer*, in Europe for the purpose of filing reports written 'from the radical point of view',[17] the briskly active Henrietta has duties that the narration admits her to be quite capable of performing.

In a way she threatens to pre-empt the extended literary structure in which she appears. So it is fitting that she should at first be presented as though she were the very embodiment of her particular profession, as if there were no distinction to be made between who she is and what she does. Henrietta impresses Ralph Touchett, who may be as close as the novel comes to a moral touchstone, as being 'as crisp and new and comprehensive as a first issue before the folding. From top to toe she probably had no misprint.' But she also strikes him 'as not at all in the large type, the type of horrid "headings", that he had expected'.

Henrietta has the journalist's right of scrutiny. Her eye 'rested without impudence or defiance, but as if in conscious exercise of a natural right, upon every object it happened to encounter', yet Touchett comes to believe that 'it would be a sovereign injustice to the correspondent of *The Interviewer* to assign a dishonourable motive to any act of hers'. In contrast, the villain of the book, Gilbert Osmund, sees her as 'a new steel pen – the most odious thing in nature', while its heroine, Isabel Archer, though she knows journalism to be 'ephemeral', nevertheless esteems Henrietta's 'courage, energy and good humour'.

It is largely to Henrietta's credit that there should be not much more to her than meets the eye. She herself sees through English upper-class life with spontaneous clarity. The doubtful radicalism of Lord Warburton is put firmly in place: 'It's pleasant to own something, but inanimate objects are enough for me. I don't insist on flesh and blood and minds and consciences.' Having won the disapproval of the repellent Osmund, she continues to conduct herself with unquestioning loyalty and, for the most part, good sense. It is Henrietta who greets Isabel at Charing Cross when she arrives from Italy to be present at Touchett's deathbed, Henrietta who is the only person to speak to Isabel at the funeral, the only person to weep. Her *bêtises* – preferring the dome of the Capitol building in Washington to that of St Peter's in Rome, for example – are trivial in comparison, while her more serious lapses have a beguiling self-knowledge. 'I consider', she says, 'that my conversation refers only to the moment, like the morning papers.'

All of which makes Touchett's joke, to be appreciated posthumously, of leaving Henrietta his library 'in recognition of her services to literature' rather hard for others to enjoy. Ralph's mother suggests, unkindly, that Henrietta will use the proceeds to set up a newspaper, though she has already decided to settle in England and pursue her understanding of the 'inner life'. Throughout *Portrait* Henrietta has to bear more moral responsiblity than is reasonable, only to be blamed for inadequacy when she behaves correctly.

'Henrietta', James rued in 1908, 'must have been at that time a part of my wonderful notion of the lively.'[18] So she probably was, but her liveliness owed a fair amount to her profession. Like James's later journalists, she brims with energy and dazzles with integrity.

If James's journalists had to be acknowledged seekers after truth, he nonetheless liked to make them suffer for their presumptuousness in thinking that they knew where the truth might be found, a delusion in which they were increasingly encouraged by the booming confidence of the commercial interests they served. Long before the humiliating reviews of *Guy Domville*, James had learned to fear the power that the newspaper industry had gained in determining the success or failure of artistic ventures. *The Reverberator* (1888) shows the corrupting influence of the American press and, by the time of *The Tragic Muse* (1890), it had become very clear to James that Europe was going down the same road. An unholy alliance between publicity and investigation found its apotheosis in the 'interview', which struck James as a peculiarly insidious innovation because it perverted conversation: for James the most delicate, the most dangerous, the most precious and erotic of human activities – particularly when it involved an artist.

In an extended sequence of stories about writers which stretches from 'The Middle Years' (1893) through 'The Death of the Lion' (1894), 'The Next Time' (1895), 'The Figure in the Carpet' (1896) to 'John Delavoy' (1898), a series of young people descend on ageing but magisterial authors, eager, above all, to question. The difficulty is that they expect the author's answers to shed light on his work, a situation that becomes particularly fraught when the questioner is a professional journalist. Once or twice, they appear to be saved, ending up as the writer's private protector from all the busy-bodies. Curiously, though, as in 'The Death of the Lion', the distinguished author often gives off a certain air of fraudulence.

In 'The Death of the Lion', the author's defender, himself a journalist, rebukes another, more intrusive specimen, with 'My dear sir, the best interviewer's the best reader.' What he means presumably, as a literary critic, is that the novelist, in all his complexity, can only be known through his works. Yet the syntax of his remark allows the opposite: he who best knows the novelist will best understand the novels. The distinction between creator and creation is threatened by that ambiguity, which might in turn be a tell-tale slip by the character who perpetrates it, or an accurate reflection of the mystification that surrounds the 'Lion's' oeuvre. In fact none of James's successful writers, however talented, quite escapes the taint of pretension. Journalism was to be sacrificed to 'literature' all right, but on what grounds was 'literature' worth saving?

The most extended version of that dilemma is the long story that James published in 1903 as *The Papers*[20] – a sufficiently indicative title because it investigates the New Journalism from an historical vantage point and displays an amused familiarity with the décor of *fin de siècle* London. Close by the 'howl of the Strand', where the news-stands promise 'Astounding Disclosures', there are, James tells us, greasy pot-houses frequented by the likes of 'the greatest authority in London about the inner life of the criminal classes'. It is either in such places or along 'the gray river', whose mist encircles 'the blurred face of Big Ben', that his hero and heroine, journalists both, discuss the meaning of the press in relation to, among other things, suicide. Their names – Maud Blandy and Howard Bight – are a clear sign of how they jointly represent the limits and possibilities of their profession. They are, however, only beginning to make their way.

Bight is so far the more successful, largely because he has the confidence of an unimportant but well-known politician, Sir A. B. C.

*A woman journalist as depicted in* The Idler, *1895.*

Beadle-Muffet, KCB, and has worked with him to feed newspapers with snippets of information about his supposed activities and opinions. (Beadle-Muffet's 'alleged position on the date of the next school-treat of the Chelsea Cabmen's Orphanage' is Bight's facetious example to Blandy.) Blandy, a 'New Woman', is yet to be published. The two young journalists conduct their courtship by discussing their *métier*, reflecting in particular on Beadle-Muffet's extraordinary ability to remain in the public eye without ever actually doing anything. Reaching for the political paradox that underlies the story as a whole, they contemplate the spectacle of newspaper publicity turning negative beings into positive personalities, absence from action becoming presence in print.

Such thoughts lead them to play with a hypothesis: what if Beadle-Muffet should discover, for reasons they cannot at first dream up, that he urgently needs to escape from the publicity that he has so assiduously cultivated? No sooner is the scenario proposed than it occurs. He does vanish – but his disappearance, just as they had anticipated, serves merely to increase the number of references to him in the papers. A speculation grows: there are rumours that he may have died, committed suicide perhaps.

Blandy begins to worry that Bight may have somehow played a part in creating the mystery. She loves the glamour of Bight the journalist, but will only marry him if she is sure that he does not take undue pleasure in manipulation. And Bight, though he enjoys the opportunities for indulging cruel ironies that his job provides, wants Blandy to join him in chucking the papers to take up what they call, in embarrassed mock Cockney, more 'littery' work.

Two other characters contribute to the complications. Mortimer Marshal is an unsuccessful author prepared to go to any lengths to gain attention, as far as following Beadle-Muffet in a sham (or even literal) suicide. In the world of 'the papers' it is acknowledged that to be reported dead whilst still alive would be the ultimate gratification for the publicity-fed personality. It would indeed be to 'have your cake and eat it'; in biblical terms, to be 'lost and found'.

In addition to Mortimer Marshal there is Mrs Chormers, whom the reader never meets, the woman Beadle-Muffet wants to marry. Both Chormers and Marshal grant interviews to Blandy. Her conversation with the man is published, but Blandy withholds her interview with the woman at a time when it would be irresistible to any editor, feeling it to be too intimate for publication.[21] For this act of self-sacrifice she is blamed by Mrs Chormers herself, who sees Blandy's well-meaning reticence as a betrayal of her confessional trust.

Within the torsions and turnabouts of mature James, satirical duties frequently intertwine with sympathetic impulses. There was little that James did not know about the New Journalism and its less reputable progeny, and that he was not prepared to ridicule. Conscious that the quantity of cheap information was proliferating along with the multiplicity of outlets, he has Mortimer Marshal subscribing to thirty-seven press-cutting agencies in England and America. When Marshal still finds no mention of his name James makes Bight waggishly suggest that the solution might be for Marshal to submit letters protesting at their failure to report him. Blandy is struck by the neatness of this idea, but can see the flaw: the papers would be 'afraid, for they do guarantee, you know, that there's something for everyone. They claim it's their strength – that there's enough to go round. They won't want to show that they break down.'

Blandy and Bight finally come together with shared confessions of ignorance in the Beadle-Muffet affair, and with a mutual renunciation of the journalism that purports to have 'something for everyone', they turn instead to the 'littery'. But the defensive irony with which they continue to refer to popular 'tiles' and 'plys' allows James to leave some doubt as to how their particular form of 'literature' will improve on the journalism they now despise. Apart from the fact that he appears not to be dead, the outcome of the Beadle-Muffet affair is never disclosed. His story may be 'too good for a ply', as Blandy originally observed, but it would take an exceptional kind of fiction to disclose the true factitiousness of the supposedly democratic press. James had been trying to write it for years.

## THE UNREADABLE AND THE UNREAD

For Shaw a *métier*, for James a theme, for Wilde journalism was a means. He shamelessly pursued his career as a writer, all the while showing absolute disdain for the force that propelled it. Wilde always knew the value of a signature and came out against anonymity early on, perhaps because he feared an extended period of nameless reviewing in the newspapers. 'The English journals', he told a French interviewer in 1882,

> are much more serious and earnest in their tone than yours. But a man who has a name that is valuable will not be an English journalist. English newspaper articles are written anonymously. A good writer can get no credit for good work, and so will not write for an English paper. The proprietor is everything, the writer nothing there. In France, where the writers sign their names, better men become journalists.[22]

Temperamentally at odds with the straight face of English journalism, Wilde developed the habit, as soon as he had established his own name, of undermining its pomposities by insinuating his distinctive presence into its columns on every possible occasion. Recognizing the competitiveness of the professional situation, Wilde nominated himself as the journalist's natural butt and mocking colleague. In the eighties, he made his living mainly by writing for the papers. He moved in journalistic circles and interested himself in the daily output of print. He even became an editor – running the *Woman's World* from 1887 to 1889. By the early nineties, though, Wilde was sufficiently secure as a literary writer, if increasingly vulnerable in his private life, to recognize the press as a direct threat, and he began to refer to journalism as the absolute enemy, representing precisely the wrong kind of social criminality.

'Journalism is a terrible cave where the divine become tainted', he warned Richard Le Gallienne in 1893, adding as a concession to an

ephemeral medium, 'for a moment only'.[23] Invited to contribute an
article attacking the term '*fin de siècle*', he snapped back: 'I never write
"slashing" articles: slash does not seem to me to be a quality of good
prose ... But perhaps your letter was intended for someone else. It seems
to me to be addressed to a journalist, not to an artist.'[24] Not that he was
averse to using newspaper controversy for publicity purposes, a
technique that went back to his American tour of 1881–2.[25] In 1890 he
responded to hostile, moralistic reviews of *Dorian Gray* with long,
brilliant, and irresistibly publishable letters, in which he simultaneously
claimed and disclaimed responsibility for the novel by insisting that it
was an entirely 'perfect' work of art, and therefore beyond the reach of
'the absurd terms used by modern journalism'.[26] To the *St James's
Gazette* he wrote protesting at their description of *Dorian Gray* as an
'advertisement' for its author: 'Of all men in England I am the one who
requires least advertisement. I am tired to death of being advertised. I
feel no thrill when I see my name in a paper.'[27]

Just as Wilde wrote to newspapers rebuking their right to criticize
him, thereby goading them into further attention, when he gave
interviews, which he did quite frequently, he made a point of reproving
the reporter. 'Bad manners', he said, 'make a journalist.' As he was at
heart the politest of men, this attitude rarely caused serious offence. Like
James, he saw the interview as a scene of psychic confrontation, a test of
sensibility for the interviewer as much as for the victim. By interviewing
artists a journalist might learn what it was like to be one. If the
interviewer was a young man the opportunity for a little friendly
induction was an added bonus, and had always been so, even when Wilde

---

### A CORRESPONDENCE.
(Telegram, Feb. 23.)

To O—— W——, Esq.

Will you review a new and dangerous French play called " Salome "
for me ?—Ed. *P.M.B.*

(Telegram, Feb. 23 )

To Editor, *Pall Mall Budget*, London.

My Dear Sir,—I could not criticise perfection ; you must Hire some-
body to do that.

O—— W——.

---

*The exchange – which may be fake or facsimile – appeared in the* Pall Mall
Budget *on 2 March 1893.*

himself had only been in his twenties. A young American journalist who called on the great Aesthete in his Boston hotel in 1882 was advised to learn French and instructed as to what books to read. 'In fact I interviewed him', the intended interviewee confessed – to another newspaper. And paid him too: 'I gave him an orange and then sent him away. What he did with the orange I don't know; he seemed pleased to get it.'[28]

More than a decade later Wilde was still swapping roles. Cornered coming out of his St James's club by a young man from the *Sketch* on the morning after the first night of *An Ideal Husband*, he held forth on the theatre, dramatic criticism and the outrageous demands that the public made upon creative artists.

*'I'm afraid you don't like journalists?' I remarked nervously.*

'The journalist is always reminding the public of the existence of the artist. That is unnecessary of him. He is always reminding the artist of the existence of the public. That is indecent of him.'

*'But we must have journalists, Mr Wilde.'*

'Why? They only record what happens. What does it matter what happens? It is only the abiding things that are interesting, not the horrid incidents of everyday life.'[29]

Luckily, in Wilde's benign dispensation, there was some hope – the signs being right – even for the man from the *Sketch*.

*'We shook hands, and Mr. Wilde, giving me a glance of approval, said*: 'I am sure that you must have a great future in literature before you.'

*'What makes you think so?' I asked, as I flushed with pleasure at the prediction.*

'Because you seem to be such a very bad interviewer. I feel sure that you must write poetry, I certainly like the colour of your necktie very much.'

The interview ending, a more promising relationship – both romantic and literary – presumably opens up.

Wilde's insistence that art could free people from the tyranny of fact was invariably coupled with an attack on the medium that gave fact priority. Journalism reduced writing to mere record and, ultimate ignominy, made authors subservient to universal opinion. 'There is much to be said in favour of modern journalism', observes 'Gilbert', one of Wilde's surrogates. 'By giving us the opinions of the uneducated, it keeps us in touch with the ignorance of the community. By carefully chronicling the current events of contemporary life, it shows us of what very little importance such events really are. By invariably discussing the unnecessary, it makes us understand what things are requisite for culture, and what are not.' Newspapers, Gilbert feels, 'give us the bald, sordid, disgusting facts of life', while the New Journalism 'is but the old vulgarity "writ large"'.[30]

Carrying out in public a private conversation with himself was a device that Wilde used for his two major aesthetic statements, 'The Critic as Artist' and 'The Decay of Lying'. Throughout 'The Critic' Gilbert and Ernest repeatedly exchange the positions of interviewer and interviewee. With delighted complicity they badger each other with questions intended for elegant repudiation. By demoting mere 'opinion', Gilbert maintains that criticism can be seen as an art. Ernest comments that in classical times there was 'no ridiculous journalism monopolizing the seat of judgement when it should be apologizing in the dock'. Gilbert distances himself by replying that it is certainly not his business to defend modern newspaper criticism: 'It justifies its own existence by the great Darwinian principle of the survival of the vulgarest. I have merely to do with literature.' Challenged by Ernest to perform the ritual exercise of distinguishing literature from journalism, Gilbert comes up with the nineties' best and least helpful answer: 'Journalism is unreadable and literature is not read. That is all.'[31]

It was not all, of course, as Wilde was perfectly well aware. The immediate task was to make literature as pleasurable a read as journalism but less egregiously accessible. At a time when the journalist was making a noisy entrance, the artist had better slip into the wings, and return in a mask. Like Shaw, though with an even greater theatrical sense, Wilde realized that in order to stay in circulation he would have to provide his own copy, and his interviews were always, in a sense, collaborations.

On at least one occasion he went further and virtually, perhaps literally, interviewed himself. The piece appeared in the *St James's Gazette* under the title 'Mr Oscar Wilde on Mr Oscar Wilde' and was concocted with the help of Robert Ross.[32] Published on 18 January 1895, it alluded to the opening of *An Ideal Husband* – a memorable night when Wilde had been called in the interval to the Prince of Wales's box for royal compliments and then, at the curtain, responding to cries of 'Oscar!' from the rest of the audience, out on to the stage itself. There was also mention of an imminent trip to Algiers – traditional hunting-ground of the homosexual hedonist.

The heightened flamboyance of the public pose was accompanied by an increased daring in Wilde's private conduct. Yet, as he attempts to persuade his *alter ego* in the interview, 'The personality of the artist is not a thing that the public should know anything about. It is too accidental.' On the other hand, 'Humility is for the hypocrite, modesty for the incompetent. Assertion is at once the duty and privilege of the artist.' It was journalists, not artists, who said that the duty of a writer was to please the public; but too many London theatre critics believed that the artist had a duty to please only them. Nor did the range of characters required by a play prevent a true stylist – Shakespeare, Ibsen, Dumas, Wilde – from 'dominating' his own work.

It is hard to say which Wilde feared most: mediocrity, intrusion or neglect. The self-interview technique protected him from all three, and allowed him to shed light upon the coercive procedures of journalism. No one should have wanted to disappear among 'our readers' after reading Wilde on the subject of the press: the risk of misrepresentation was too great. By a similar token Wilde took, wherever possible, steps to script himself. Many of his best-known remarks are not so much reported speech as sayings previously prepared for print. Yeats was to marvel that his sentences seemed to have been written 'overnight with labour and yet all spontaneous'.[33] An impromptu wit could take no chances.

At the end of the self-interrogation of 18 January 1895, Wilde asked the half-imagined journalist how he 'managed' his interviews and, in the subsequent exchange, deviously confessed the narcissism of the whole enterprise. 'Oh, Pitman', came the answer. 'Is that your name?' Wilde affected to ask, feigning misunderstanding. 'It's not a very *nice* name.' It was, of course, the name of the shorthand system used by reporters whose job it was simply to reproduce other people's words.

Wilde's final joke not only put journalists neatly in their place but gave him a chance to indulge his own obsession with onomastic convention. A genuine formalist who believed that words anticipate their reference, Wilde thought that the best, the most appropriate names – Ernest, for example – had to be lived up to. The preoccupation long precedes his most famous play on names. As Lord Henry Wotton pronounces, 'Names are everything.' 'John is an admirable name,' Wilde wrote to a journalist who had misnamed him in a review, 'Popes and Princes, wicked or wonderful, have been called John. John has been the name of several eminent journalists and criminals. But John is not amongst the delightful names given to me at my birth.'[34]

Pope and prince, journalist and criminal: through his appreciation of each and every social role the artist strove to preserve his special self, his unique name. For Wilde knew, too, that the right to publish under one's own name, however coveted by journalists, offered the artist no more than a further opportunity for fiction. If an artist really did have the 'multiple personality' that Wilde liked to maintain, then any single signature would be simultaneously genuine and fake, the truth and a lie. With the future of 'literature' at stake, nobody's words were to be trusted.

# NOTES

## INTRODUCTION

Holbrook Jackson's *The Eighteen Nineties* has been several times reprinted, most recently in 1988, with an introduction by Malcolm Bradbury (London: Cresset Library). It remains unchallenged in its scope. The modern tendency to concentrate upon individual themes or trends has produced books that cast a different, more specialized light upon the decade. The most influential has been Frank Kermode's *Romantic Image* (London: Routledge and Kegan Paul, 1957), which did much to re-establish the reputation of Arthur Symons and to indicate the origins of Yeats's mature style. The importance of the nineties as the culmination of Victorian aesthetics is confirmed in William Gaunt's *The Aesthetic Adventure* (London: Jonathan Cape, 1945) and Graham Hough's *The Last Romantics* (London: Duckworth, 1947). For studies of the theory and practice of a closely related topic, 'The Decadence', see *Decadence and the 1890s*, Stratford upon Avon Studies No. 17 (London: Edward Arnold, 1979), ed. Ian Fletcher, with its comprehensive bibliography; a supplement to Linda Dowling's *Aestheticism and Decadence: A Selective Annotated Bibliography* (New York: Garland Publishing, 1977). The major full-length studies of the subject are Barbara Charlesworth, *Dark Passages: The Decadent Consciousness in Victorian Literature* (Madison and Milwaukee: University of Milwaukee, 1965); J. E. Chamberlin, *Ripe was the Drowsy Hour: The Age of Oscar Wilde* (New York: The Seabury Press, 1977); R. K. R. Thornton, *The Decadent Dilemma* (London: Edward Arnold, 1983); John R. Reed, *The Decadent Style* (Athens, Ohio: Ohio University Press, 1985); Linda Dowling, *Language and Decadence in the Victorian Fin de Siècle* (Princeton: Princeton University Press, 1986). Wilde dominates scholarship as he did his times: see the bibliographical essays by Ian Fletcher and John Stokes in *Anglo-Irish Literature: a Review of Research* (New York: MLA, 1976) and *Recent Research on Anglo-Irish Writers* (New York: MLA, 1983). No single biographical work compares with Richard Ellmann's magnificent *Oscar Wilde* (London: Hamish Hamilton, 1987), cited hereafter as Ellmann. There are several anthologies with useful introductions and annotations: *Aesthetes and Decadents*, ed. Karl Beckson (New York: Random House, 1966; revised, enlarged edition: Chicago: Academy, 1981); *Poetry of the Nineties*, ed. R. K. R. Thornton (Harmondsworth: Penguin Books, 1970); *Writing of the Nineties*, ed. Derek Stanford

(London: Dent, 1971); *The Aesthetes,* ed. Ian Small (London, Boston and Henley: Routledge and Kegan Paul, 1979); *Strangeness and Beauty,* ed. Eric Warner and Graham Hough (Cambridge: Cambridge University Press, 2 vols, 1983). Important books on individual authors will be cited as and when their names appear in the text.

1. *Star,* 15 February 1898. The ballet is described in C. W. Beaumont, *Complete Book of Ballets* (New York: Putnam's, 1938), pp. 629–31.
2. I am thinking here of John Goode's essay, 'The Decadent Writer as Producer' in *Decadence and the 1890s,* Stratford upon Avon Studies No. 17 (London: Edward Arnold, 1979), pp. 109–29; Allon White, *The Uses of Obscurity* (London: Routledge and Kegan Paul, 1981); Nigel Cross, *The Common Writer* (Cambridge: Cambridge University Press, 1985); Regenia Gagnier, *Idylls of the Marketplace: Oscar Wilde and the Victorian Public* (London: Scolar Press, 1987).
3. *The Eighteen Nineties* (1988), p. 157.
4. Ibid., p. 158.
5. Katherine Lyon Mix, *A Study in Yellow: The Yellow Book and Its Contributors* (Lawrence and London: University of Kansas Press and Constable and Company Ltd, 1960), p. 14. Symons's status as the true prophet of the *fin de siècle,* and echo of its obsessions, has always been known. His presence has recently become more concrete as a result of Karl Beckson's full-scale biography, *Arthur Symons: A Life* (Oxford: Clarendon Press, 1987), cited hereafter as Beckson.
6. *The Oxford Book of Modern Verse 1892–1935* (Oxford: Clarendon Press, 1936), 'Introduction', p. xi.
7. Ellmann, p. 285.
8. In *The Modes of Modern Writing* (London: Edward Arnold, 1977) David Lodge uses it to suggest distinctions between literature and journalism.

## 1   'IS IT A REVOLUTION?'

The history of the press – of particular imprints and overall tendencies, with all their various cultural meanings and political alignments – is now a secure academic pursuit. A good sampling of modern approaches can be had from George Boyce, James Curran, Pauline Wingate, *Newspaper History: from the 17th Century to the present day* (London: Constable, 1978), which includes an exceptional essay by Anthony Smith, 'The long road to objectivity and back again: the kinds of truth we get in journalism' (pp. 153–72). The phenomenon of the New Journalism is sometimes related to the effects of the Education Act of 1870 in terms of its audience and to American models for its style of presentation. At least as important, though harder to define, are the determining shifts in social attitudes and in class formation that took place in the late nineteenth century. Alan J. Lee, *The Origins of the Popular Press in England* (London: Croom Helm, 1976) is particularly good on the relationship of the press to ideology. The most recent full-scale study, Lucy Brown's *Victorian News and Newspapers* (Oxford: Clarendon Press, 1985), cited hereafter as Brown, stresses, with considerable persuasiveness, the economic context of newspaper history. Political theory at the turn of the century and after is analysed by Michael Freeden, *The New Liberalism* (Oxford: Clarendon Press, 1978). All the classic liberal assumptions can be seen at work in the contemporary survey, H. W. Massingham, *The London Daily Press* (London: The Religious Tract Society, 1892), while the history of the *Pall Mall Gazette* (which dropped its support for the Liberals in 1892) is told in J. W. Robertson Scott, *The Life and Death of a Newspaper* (London: Methuen and Co., 1952). Stephen Koss traces, probably definitively, the negotiations between the press and parliamentary politics in *The Rise and Fall of the Political Press in Britain* (Chapel Hill and London: University of North Carolina Press, 1981–84, 2 vols).

Raymond Williams's major statement on the place of newspapers in literary history is *The Long Revolution* (London: Chatto and Windus, 1961), but he also contributed an essay on 'The press and popular culture' to Boyce, Curran and Wingate, *Newspaper History*. Williams always insisted that complaints about the cheapening and vulgarisation of communication by new media were perennial, and the reminder was always salutary.

1. Ellmann, p. 450.
2. Holbrook Jackson, *The Eighteen Nineties*, p. 62.
3. Ellmann, p. 288.
4. Henry James, *The Scenic Art*, ed. Allan Wade (London: Rupert Hart-Davis, 1949), p. 197. For the first night of *Guy Domville* see H. G. Wells's account, reprinted in *Henry James. Interviews and Recollections*, ed. Norman Page (London: Macmillan, 1984), pp. 63–6.
5. London: W. Heinemann.
6. 'A Degenerate's View of Nordau', *Liberty* (New York), 27 July 1895, pp. 2–10. Revised, with a new introduction, as *The Sanity of Art* (London: The New Age Press, 1908).
7. Among the more notable reviews are those in the *Bookman*, April 1895; *Daily Telegraph*, 22 February 1895; *Graphic*, 30 March 1895; *Pall Mall Gazette*, 25 February 1895; *Spectator*, 2 March 1895; *Westminster Gazette*, 25 February 1895. There is a comprehensive survey in an American dissertation: Milton P. Foster, *The Reception of Max Nordau's 'Degeneration' in England and America*, University of Michigan, 1954.
8. Ellmann, p. 434.
9. Richard Whittington-Egan and Geoffrey Smerdon, *The Quest of the Golden Boy* (London: The Unicorn Press, 1960), p. 215. The 'Is Christianity Played Out?' letters ran through January 1893 and beyond. They inspired a book, *The Religion of a Literary Man*, published later that year.
10. 'An Optimist', *Daily Chronicle*, 12 August 1895.
11. 'X. Y. Z.', *Daily Chronicle*, 13 August 1895.
12. 'The New Hedonism', *Fortnightly Review*, March 1894, pp. 377–92. Also

see the *Speaker*, 15, 22, and 29 December 1894. In the *Westminster Gazette*, 23 October 1894, Grant Allen had answered his own rhetorical question, 'Are we Decadent?', with 'Our age is the most original, the most individual, the most lawless that ever existed. It swarms with personalities. It abounds in impulse. The very decadents themselves are far, far removed from all real signs of decadence. What could be more vigorous than our Oscar Wildes and the New English Art Club?'

13. *Daily Chronicle*, 10 August 1895.

14. *Daily Chronicle*, 13 August 1895.

15. *Daily Chronicle*, 12 August 1895.

16. *Understanding Brecht* (London: New Left Books, 1973), pp. 89–90.

17. For information on W. T. Stead (1849–1912), see Raymond L. Shults, *Crusader in Babylon. W. T. Stead and the Pall Mall Gazette* (Lincoln: University of Nebraska, 1972). Stead was editor of the *Pall Mall Gazette* from 1883 to 1890, and editor of the *Review of Reviews* from 1890 to 1912. For H. W. Massingham see Alfred F. Havighurst, *Radical Journalist. H. W. Massingham (1860–1925)* (London: Cambridge University Press, 1974). Massingham was editor of the *Star* in 1890, assistant editor of the *Daily Chronicle* in 1892, editor from March 1895 until November 1899. For T. P. O'Connor see Hamilton Fyfe, *T. P. O'Connor* (London: George Allen and Unwin, 1934). O'Connor was founder editor of the *Star*, the *Sun* and *T. P.'s Weekly*, and a nationalist MP from 1885 to 1929.

18. 'The Pall Mall Gazette', *Review of Reviews*, February 1893, pp. 139–56, p.151.

19. H.G. Wells, *Anticipations* (London: Chapman and Hall, 1902), pp. 162–3.

20. Olive Anderson, *Suicide in Victorian and Edwardian England* (Oxford: Clarendon Press, 1987), pp. 245–6.

21. Havighurst, *Radical Journalist*, p. 22. It is suggested that the idea originated with Massingham.

22. *The Letters of Oscar Wilde*, ed. Rupert Hart-Davis (London: Hart-Davis, 1962), pp. 257–301. Cited hereafter as *Letters*.

23. 27 May 1895.

24. For more information on *Degeneration* see the summary in Adrian Poole, *Gissing in Context* (London: Macmillan, 1975), pp. 20–1; Tom Gibbons, *Rooms in the Darwin Hotel* (Nedlands: University of Western Australia Press, 1973) – the best book on the influence of evolutionist ideas on literary critics; Robert A. Nye, *Crime, Madness and Politics in Modern France. The Medical Concept of National Decline* (Princeton, New Jersey: Princeton University Press, 1984) – general information on Morselli, Ferri, Lombroso etc.; and J. Edward Chamberlin and Sander L. Gilman (eds), *Degeneration: The Dark Side of Progress* (New York: Columbia University Press, 1985).

25. Max Nordau, *Degeneration* (London: W. Heinemann, 1895) p. 24.

26. Janet E. Hogarth, 'Literary Degenerates', *Fortnightly Review*, April 1895, pp. 586–92, p. 592. This is only one of several full-length discussions: D. F.

Hannigan, 'Sex in Fiction', *Westminster Review*, June 1895, pp. 616–25; James Ashcroft Noble, 'The Fiction of Sexuality', *Contemporary Review*, April 1895, pp. 490–8; Hugh E. M. Stutfield, 'Tommyrotics', *Blackwood's Magazine*, June 1895, pp. 833–45.

27. T. Clifford Allbutt, 'Nervous Diseases and Modern Life', *Contemporary Review*, February 1895, pp. 210–31, p. 224.

28. Ibid., pp. 214–15.

29. 2 February 1895, p. 127.

30. *Punch*, 11 May 1895.

31. 13 April 1895, p. 403. The most celebrated version of this cry is H. D. Traill's 'Not to be "new" is, in these days, to be nothing', *The New Fiction and Other Essays on Literary Subjects* (London: Hurst and Blackett, 1897), p. 1.

32. Evelyn March Phillipps, 'The New Journalism', *New Review*, August 1895, pp. 182–9, p. 182.

33. *The Rise of the Political Press*, 1, p. 343. Certainly Robert Buchanan entitled his 1877 attack on society gossip sheets like *Vanity Fair*: 'Sign of the Times. 1. The Newest Thing in Journalism', *Contemporary Review*, September, pp. 678–703.

34. 'Up to Easter', *The Nineteenth Century*, May 1887, reprinted in Matthew Arnold, *The Last Word*, ed. R. H. Super (Ann Arbor: The University of Michigan Press, 1977), pp. 190–209, p. 202.

35. 'On Translating Homer', Matthew Arnold, *On the Classical Tradition*, ed. R. H. Super (Ann Arbor: University of Michigan Press, 1960), p. 140.

36. For details of the changing costs of newspaper production see Brown, pp. 12, 30, 86.

37. Ibid., p. 35.

38. Ibid., pp. 12–13.

39. Holbrook Jackson, *The Eighteen Nineties*, pp. 61–2.

40. 'The New Journalism', *New Review*, October 1889, pp. 423–34, p. 430.

41. 'Government by Journalism', *Contemporary Review*, May 1886, pp. 653–74, p. 669.

42. *Pall Mall Gazette*, 16 January 1888.

43. *Star*, 17 January 1888.

44. Anthony Smith in *Newspaper History*, p. 168.

45. 'Government by Journalism', p. 671.

46. For an account of 'The Maiden Tribute' see Shults, *Crusader in Babylon*, pp. 63–6.

47. Brown, p. 23.

48. For 'The Bitter Cry', see Shults, *Crusader in Babylon*, pp. 49–50.

49. See 'The Press and the Public', *Pall Mall Gazette*, 28 July 1885, but for Stead's attack on mere gossip see 'Pecksniff and Poison', *Pall Mall Gazette*, 16 December 1886.

50. 'Art and the Daily Paper', *The Nineteenth Century*, October 1897, pp. 653–62, p. 657.

51. *Pall Mall Gazette*, 23 August and 31 December 1884.
52. Brown, pp. 160–2.
53. 'Government by Journalism', *Contemporary Review*, p. 655.
54. Massingham, *The London Daily Press*, p. 34.
55. Anderson, *Suicide in Victorian and Edwardian England*, p. 246.
56. *Daily Chronicle*, 3 August 1895.
57. William Arthur Bentley, *Daily Chronicle*, 15 August 1895.
58. J. A. Spender (1862–1942), assistant editor of the *Pall Mall Gazette* in 1892, a writer on the *Westminster Gazette* from 1893, its editor from 1896. See J. A. Spender, *Life, Journalism and Politics* (London: Cassell and Co., 1927) and Wilson Harris, *J. A. Spender* (London: Cassell and Co., 1946).
59. London: 'Westminster Gazette' Office.
60. London: Swan Sonnenschein and Co.
61. George and Weedon Grossmith, *The Diary of a Nobody* (Harmondsworth: Penguin Books, 1965), p. 89.
62. *The New Fiction*, p. vii.
63. Brown, pp. 77 and 79.
64. *The Woman Who Did* (London: John Lane, 1895), p. 151.
65. Ibid., p. 152.
66. *The New Fiction*, p. 103.
67. *Keynotes* (London: Elkin Mathews and John Lane, 1893), pp. 88–9.
68. *Discords* (London: Elkin Mathews, 1894), p. 239.
69. Evelyn March Phillipps, 'The New Journalism', p. 187.
70. Ibid.
71. *The New Fiction*, p. 101.
72. 'The Decadent Movement in Literature', *Harper's New Monthly Magazine*, November 1893, p. 867.
73. *A Full and True Account of the Wonderful Mission of Earl Lavender* (London: Ward and Downey Ltd., 1895), p. 277.
74. *Complete Works of Oscar Wilde* (London and Glasgow: Collins, 1971), pp. 491, cited hereafter as *Works*.
75. London: Hermes Press, 1905.
76. Henry Maudsley, *The Pathology of Mind. A Study of its Distempers, Deformities, and Disorders* (London: Macmillan and Co., 1895). This edition has a complicated but significant publishing history. The first edition of *The Physiology and Pathology of Mind* had appeared in 1867 and was several times reprinted in various formats in the 1870s. According to Maudsley himself the 1895 edition was 'virtually new... the text entirely re-written' (Preface). It therefore represents Maudsley's current thinking on such topics as the link between madness and what he saw as aberrant sexuality. That Maudsley was treated with some scepticism by Shaw in *The Sanity of Art* ('Dr. Maudsley is a clever and cultivated specialist in insanity, who has written several interesting books, consisting of repetitions, amplifications and historical illustrations of the same idea ...'), does nothing but confirm Maudsley's claim to conventional wisdom. As Peter

Gay puts it: 'Maudsley was a sniffer of trends, a commentator on fashionable concerns ...' *The Bourgeois Experience I. Education of the Senses* (Oxford: Oxford University Press, 1984), p. 213. Maudsley is also discussed by Elaine Showalter in *The Female Malady: Women, Madness and English Culture. 1830–1980* (London: Virago, 1987).

77. Maudsley, *Pathology of Mind*, p. 24.
78. *Works*, p. 1039.
79. *Around Theatres* (London: Rupert Hart-Davis, 1953), p. 576.
80. 'Diminuendo', *The Works of Max Beerbohm* (London: John Lane, The Bodley Head; New York: Charles Scribner and Sons, 1896), p. 159.
81. 'Bread and the Circus', *The Yellow Book*, 7, October 1895, pp. 235–57, p. 247.
82. The phenomenon has been widely observed by American and Continental critics: Marshall McLuhan, for example, in *The Mechanical Bride* (London: Routledge and Kegan Paul, 1951). English critics have been more intrigued by the possible influence of journalism upon modernist prose style, but their attempts to put these on a firm footing have been provisional. Malcolm Bradbury volunteers that 'The change in language can be followed out from those basic, almost invisible usages of journalism – in for instance the columns of *Answers* and *Tit-Bits*, where in the encapsulated sentence and the brief paragraph experience was being redefined ...', *The Social Context of Modern English Literature* (Oxford: Basil Blackwell, 1971), p. 32.
83. *Fleet Street Eclogues* (London: Elkin Mathews and John Lane, 1893), pp. 4–5.
84. 'A New Guide to Journalism', *Saturday Review*, 8 August 1903, p. 165.
85. Brown, p. 252.
86. *Fleet Street Radical. A. Gardiner and the 'Daily News'* (London: Allen Lane, 1973), p. 30.
87. Ibid., pp. 32–3.

## 2 'IT'S THE TREATMENT NOT THE SUBJECT'

For the English response to French Impressionist painting the main sources are Douglas Cooper's introductory essay to *The Courtauld Collection* (London: Athlone Press, 1954) and Kate Flint, *Impressionists in England. The Critical Reception* (London: Routledge and Kegan Paul, 1984). For the specific case of Degas see Ronald Pickvance, '*L'Absinthe* in England', *Apollo*, May 1963, pp. 395–8; for a thorough investigation of pre-modernist critical attitudes see Jacqueline V. Falkenheim, *Roger Fry and the Beginnings of Formalist Art Criticism* (Ann Arbor, Michigan: UMI Research Press, 1980); and for a particularly intelligent study of the main trends in late nineteeth-century art see Linda Nochlin, *Realism* (Harmondsworth: Penguin Books, 1971). The most interesting memoir is by a minor artist: Alfred Thornton, *The Diary of an Art*

*Student in the Nineties* (London: Sir Isaac Pitman and Sons Ltd, 1938). Two essays by D. J. Gordon pose the essential questions and begin to provide some of the answers: 'Aubrey Beardsley at the V. and A.', *Encounter*, October 1966 and 'Dilemmas: *The Studio* in 1893–4', *Studio International*, April 1968, pp. 175–9. The most significant books on individual figures will be given when their names appear in the text.

1. Walter Sickert (1860–1941). See Wendy Baron, *Sickert* (London: Phaidon Press, 1973); Lilian Browse, *Sickert* (London: Hart-Davis, 1960); Denys Sutton, *Walter Sickert: A Biography* (London: Michael Joseph, 1976).

2. Philip Wilson Steer (1860–1942). See D. S. MacColl, *Steer* (London: Faber and Faber Ltd, 1945); Bruce Laughton, *Philip Wilson Steer* (Oxford: Clarendon Press, 1971).

3. George Moore (1852–1933). Novelist, playwright and, in the nineties, art critic. *Modern Painting* (London: Walter Scott, 1893) collects much of his art journalism from the period. Moore's contribution to the understanding of French painting is controversial – see Cooper, *Courtauld Collection*.

4. R. A. M. Stevenson (1847–1900). The cousin of R. L. Stevenson, educated at Cambridge and Edinburgh School of Art. Between 1879 and 1885 he studied painting in France and London; from 1888 to 1892 he wrote for various journals including the *Magazine of Art* and the *Saturday Review*. Later he became art critic of the *Pall Mall Gazette* and Professor of Fine Art at University College, Liverpool. Stevenson's most important work, the product of an obsession, is *The Art of Velasquez* (London: George Bell, 1895), reprinted in an enlarged edition in 1899 and again in 1962 with a biographical study of the author by Denys Sutton (London: G. Bell and Sons).

5. D. S. MacColl (1859–1948). Painter and writer. Studied at the Westminster School of Art and the Slade school. At University College, London until 1881, and at Lincoln College, Oxford from 1881–4 where he was a founder of *The Oxford Magazine*. (See 'Early Days of *The Oxford Magazine*', *The Oxford Magazine*, 19 January 1933, pp. 294–6 and 'Birth-pangs of *The Oxford Magazine*', *The Oxford Magazine*, 16 November 1944, pp. 54–6). Won the Newdigate Prize in 1882. Graduated in 1884. Travelled in Europe from 1887–9. Art critic of the *Spectator* from 1890–5, and of the *Saturday Review* from 1896. Member of the New English Art Club. Keeper of the Tate Gallery from 1906–11 and of the Wallace Collection from 1911–24. A selection of his critical essays, some of them dating back to the nineties, appeared in 1931: *Confessions of a Keeper* (London: A. Maclehose and Co.). MacColl also wrote an encylopaedic survey of *Nineteeth Century Art* (Glasgow: James Maclehose and Sons, 1902). Autobiographical essays appeared under the title 'A Batch of Memories' in the *Week-End Review*, 20 December 1930, pp. 911–13; 17 January 1931, pp. 66–7; 31 January 1931, pp. 138–40; 21 February 1931, pp. 251–2; 21 March 1931, pp. 432–3; 11 April 1931, pp. 533–4; 9 May 1931, pp. 684–5; 13 June 1931, pp.

879–80; 18 July 1931, pp. 71–2; 15 August 1931, pp. 192–3; 24 October 1931, pp. 508–9; 12 December 1931, pp. 759–60; and as 'Memories of the Nineties' in *The London Mercury*, January 1939, pp. 287–96. MacColl's papers are now housed in the Library of the University of Glasgow.

6.  'Degas determines to find new subjects – new effects' in the *Standard*, 25 April 1883, for example.

7.  'In poetry and painting, the situation predominates over the character; in sculpture, the character over the situation.' Walter Pater, *Studies in the History of the Renaissance* (London: Macmillan, 1873), p. 215.

8.  The formulation had been current for at least a decade before the Degas row blew up in 1893. For example, according to Frederick Wedmore in 1883, Degas knew that 'the final basis of artistic reputation is not the subject that is treated, but the capacity to treat it'. ('The Impressionists', *Fortnightly Review*, Jan.–June 1883, p. 79). Or, again, from the *Whitehall Review*, 2 May 1883, p. 10: 'We know of course that a man is behind the times who thinks the subject of a picture a matter of any moment, that it is the skill in expression and not the thing expressed that is of any importance.' MacColl's extended statements on the topic are 'Subject and Technique', *Spectator*, 25 March 1893, pp. 387–8 and 'Notes on a Recent Controversy', *Spectator*, 1 April 1893. Both he and Moore continued on the theme throughout April 1893.

9.  *The New Fiction*, p. 5.

10.  *Speaker*, 25 February 1893.

11.  *Speaker*, 25 March, 1 and 8 April 1893.

12.  *Spectator*, 25 February 1893.

13.  *The New Fiction*, p. 1.

14.  John Ruskin, *Works, Library Edition*, eds. E. T. Cook and Alexander Wedderburn (London: George Allen, 1903–12), 5, p. 31.

15.  *The Gentle Art of Making Enemies* (London: W. Heinemann, 2nd and enlarged edition, 1892), p. 127.

16.  'The Logic of Painting', *Albemarle*, September 1892, p. 6.

17.  *Spectator*, 1 April 1893.

18.  *Spectator*, 26 November 1892. For the 'handling' debate with Moore see the *Speaker*, 3 December 1892, pp. 677–8, and *Spectator*, 24 December 1892, pp. 925–6.

19.  *The New Fiction*, p. 3.

20.  Ibid., p. 5.

21.  1 April 1893.

22.  D. S. MacColl, 'The Beardsleys', *Manchester Guardian*, 18 March 1948, p. 3. The main sources for the French trips of 1893 and 'the art coterie' are MacColl in *The London Mercury*, January 1939; Elizabeth Robins Pennell, *Nights* (London: Heinemann, 1916), pp. 227–303 and *The Life and Letters of Joseph Pennell* (London: Ernest Benn, 1930), 1, pp. 252–7; and Thornton's *Diary*.

23.  MacColl, 'Memories of the Nineties', p. 29.

24. Thornton, *Diary*, p. 37.

25. MacColl, 'The Beardsleys'. The report of Moore writing about his book is in 'Memories of the Nineties'.

26. MacColl, 'Memories of the Nineties'.

27. MacColl, 'The Beardsleys'.

28. D. S. MacColl, *Poems* (Oxford: Basil Blackwell, 1940), p. 100.

29. MacColl, 'Memories of the Nineties', p. 293. For Giverny and Vétheuil see Logan Pearsall Smith, *Unforgotten Years* (London: Constable and Co., 1938), pp. 190–4.

30. Thornton, *Diary*, pp. 47–8.

31. Frances Spalding, *Roger Fry* (London: Granada, 1980), p. 44.

32. MacColl, 'Memories of the Nineties', p. 293.

33. Thornton, *Diary*, p. 99.

34. MacColl, 'Memories of the Nineties', p. 292.

35. *Manchester Guardian*, 9 December 1893.

36. Ibid. MacColl wrote on Sickert in the *Spectator*, 2 March 1895, pp. 295–6.

37. 'A Diary of Moods', *Speaker*, 9 December 1893, pp. 640–1.

38. Fry in *The Cambridge Review*, 22 June 1893, reprinted in *The Cambridge Mind* (London: Jonathan Cape, 1970), p. 214, MacColl in the *Spectator*, 18 November 1893, p. 131.

39. *Spectator*, 28 December 1895.

40. See his collected journalism, *A Free House* (London: Macmillan, 1947), ed. Osbert Sitwell.

41. *Spectator*, 18 May 1895, p. 683.

42. Ibid., 11 January 1896, p. 51.

43. *Spectator*, 18 January 1896. The article is part of a series on 'The Old Masters': *Spectator*, 18 January 1896, pp. 84–5; 1 February 1896, pp. 167–9; 8 February 1896, pp. 204–5.

44. *Pall Mall Gazette*, 17 December 1895.

45. *Velasquez*, p. 71.

46. Ibid., p. 157.

47. *Nineteenth Century Art*, pp. 165–6.

48. Ibid., p. 147.

49. Ibid., p. 164.

50. Ibid., p. 153. According to Falkenheim, in his later disagreements with Roger Fry over Post-Impressionism, MacColl retained his interest 'in the tangible results of sense stimulation [he] does not think that essences and concepts of objects are possible subjects for the artist. He believes that the artist can only paint what can already be seen.' Falkenheim, *Roger Fry*, p. 38.

51. The Beardsley essay is in R. A. Walker, *A Beardsley Miscellany* (London: Bodley Head, 1949), pp. 17–32.

52. Ibid., p. 18.

53. Ibid., p. 21.

54. P. Villars, 'A Foreign Artist and Author in England. Ramsgate and

Margate', *The Art Journal*, December 1888, pp. 366–71, p. 367.

55. *Speaker*, 3 March 1894.
56. Ellmann, p. 225.
57. *The Gentle Art of Making Enemies*, p. 144.
58. *The Whirlwind*, 19 July 1890, p. 51.
59. *Spectator*, 2 April 1892, p. 465.
60. *Modern Painting*, p. 22.
61. 2 April 1892, p. 464.
62. Paul Meier, 'An Unpublished Lecture of William Morris', *International Review of Social History*, 16 (1971), pt. 2, p. 11.

## 3 'PRUDES ON THE PROWL'

The history of the music-hall now attracts many students, both academic and 'amateur'. The standard reference works are Diana Howard, *London Theatres and Music-Halls 1850–1950* (London: Library Association, 1970) and Laurence Senelick, David F. Cheshire and Ulrich Schneider, *British Music-Hall 1840–1923: A Bibliography and Guide to Sources with a Supplement on European Music-Hall* (Hamden, Connecticut: Archon Books, 1981). They can be usefully complemented by a number of popular histories including Clarkson Rose, *Red Plush and Greasepaint* (London: Museum Press, 1964); Daniel Farson, *Marie Lloyd and Music Hall* (London: Tom Stacey, 1972); Joe Mander and Raymond Mitchenson, *British Music-Hall* (London: Gentry Books, rev. ed. 1974); D. F. Cheshire, *Music Hall in Britain*, 1974; Peter Leslie, *A Hard Act to Follow* (New York and London: Paddington Press Ltd, 1978). Sometimes contemporary memoirs manage to be both opinionated and evasive at the same time and require special interpretation: two good examples are Percy Fitzgerald, *Music-Hall Land* (London: Ward and Downey, 1890) and W. R. Titterton, *From Theatre to Music Hall* (London: Stephen Swift and Co. Ltd, 1912).

Modern sociological studies of the place of the music-hall in Victorian culture are well represented by Peter Bailey, *Leisure and Class in Victorian England* (London: Routledge, 1978); Peter Bailey (ed.), *Music Hall: The Business of Pleasure* (Open University Books, 1986); J. S. Bratton, *Music Hall: Performance and Style* (Open University Books, 1986); Peter Davison, *Contemporary Drama and the Popular Dramatic Tradition in England* (London: Macmillan, 1982). Also see Laurence Senelick, 'Politics as Entertainment: Victorian Music Hall Songs', *Victorian Studies*, December 1975, pp. 149–80, and Gareth Stedman Jones's important article, 'Working-Class Culture and Working-Class Politics in London, 1870–1900', *Journal of Social History*, Summer 1974, pp. 490–7, reprinted in *Popular Culture*, ed. B. Waites etc. (London: Croom Helm, 1982). Recent ideological analysis is often significantly at variance with the intellectual opinions expressed at the time. Compare Stedman Jones with, for instance, Elizabeth Robins Pennell, 'The Pedigree of the Music-Hall', *Contemporary Review*, April 1893, p. 575–83 or, for that matter, with T. S. Eliot's famous obituary of Marie Lloyd (*Criterion*, January 1923, pp. 192–5).

The 'Prudes' affair itself is mentioned in most books on the halls and, with some detail, in E. S. Turner, *Roads to Ruin: The Shocking History of Social Reform* (London: Michael Joseph, 1966). Robert Machray's *Night Side of London* (London: John McQueen, 1902) shows that the Promenade was still in business in the new century and has one of the very few sketches. John Elsom's *Erotic Theatre* (London: Secker and Warburg, 1973) discusses more generally the relation of modern dance to sexual provocation. For excellent photographs of theatre buildings see Victor Glasstone, *Victorian and Edwardian Theatres* (London: Thames and Hudson, 1975). My reading of the work of Walter Sickert and of Joseph Pennell has been strongly influenced by the arguments in T. J. Clark's brilliant study of French Impressionist art, *The Painting of Modern Life* (London: Thames and Hudson, 1985). I have also benefited from reading an unpublished thesis housed in the Department of English, University of Reading: *Some Literary and Visual Responses to the Music-Hall, 1890–1910* by Rosemary Neal.

1. The Reverend Stewart Headlam. For information on Headlam see F. J. Bettany, *Stewart Headlam. A Biography* (London: John Murray, 1926); Ian Brittain, *Fabianism and Culture* (Cambridge: Cambridge University Press, 1982) and T. H. Gibbons, 'The Reverend Stewart Headlam and the Emblematic Dancer', *British Journal of Aesthetics*, 5, 4 (1965), pp. 329–40.
2. Mrs Chant's own pamphlet, *Why We Attacked the Empire* (London: Horace Marshall and Son, 1895) has transcripts of the hearings. Guy Thorne, *The Great Acceptance. The Life Story of F. N. Charrington* (London: Hodder and Stoughton, 1912) gives details of earlier skirmishes between temperance organizations and the halls.
3. All the quotations in this paragraph come from the *Daily Telegraph*, 11 October 1894.
4. 18 October. Was this Winston Leonard Spencer Churchill? Another initialled letter from him to the *Westminster Gazette* on the subject was also printed on the 18th. Randolph S. Churchill, *Winston S. Churchill*, 1, *Youth 1874–1900* (London: Heinemann, 1966), p. 234, says that a letter to the *Daily Telegraph* went unpublished, yet this item certainly bears his father's initials and expresses some plausibly Churchillian sentiments.
5. Information from the *Daily Telegraph* throughout October.
6. *Daily Telegraph*, 18 October 1894.
7. *Daily Telegraph*, 26 October 1894.
8. See Randolph Churchill, *Winston S. Churchill*.
9. *Sunday Times*, 9 December 1894.
10. *Bernard Shaw Collected Letters 1898–1910*, ed. Dan. H. Laurence (London: Max Reinhardt, 1972), p. 34.
11. Letter to the *Pall Mall Gazette*, 16 October 1894.
12. *Pall Mall Gazette*, 15 October 1894.
13. *Saturday Review*, 10 November 1894, p. 502.
14. *Star*, 7 May 1892.

15. *St James's Gazette*, 16 December 1892.
16. F. E. Hardy, *The Life of Thomas Hardy*, 2 (London: Macmillan, 1930), p. 14.
17. 'A Spanish Music-Hall', *Fortnightly Review*, May 1892, pp. 716–22, reprinted in *Cities, Sea-Coasts and Islands* (London: W. Collins Sons and Co. Ltd, 1918).
18. *London Nights* (London: L. Smithers, 1895, poem dated 17 May 1893), and in Symons's *Collected Works*, p. 170.
19. *Orchids* (London: Leonard Smithers, 1896), p. 20.
20. *Pall Mall Gazette*, 17 October 1894. Also see Beckson, pp. 110–11.
21. A letter to Edmund Gosse of 15 December 1893; see Beckson, p. 103.
22. 'The New Ballet at the Alhambra', *Sketch*, 3 October 1894, p. 57.
23. *Pall Mall Gazette*, 24 August 1893.
24. 'At the Empire', *Sketch*, 7 June 1893, p. 301.
25. See Beckson, chapter 7.
26. 'At the Alhambra. Impressions and Sensations', *Savoy*, no. 5, September 1896, pp. 75–83, p. 75.
27. *The Letters of Beardsley*, ed. Henry Maas, J. L. Duncan and W. E. Good (London: Cassell, 1970), p. 300.
28. According to Shaw in *Our Theatres in the Nineties* (London: Constable and Co., 1932), 2, p. 103.
29. Shaw, ibid.
30. *Around Theatres* (London: Rupert Hart-Davies, 1953), pp. 32–4. For Beerbohm's early penchant for young female performers see David Cecil, *Max* (London: Constable, 1964), pp. 55 and 80.
31. See Anna Robins, 'Feuds and Fashions at the New English Art Club', Catalogue of *The New English Art Club Centenary Exhibition* (London: Christie's, 1986), p. 6.
32. F. Anstey, 'London Music Halls', *Harpers Magazine*, January 1891, pp. 190–202.
33. Elizabeth Robins Pennell, *The Life and Letters of Joseph Pennell* (London: Ernest Benn, 1930), 1, pp. 215–16.
34. Anstey, 'London Music Halls', p. 202.
35. For the Progressives see Norman and Jeanne MacKenzie, *The First Fabians* (London: Weidenfeld and Nicolson, 1977). The 'New London' series is outlined in Elizabeth Pennell, *Joseph Pennell*.
36. See Joseph Pennell, *Adventures of an Illustrator* (London: Fisher Unwin, 1925).
37. 'New London', *Daily Chronicle*, 28 February 1895.
38. Ronald Pickvance, 'Sickert at Brighton', *Apollo*, July 1962, pp. 404–5, p. 404. Sickert's 'The Old Bedford' was shown at the London Impressionists' exhibition in 1889. Also see R. Pickvance, 'The Magic of the Halls and Sickert', *Apollo*, April 1962, pp. 107–15, and the various biographies listed in the note to chapter 2. Sickert's 'Oxford Music-Hall' is printed in Mander and Mitchenson, *British Music-Hall*, p. 69.

39. *Pall Mall Gazette*, 28 June 1895.
40. 'Impressionism – What it Means', *Albemarle*, August 1892, pp. 47–51, p. 51.
41. 'The Logic of Painting', *Albemarle*, September 1892, pp. 85–90.
42. *Pall Mall Gazette*, 28 January 1895.
43. *Hawk*, 17 December 1889, p. 671.
44. *Spectator*, 26 November 1892.
45. *Spectator*, 2 March 1895.
46. From a letter to the press quoted by Pickvance, 'The Magic of the Halls and Sickert', p. 109.
47. 'Modern Realism in Painting', in André Theuriet, *Jules Bastien-Lepage* (London: T. Fisher Unwin, 1892), pp. 136–7.
48. Mander and Mitchenson, *British Music-Hall*, p. 11. The earlier history of *poses plastiques* is described in Richard D. Altick, *The Shows of London* (Cambridge, Mass: The Belknap Press of Harvard University Press, 1978), pp. 345–9.
49. *Daily Telegraph*, 11 October 1894.
50. 'Licensing London's Entertainments', *Westminster Gazette*, 10 October 1894.
51. 'Purity or Prudery', *Westminster Gazette*, 15 October 1894.
52. *Our Theatres in the Nineties*, 1, pp. 79–86.
53. *New Review*, November 1894, pp. 461–70, a symposium which included statements by George Edwardes of the Empire, Arthur Pinero, W. Alex Coote and others as well as Symons. Symons also wrote about the 'Living Pictures' in the *Sketch*, 1 January 1894, and the *Star*, 30 August 1900.
54. *New Review*, p. 465.
55. *Our Theatres in the Nineties*, 1, p. 86.
56. Cheshire, *Music Hall in Britain*, p. 41.
57. *New Review*, p. 465.
58. For the history of the symbolist dancer see Frank Kermode, *Romantic Image*; Frank Kermode, 'Poet and Dancer before Diaghilev', *Puzzles and Epiphanies* (London: Routledge and Kegan Paul, 1963), pp. 1–28; Ian Fletcher, 'Symons, Yeats and the Demonic Dance', *London Magazine*, 7, no. 6 (1960), pp. 46–60.
59. *Around Theatres*, p. 429.
60. 'The New Ballet at the Alhambra', *Sketch*, 17 October 1894, p. 557.
61. 'The New Ballet at the Empire', *Sketch*, 4 October 1893, p. 488.
62. 'The New Ballet at the Alhambra', *Sketch*, 7 August 1895, p. 77.
63. 'A Ballet Rehearsal. By a Casual Spectator', *St James's Gazette*, 16 December 1892.
64. *Our Theatres in the Nineties*, 3, p. 11.
65. 'A Famous Dancer', *Star*, 22 January 1894.
66. 'Cyrene at the Alhambra', *Sketch*, 5 April 1893, p. 610.
67. 'Serpentine Dancing', *Star*, 2 August 1892.
68. 'A New Tivoli Dance', *Star*, 28 November 1892.

69. *Our Theatres in the Nineties*, 3, p. 12. Shaw had written warmly about dancers in his early unpublished novel *Immaturity*.

70. *Around Theatres*, p. 431.

71. *Speaker*, 20 August 1892, p. 227.

72. *The Artist as Critic*, ed. Richard Ellmann, p. 114.

73. Review of Hugues Le Roux and Jules Garnier, *Acrobats and Mountebanks*, in *Athenaeum*, 22 February 1890, p. 239. Acrobats are a true obsession of the European *fin de siècle*, linking Degas with Steer, Toulouse-Lautrec with Beardsley. The German playwright Frank Wedekind founded his aesthetic upon the 'elasticity' of the tight-rope walker. Shaw put a lady acrobat into *Misalliance* (1910). For further guidance to the field see Jean Starobinski, *Portrait de l'artiste en saltimbanque* (Geneva: Albert Skira, 1970).

74. '"Acrobatics" at the Empire', *Star*, 6 February 1892.

75. Ibid.

76. *Our Theatres in the Nineties*, 2, p. 126.

77. *Around Theatres*, p. 33.

78. '"Acrobatics" at the Empire'.

79. 'Stéphane Mallarmé', *Fortnightly Review*, November 1898, pp. 677–85, p. 679.

80. Ellmann, p. 324.

81. 'The training of the Contortionist', *Pall Mall Gazette*, 11 August 1892. Symons also wrote on Petrescue in 'She Walks on her Hands', *Star*, 5 March 1892.

82. 'Human eels', *Star*, 9 July 1892. Symons also wrote on the Rowe brothers in 'The training of the Contortionist'.

83. *A Beardsley Miscellany*, p. 25.

84. 'The Evolution of the Music-Hall', *Speaker*, 27 July 1895.

85. In 'The Music-Hall of the Future', *Pall Mall Gazette*, 13 April 1892.

86. 'The Modern Actor', *Albemarle*, July 1892, pp. 20–4.

87. See *Daily Chronicle*, 30 October 1894.

88. *Our Theatres in the Nineties*, 3, p. 355.

89. 'The Older and Better Music-Hall' and 'Idolum Aularum', *Around Theatres*, pp. 298–301 and pp. 414–18.

90. 'The Music-Halls', *Star*, 19 October 1891.

91. Martha Vicinus's excellent chapter on the music-hall in *The Industrial Muse* (London: Croom Helm, 1974), for example.

92. 'Arthur Roberts', *Star*, 2 July 1893.

93. *Albert Chevalier, A Record by Himself* (London: John Macqueen, 1896), p. 135.

94. 'Chevalier's Return', *Star*, 20 September 1893. Symons also wrote on Chevalier in 'The Coster's Laureate – Mr Albert Chevalier', *Black and White*, 18 June 1892, p. 784.

95. *More Theatres* (London: Rupert Hart-Davis, 1969), p. 497.

## 4  'OUR DARK PLACES'

It was because the Victorian reformers knew prisons to be secret silent places carefully hidden from public view that they put so much energy and commitment into meticulous description. Philip Priestley's *Victorian Prison Lives* (London: Methuen, 1985) anthologizes the testimonies of the prisoners themselves, and has bibliographical information. Francis Scougal (pseud. of Felicia Mary Frances Skene), *Scenes from a Silent World* (Edinburgh and London: Blackwoods and Sons, 1889), is a wide-ranging survey made up of articles which originally appeared in *Blackwood's*. The gradual impact of Continental ideas of the criminal can be observed in the volumes of *The Criminology Series* edited by the Reverend W. D. Morrison (see below) for T. Fisher Unwin: *The Female Offender* by Cesare Lombroso and William Ferrero (London: 1895), *Criminal Sociology* by Enrico Ferri (London: 1895), and *Juvenile Offenders* by Morrison himself (London: 1896). Morrison was also the author of *Crime and its Causes* (London: Swan Sonnenschein, 1891). These are the works that provide the evidence against which to test the influential theories of Michel Foucault in *Discipline and Punish* (London: Allen Lane, 1977).

There are unusual historical readings of *The Ballad of Reading Gaol* and *De Profundis*, along with additional bibliographical material, in Regenia Gagnier, *Idylls of the Marketplace*.

1. *Daily Chronicle*, 23, 25, 29 January. The subsequent correspondence ran until 8 February.
2. Sir Edmund du Cane (1830–1903), Chairman of Commissioners of Prisons, Chairman of Directors of Prisons, Inspector-General of Military Prisons, Surveyor General of Prisons. Author of *The Punishment and Prevention of Crime* (London: Macmillan, 1885).
3. For H. W. Massingham see Havighurst, *Radical Journalist*.
4. W. D. Morrison (1852–1943). A prominent prison reformer who had been writing on the subject in the *Daily Chronicle* since 1891, his 'Are Our Prisons a Failure?' was printed in the *Fortnightly Review*, April 1894, pp. 459–69. Chaplain at Wandsworth Prison since 1887, he later worked as a priest in Marylebone. In May 1898 he contributed another article to the *Fortnightly Review* (pp. 781–9) which referred to Wilde without naming him. See Ellmann, p. 464.
5. John Burns (1858–1943). A prominent member of the Labour movement who served six months' imprisonment in 1888 as a result of his involvement in the 'Bloody Sunday' demonstrations in Trafalgar Square on 13 November 1887. A New Unionist, Burns led the London Dock Strike in 1889 and worked with the 'Progressives' on the LCC. He was elected to Parliament for Battersea in 1892 as an Independent Labour candidate, re-elected in 1895, and served in the Liberal Government of 1906–14.

6. *Daily Chronicle*, 23 January 1894. For Lombroso, see Robert A. Nye, *Crime, Madness and Politics*.

7. *Daily Chronicle*, 25 January 1894.

8. Ibid.

9. *Daily Chronicle*, 23 January 1894.

10. *Daily Chronicle*, 25 January 1894.

11. *Daily Chronicle*, 29 January 1894.

12. Ibid.

13. The quote is from the *Report from the Departmental Committee on Prisons*, April 1895, p. 8.

14. *Works*, p. 1204.

15. Edward Carpenter (1844–1929). Poet, socialist and life-long advocate of sexual liberation. See Chushichi Tsuzuki, *Edward Carpenter, 1844–1929* (Cambridge: Cambridge University Press, 1980), and Sheila Rowbotham and Jeffrey Weeks, *Socialism and the New Life: The Personal and Sexual Politics of Edward Carpenter and Havelock Ellis* (London: Pluto Press Ltd, 1977).

16. *Civilisation – Its Cause and Cure* (London: George Allen and Unwin, 1889).

17. *Prisons, Police and Punishment* (London: Arthur C. Fifield, 1905), pp. 100–1.

18. *Letters*, p. 835.

19. *Prisons, Police and Punishment* (1905), p. 41. Carpenter had written to the *Star* in defence of Wilde in 1895. See Tsuzuki, *Edward Carpenter*, p. 213.

20. Prince Peter Kropotkin (1842–1921). Russian exile and anarchist. His works include *In Russian and French Prisons* (London: Ward and Downey, 1887) and *Memoirs of a Revolutionist* (London: Smith, Elder and Co., 1899), 2 vols.

21. *Letters*, p. 488.

22. *In Russian and French Prisons*, p. 346.

23. Ibid., p. 366.

24. Havelock Ellis (1859–1939). See Rowbotham and Weeks, *Socialism and the New Life*, and Phyllis Grosskurth, *Havelock Ellis. A Biography* (London: Allen Lane, 1980).

25. *The Criminal* (London: Walter Scott Ltd, 1895), p. 223.

26. See *Letters*, p. 523. In 1898 Wilde made sure that Morrison had a copy of *The Ballad of Reading Gaol*, see *Letters*, p. 704.

27. Ibid., p. 578.

28. Ellmann, pp. 498–9.

29. *Letters*, pp. 568–74.

30. Ibid., pp. 722–6.

31. Ibid., p. 650, pp. 733–4.

32. Ibid., p. 704.

33. *Daily Chronicle*, 15 February 1898.

34. Ellmann, p. 191.

35. 'Le crime, dont l'animal humain a puisé le goût dans le ventre de sa mère, est originellement naturel,' 'Eloge du Maquillage', *Le peintre de la vie moderne, Oeuvres Complètes* (Paris: Editions du Seuil, 1968), p. 562.

36. *Letters*, p. 767.

37. *Works*, pp. 993–1008. The Chatterton piece was never published, but there are manuscript notes in the W. A. Clark Library, Los Angeles.

38. See John Stokes, 'Wilde on Dostoevsky', *Notes and Queries*, June 1980, pp. 215–16.

39. *Works*, p. 1103.

40. See, for instance, Helen Zimmern, 'Professor Lombroso's New Theory of Political Crime', *Blackwood's Magazine*, February 1891, pp. 202–11.

41. *Works*, p. 340.

42. E. H. Mikhail, *Oscar Wilde, Interviews and Recollections* (London: Macmillan, 1979), 1, p. 233.

43. *Letters*, pp. 401–6.

44. Ibid., p. 695.

45. *More Letters of Oscar Wilde*, ed. Rupert Hart-Davis (London: John Murray, 1985), p. 165.

46. Ibid., p. 153.

47. *Letters*, p. 654.

48. *Saturday Review*, 12 March 1898, pp. 365–6, reprinted in *Oscar Wilde: The Critical Heritage*, ed. Karl Beckson (London: Routledge and Kegan Paul, 1970), p. 219.

49. *The Oxford Book of Modern Verse*, p. vii.

50. *More Letters*, p. 152. Also see Richard Perceval Graves, *A. E. Housman: The Scholar-Poet* (London: Routledge and Kegan Paul, 1979), pp. 113–14.

51. *The Academy*, 26 February 1898, p. 236, reprinted in *Oscar Wilde: The Critical Heritage*, pp. 211–13.

52. *Letters*, p. 712.

53. *Works*, pp. 843–60.

54. Gagnier (*Idylls of the Marketplace*, p. 195), writes of the poem's 'collective' form. I argue that the form continually buckles under the weight of alienated social reality that it has to bear.

55. From reports of the guardsman's trial in the *Reading Observer*, 20 June 1895. The *Daily Chronicle* records that 'Wooldridge walked to the scaffold with the firmness which had characterised his demeanour throughout' (8 July 1896).

56. That the condemned man 'often said that he was glad/the hangman's hands were near' was later confirmed by the guardsman's foster sister, who made a point of recording that the prisoner died in a spirit of Christian repentance. Her statement is bound in with a copy of the poem in the British Library at Cup 400 c 15.

57. *Letters*, p. 676.

58. Ibid., p. 679.

59. *Works*, p. 1080.

60. *Without Apology* (London: Martin Secker, 1938), p. 49.
61. Ibid., pp. 46–7.

## 5 'TIRED OF LIFE'

Books on suicide, even the most theoretical, tend to read like anthologies. This is a subject that continually strains against the categories imposed upon it, and seems impossible to contain within a single definition. A classic English example, a dossier of case-histories, is Forbes Winslow, *The Anatomy of Suicide* (London: Renshaw, 1840). Jack B. Douglas, *The Social Meanings of Suicide* (Princeton, New Jersey: Princeton University Press, 1967) is accessible and comprehensive, while Al Alvarez, *The Savage God* (London: Weidenfeld, 1971) is enlightening on the literary implications. There are interesting comparisons to be made between a modern like Alvarez and a high Victorian like G. H. Lewes, who wrote on the subject in the *Westminster Review*, July 1857, pp. 52–78. Emile Durkheim's *Le suicide* appeared in French in 1897 but was not available in English until 1952. Durkheim was in any case imposing order and method on a field already mapped out by Morselli (see below), and it is often said that Durkheim's categories – the 'anomic' suicide, for example – reflect the *fin de siècle* mood in which he was working. Olive Anderson's *Suicide in Victorian and Edwardian England* (Oxford: Clarendon Press, 1987), cited hereafter as Anderson, is a major re-examination of the whole subject which includes an important discussion of the case of Edward Clark (pp. 242–54 and p. 369). Anderson refers to literary material throughout her book, but generally as an indication of attitudes. My main concern, in contrast, is with the ways in which ideas about suicide inspired new literary structures and techniques. I make no attempt to deal with every literary suicide – whether of author or of character – at the end of the century. W. E. Henley, George Moore, Amy Levy and A. E. Housman all wrote poems on the theme.

1. 'The Decadent Movement in Literature', *Harper's New Monthly Magazine*, November 1893, p. 867.
2. *Daily Chronicle*, 23 August 1893.
3. *Daily Chronicle*, 19 August 1893.
4. 'Suicide and the Press', *Speaker*, 26 August 1893, pp. 207–8.
5. Beckson, p. 139.
6. 'Romantic Tragedy Near Canterbury', *Daily Chronicle*, 12 June 1893, recalled in the issue of 16 August, together with the story of the boy.
7. John Page Hopps, *Daily Chronicle*, 19 August.
8. Harry Cocking, *Daily Chronicle*, 22 August.
9. Holden Sampson, *Daily Chronicle*, 17 August.
10. George O'Byrne, *Daily Chronicle*, 18 August.
11. Walker E. Treacher, *Daily Chronicle*, 18 August.
12. J. Morrison Davidson, *Daily Chronicle*, 23 August.
13. Anderson, p. 257, describes the letters as 'sermons'.

14. See Anderson, p. 9.

15. London: Kegan, Paul and Co., 1881, p. 15.

16. The usefulness of statistics, cautiously handled, is re-asserted by Anderson, p. 2, who has shown that although national averages 'can never establish what the suicidologist would most like to know: the real scale of suicide and its causes', it is possible to 'get behind' them to the experience of ordinary people by studying more localized records, including coroner's papers.

17. Henry Morselli, *Suicide. An Essay on Comparative Moral Statistics* (London: C. Kegan Paul, 1881), p. 354.

18. London: H. K. Lewis, 1885, p. 84.

19. S. A. K. Strahan, *Suicide and Insanity* (London: Swan Sonnenschein and Co., 1893), p. 61. A further example of the preoccupation: William Ferrero, 'Suicide among Women', *New Review*, December 1894, pp. 637–46.

20. *The World as Will and Idea* (London: Trubner and Co., 1883–6), 3 vols., 1, pp. 514–15.

21. For Schopenhauer's influence in England see Patrick Gardiner, *Schopenhauer* (Harmondsworth: Penguin Books, 1963) and Bryan Magee, *The Philosophy of Schopenhauer* (Oxford: Clarendon Press, 1983).

22. Arthur Schopenhauer, 'On Suicide', *Studies in Pessimism* (London: Swann Sonnenschein and Co., 1891), p. 224.

23. *Daily Chronicle*, 18 August.

24. *Daily Chronicle*, 21 August.

25. *Daily Chronicle*, 19 August.

26. Anderson, p. 369.

27. November 1891, pp. 463–9.

28. *Collected Letters*, pp. 315–19.

29. *The Quintessence of Ibsenism* (London: Walter Scott, 1891), p. 11.

30. All the suicides in Hardy's novels are discussed in Frank R. Giordano Jun., *'I'd Have My Life Unbe'. Thomas Hardy's Self-destructive Characters* (University of Alabama Press, 1984). Giordano points out that Hardy read an essay on 'The Ethics of Suicide' in the *Saturday Review* in 1876, but otherwise tends to apply Durkheim's categories. Hardy's greatest contribution to the literature of suicide is his poem 'Standing by the Mantelpiece'.

31. Mrs Oliphant, 'The Anti-Marriage League', *Blackwood's Magazine*, January 1896, reprinted in *Thomas Hardy: The Critical Heritage* (London: Routledge and Kegan Paul, 1970), p. 261. As the *Illustrated London News* remarked, 'We all know perfectly well that baby Schopenhauers are not coming into the world in shoals' (*Thomas Hardy: The Critical Heritage* p. 275). Perhaps not, yet the *Speaker* (19 May 1894, p. 678) did report the real-life story of the eighteen-year-old daughter of a Chertsey bricklayer who gave poison to her nine-year-old sister and then took it herself because 'she thought the family (which had lost its mother) ill-managed'. 'I cannot stand this any longer', she wrote in a farewell letter to her father, 'I am treated like dirt.'

32. *Jude the Obscure*, ed. Patricia Ingham (Oxford: Oxford University Press,

1985), p. 355.
33. Ibid., p. 70.
34. *The Savoy*, reprinted in *Hardy: Critical Heritage*, p. 307.
35. A category that sometimes included the 'Socialist idealist suicide'. In
    January 1895 a young plumber was charged at Southwark with attempting
    to kill himself with a dose of laudanum. A letter was found, addressed 'To
    Society':

> With these few remarks I have attempted to show that the act I am about to
> commit is neither insane, selfish, nor cowardly. I have retired from the battle of
> life, weary of its selfishness, its cant, and its shams, weary of its brute struggle
> for existence, its misery, poverty and degradation; the crushing of what is noble
> and good, the fostering of what is ignoble and bad. For many years I have had
> the opinion that the life of the wage earner, under the present economic
> conditions, was not worth living, which opinion led me to one ineffectual
> attempt at self-destruction. But on my conversion to Socialism my life was filled
> with new hopes. I saw new possibilities and resolved that so long as I had the
> power I would strive and help to bring about that inevitable transformation
> which will beautify the world. But meanwhile the struggle is hard, and society
> has refused to allow me to exist except under conditions which are utterly
> intolerable to me. As society refuses my claim to be one of its useful members, I
> contend that it has no reasonable claim on me, either in respect of its laws or its
> obligations, and therefore leaves me free to dispose of my only property (my
> life) in whatsoever way I choose, and as the bidder (Death) offers a good
> bargain, I have decided to close with him .... But we know nothing of any realm
> beyond the end of life. Then, whilst life lasts let us try to add to its value by
> changing its conditions, and by human affection endeavour to make each life
> happy. By these means, and by none other, will suicide be avoided.
>
> *(Pall Mall Gazette*, 21 January 1895).

36. Even Anderson, p. 14, who is prepared to analyse statistics, stipulates that
    her investigation 'proposes to accept without more ado that the real scale
    of suicide is as uncertain in the past as it is in the present'.
37. A. N. P., *Daily Chronicle*, 17 August.
38. 'Hopeful', *Daily Chronicle*, 19 August.
39. 26 August 1893, p. 207.
40. 19 May 1894, p. 678.
41. See Anderson, p. 217. The reporting of suicides in the nineties – in grouped
    paragraphs – can be seen as transitional between the old-fashioned, mid-
    Victorian reliance upon short but space-filling individual reports, and the
    use of cross-headings by Edwardian tabloids to inflate a single incident. See
    Anderson, p. 252.
42. *Pall Mall Gazette*, 23 August 1895.
43. *Pall Mall Gazette*, 2 April 1895.
44. *Our Theatres in the Nineties*, 1, p. 85. There are similar jokes in Robert
    Hichens's 1894 satire *The Green Carnation*:

> 'Hope springs eternal in the human breast,' Mrs Windsor said, with a little air of
> aptness.

'That is one of the greatest fallacies of a melancholy age,' Esme answered, arranging the huge moonstone in his tie with a plump hand; 'suicide would be the better word. *The Second Mrs Tanqueray* has made suicide quite the rage. A number of most respectable ladies, without the vestige of a past among them, have put an end to themselves lately, I am told. To die naturally has become most unfashionable, but no doubt the tide will turn presently.'

'I wonder if people realise how dangerous they may be in their writings,' said Lady Locke.

'One has to choose between being dangerous and being dull. Society loves to feel itself upon the edge of a precipice, I assure you. To be harmless is the most deadly enemy to social salvation ....

'I suppose Ibsen is responsible for a good deal,' Mrs Windsor said, rather vaguely.

(London: *Unicorn Press*, 1949, p. 59)

45. See Anderson, pp. 207–13.
46. *Daily Chronicle*, 18 August 1893.
47. *Daily Chronicle*, 21 August 1893.
48. *The Suicide Club* appeared in *New Arabian Nights* (London: Chatto and Windus, 1882), 2 vols. There were certainly reports of real-life 'Suicide Clubs': for example, 'Suicide Clubs and other Curiosities in Self-Destruction' in the *Westminster Gazette*, 2 October 1894. D. S. MacColl records a Suicide Club among his fellow undergraduates at University College in the 1870s (*Weekend Review*, 21 March 1931, pp. 432–3). But it seems that the idea of the Suicide Club was suggested to R. L. Stevenson by his cousin R. A. M. Stevenson. (*The Art of Velasquez*, ed. Denys Sutton, p. 10.)
49. *Prince Zaleski* (London: John Lane, 1895), references on pp. 126, 140–1, 143, 146–7.
50. The following information is from David Crackanthorpe, *Hubert Crackanthorpe and English Realism in the 1890s* (Columbia and London: University of Missouri Press, 1979).
51. John Adlard, *Owen Seaman. His Life and Work* (London: The Eighteen Nineties Society, 1977), p. 5.
52. Morselli, *Suicide*, p. 181.
53. *Poems of Ernest Dowson*, ed. Mark Longaker (Oxford: Oxford University Press, 1962), p. 72.
54. *Wreckage* (London: William Heinemann, 1893).
55. *Star*, 2 January 1897.
56. David Crackanthorpe, *Hubert Crackanthorpe*, p. 145.
57. *Vignettes* (London and New York: John Lane, 1896).
58. H. Montgomery Hyde, *Oscar Wilde. A Biography* (London: Methuen, 1976), p. 106. Ellmann, p. 215, connects this story with Wilde's interest in the macabre French poet Maurice Rollinat, and gives other instances of Wilde's thoughts turning to the subject of suicide as he walked along the Seine. See Ellmann, pp. 531 and 540.
59. Morselli, *Suicide*, p. 181.

60. Information on the morgue can be gained from such works as *The Tit-Bits Guide to Paris and the Exhibition* (London, 1889) and *The Anglo-American Guide to Exhibition Paris 1900* (London: Heinemann) – and from fiction. Jules Janin's *L'An mort*, which featured a scene in the morgue, was first published in 1829 and many times reprinted. There was also a novel in English entitled *Keeping Afloat* (1863). Dickens was a regular visitor: see Andrew Sanders, *Charles Dickens, Resurrectionist* (London: Macmillan, 1982). So was Henry Irving: see Lawrence Irving, *Henry Irving* (London: Faber and Faber, 1961), p. 498. By the nineties, however, the most famous *vignette*, certainly known to Wilde (see *Works*, p. 1006), was in Zola's *Thérèse Raquin*. A cult developed around 'L'Inconnue de la Seine', the death-mask of a beautiful young girl whose body had been dredged from the river. When Beardsley, his sister, the Pennells *et al.* visited Paris in the spring of 1893 MacColl bought a cast of the mask, hung it on a tree in the *bois* where they lunched: 'and the Beardsleys worshipped'. ('The Beardsleys', *Manchester Guardian*, 18 March 1948). Also see Alvarez, *Savage God*, pp. 115–17 and Sacheverell Sitwell, 'L'Inconnue de la Seine', *Lilliput*, April 1945, pp. 315–17. According to T. J. Clark, Manet's *Olympia* was often compared to a body in the morgue, a reference to a 'nameless, specifically urban, and specially horrifying death'. (*The Painting of Modern Life*, p. 289). To which one might add a certain decadent taste for beauty caught in the first stages of decomposition.

61. 'The Anonymous Dead. By a Visitor to the Morgue', *Pall Mall Gazette*, 28 December 1894.

62. 'Apparent Failure', *Robert Browning: The Poems*, ed. John Pettigrew (New Haven and London: Yale University Press, 1981), pp. 860–2, pp. 1168–9.

63. Michael Millgate, *Thomas Hardy* (Oxford: Oxford University Press, 1982), p. 165.

64. Jacob Korg, *George Gissing: A Critical Biography* (London: Methuen, 1965), p. 98.

65. *The Collected Works of Arthur Symons*, 3, Poems (London: Martin Secker, 1924), p. 36.

66. *More Letters*, p. 201.

67. Ellmann, p. 330.

68. 'The Child in the House', *Imaginary Portraits* (London: Macmillan, 1887). Also see Frank Kermode, *Romantic Image*, p. 63.

69. Mary Anderson, *A Few Memories* (London: Osgood, McIlvaine and Co., 1896), p. 231.

70. *Our Theatres in the Nineties*, 2, pp. 87–8.

71. *Works*, p. 346.

72. Ellmann, p. 549.

73. *Letters*, p. 708.

74. Ibid., p. 855.

75. Ibid., p. 185.

76. Oscar Wilde, *The Importance of Being Earnest*, ed. Russell Jackson (London: Ernest Benn, 1980), p. 51.
77. *Works*, p. 191. The story was first published in *Court and Society Review* in May 1887.
78. *Works*, p. 100.
79. Ibid., p. 160.


# 6 'ASTOUNDING DISCLOSURES'

Enquiries into the debate between literature and journalism have often focused upon disagreements between H. G. Wells and Henry James in 1911. Their exchange is in *Henry James and H. G. Wells. A Record of Their Friendship, Their Debate on the Art of Fiction, and Their Quarrel*, ed. with an introduction by Leon Edel and Gordon N. Ray (London: Rupert Hart-Davis, 1958). This is undoubtedly a significant guide to a major concern of established and very professional writers in the Edwardian period, a pointer to the formal position soon to be held by 'modernism' as well. Whether it is more than that may be doubtful. Shaw had long proclaimed himself to be a journalist rather than an artist, a position he reiterated in correspondence with James in 1909. See *The Collected Plays of Henry James*, ed. Leon Edel (London: Rupert Hart-Davis, 1949), pp. 642–7.

1. Zola's publisher, Vizitelly, was prosecuted in 1888, and again in 1889, when he was sentenced to three months' imprisonment. He died in 1894. See Clarence Dekker, *The Victorian Conscience* (New York: Twayne, 1952).
2. The sources for this material are the papers in September 1893, in particular 'A Morning with Zola', *Westminster Gazette*, 22 September 1893; 'A Chat with Emile Zola', *Daily Chronicle*, 27 September 1893; *Pall Mall Gazette*, 23 September 1893. The *Westminster Gazette* covered the visit with articles by Robert Sherard and by Vizitelly himself.
3. Address to the Congress of Journalists is based on reports in the *Daily Chronicle*, 25 September 1893 and *The Times*, 25 September 1893.
4. *Daily Chronicle*, 23 September 1893.
5. The President's address is taken from the *Daily Chronicle*, 22 September 1893.
6. The symposia on anonymity are in the *New Review*, November 1889, pp. 513–31 and March 1890, pp. 265–76. Shaw is quoted on p. 275. Also see *Collected Letters 1874–1897*, pp. 221–4 and p. 497.
7. The figures for Shaw's journalism are based on Dan H. Laurence, *Bernard Shaw: A Bibliography* (Oxford: Clarendon Press, 1983), 2. For more on Shaw see Michael Holroyd, *Bernard Shaw*, 1, 1856–98 (London: Chatto and Windus, 1988). His journalistic output in the 1880s is listed on pages 213–14.
8. *Our Theatres in the Nineties*, 2, p. 140. The *Star*, 23 September 1893, had

responded to Zola's strictures with a similarly left-handed defence of pseudonyms that failed to do their job:

> Our criticisms on the drama, literature, art and music all appear above the signatures of accomplished writers who are known to be masters of their subjects, and whose newspaper names are immediately associated in the minds of those at all versed in the world of letters with individuals. Who does not know SPECTATOR most incisive dissector of plays? etc.... Signed articles may help rare gifts to assert themselves, but anonymity will not suppress them.

9. *Our Theatres in the Nineties*, 1, p. 65.
10. 'A Degenerate's View of Nordau', pp. 63–5.
11. 'The Problem Play: A Symposium (Part V)', *The Humanitarian*, May 1895, pp. 347–52, p. 352.
12. Ibid., pp. 349–50.
13. 'Playwright Cut Playwright. Bernard Shaw on George Moore', *Star*, 27 June 1893.
14. 'Arms and the Man. Terrible Scenes at the Avenue Theatre', *Star*, 14 April 1894.
15. 'The Censorship of Plays. A Talk with Mr Bernard Shaw'.
16. *The Art of the Novel: Critical Prefaces*, with an introduction by R. P. Blackmur (London: Charles Scribner's Sons, 1935), pp. 54–5.
17. All quotations from *Portrait of a Lady* are from the *World's Classics* edition (Oxford, 1981), which prints the 1907 text.
18. *The Art of the Novel*, p. 57.
19. *The Yellow Book*, 1, April 1894, pp. 7–52, p. 23.
20. 'The Papers', *The Complete Tales of Henry James*, ed. Leon Edel, 12 (London: Rupert Hart-Davis, 1964). Virtually the only extended critical treatment of this story is David Howard's fine essay, 'Henry James and "The Papers"', in *Henry James: Fiction as History*, ed. Ian F. A. Bell (London: Vision Press, 1984), pp. 49–64.
21. An action that blurs the usual journalistic distinction between confidential conversation and interview interrogation. 'Personal confidence is the foundation of the system', W. T. Stead had written in 'The Future of Journalism', *Contemporary Review*, November 1886, pp. 663–79, p. 679. Maud Blandy proves Stead wrong by respecting his principle.
22. The *Morning Herald* (Halifax, Nova Scotia), 10 October 1882, reprinted in *Oscar Wilde: Interviews and Recollections*, ed. E. H. Mikhail (London: Macmillan, 1979), 1, p. 107.
23. *More Letters*, p. 121.
24. Ibid., p. 123.
25. Ellmann, p. 149.
26. *Letters*, p. 263.
27. Ibid., p. 257.
28. Ellmann, p. 176.

29. *Sketch*, 9 January 1895, p. 495, reprinted in *Interviews and Recollections*, pp. 239–45.
30. *Works*, p. 1049.
31. *Works*, p. 1015.
32. *Interviews and Recollections*, I, pp. 246–51. Also see *More Letters*, pp. 189–96.
33. W. B. Yeats, *Autobiographies* (London: Macmillan, 1966), p. 130.
34. *More Letters*, p. 115.

# INDEX